THE PSYCHOLINGUISTICS OF READABLE WRITING: A MULTIDISCIPLINARY EXPLORATION

THE COMMUNICATION AND INFORMATION SCIENCE SERIES
Series Editor: BRENDA DERVIN, The Ohio State University

Subseries:
Progress in Communication Sciences: Brant R. Burleson
Interpersonal Communication: Donald J. Cegala
Organizational Communication: George Barnett
Mass Communication/Telecommunication Systems: Lee B. Becker
User-Based Communication/Information System Design: Michael S. Nilan
Cross-Cultural/Cross-National Communication and Social Change: Josep Rota
International Communication, Peace and Development: Majid Tehranian
Critical Cultural Studies in Communication: Leslie T. Good
Feminist Scholarship in Communication: Lana Rakow
Rhetorical Theory and Criticism: Stephen H. Browne
Communication Pedagogy and Practice: Gerald M. Phillips
Communication: The Human Context: Lee Thayer

The Psycholinguistics of Readable Writing: A Multidisciplinary Exploration

Alice S. Horning
Rhetoric and Linguistics
Oakland University
Rochester, MI

ABLEX PUBLISHING CORPORATION
NORWOOD, NEW JERSEY

The following publishers have generously given permission to use quotations from copyrighted works:

From "Effective Ideation in Written Text: A Functional Approach to Clarity and Exigence," by B. Couture, 1986, in *Functional Approaches to Writing*. Reprinted by permission of Pinter Publishers Ltd., 25 Floral St., Covent Garden, London WC2E 9DS. All Rights Reserved.

From Appendix 3 of *Personality and the Teaching of Composition*, by G. Jensen and J. DiTiberio, 1989. Reprinted by permission of Ablex Publishing Corporation, Norwood, NJ.

From *Modern Political Systems: Europe* (2nd ed.), by R.C. Macridis and R.E. Ward, 1968. Adapted by permission of Prentice-Hall, Englewood Cliffs, NJ.

From *Toward a Grammar of Passages*, by R. Coe, 1988. Reprinted by permission of National Council of Teachers of English.

From "Readable Writing," *Journal of Advanced Composition*, Vol. 11, No. 1, 1991; and "Readability: Reading/Writing Tools for Measurement," *Journal of Advanced Composition*, Vol. 7 Nos. 1 and 2, 1987. Reprinted by permission.

From "Redundancy and Text Difficulty: A Study," *New England Reading Association Journal*, Vol. 17, 1982. Reprinted by permission.

Printed in the United States of America

Library of Congress Cataloging-in-Publication Data

Horning, Alice S.
The psycholinguistics of readable writing : a multidisciplinary exploration / Alice S. Horning.
p. cm. – (Communication and information sciences)
Includes bibliographical references and index.
ISBN 0-89391-896-2 (cloth). – ISBN 0-89391-997-7 (pbk.)
1. Rhetoric–Psychological aspects. 2. Discourse analysis–Psychological aspects. 3. Reading, Psychology of. I. Title. II. Series.
P301.5.P75H67 1992
808'.0014–dc20 92-33489
CIP

Ablex Publishing Corporation
355 Chestnut Street
Norwood, New Jersey 07648

for Bela

Contents

Acknowledgments

I would like to thank Mr. Richard Teeple for providing the illustration that appears in Chapter 1.

I am indebted to many first-year students at Wayne State University in Detroit, Michigan and colleagues there who volunteered their classes to serve as subjects in the study reported in Chapter 7, and also to many first-year students at Oakland University in Rochester, Michigan and colleagues there who gave me access to students in their classes who served as subjects in the study reported in Chapter 9.

I wish to acknowledge several forms of generous assistance from Professor Kate Kiefer of Colorado State University, in running the passages on Writer's Workbench, to provide the data reported in Chapter 8, and in providing close readings of two drafts of the complete manuscript, offering many helpful suggestions and encouragement at several important points.

The work reported in Chapter 8 was completed under the auspices of an Oakland University Faculty Research Fellowship, Spring–Summer, 1985.

I wish to thank Barbara Reetz and Carole Crum for their assistance as a second scorers in the studies in Chapters 7 and 9. I am grateful to Ms. Reetz and to Professors Daniel Fullmer and William Schwab for their assistance in the pilot study for the research reported in Chapter 10.

I am indebted to a number of colleagues who served as subjects in the study reported in Chapter 10.

In my work on this book, I have been the fortunate recipient of the generous help of many colleagues. I have asked all of the following people to read all or part of the book for me, and I have repeatedly received careful, attentive comments that were extremely helpful. My work and findings reported in the book have been greatly enriched by these responses. I am grateful to all of the following for their assistance with all or part of the manuscript: Roxanne Allen, Wallis Anderson, Jane Eberwein, Carole Crum, John DiTiberio, Linda Epstein, William Grabe, Barbara Hamilton, Van Hillard, George Jensen, Robert Kushler, Donald Morse, Paul Munsell, Lois Overbeck, Margaret Pigott, Gerald Phillips, Michael Scrivener, Ronald Sudol, Debbie Szobel-Logan, and Jack Wilson.

Responsibility for the form and content of the final manuscript is mine alone.

Introduction: The Psycholinguistics of Readable Writing: A Multidisciplinary Exploration

In *Lives on the Boundary: The Struggles and Achievements of America's Underprepared*, Mike Rose argues an eloquent case for promoting literacy in order to change the shape of American higher education. He asserts that underprepared students who can read and write in the critical way that college work requires can enter the academic realm formerly reserved for the elite. Rose speaks with authority: His personal experiences, recounted in the book, make a strong case for the potential of students from diverse cultural and socioeconomic backgrounds to become literate, and for the urgency of our need to help them achieve that potential. American education can reach this goal through an understanding of literacy in all its complexity. *The Psycholinguistics of Readable Writing* examines, from the intertwined perspectives of linguistics, psychology, reading, and writing, how readers derive meaning from written language and how writers can best facilitate an understanding of their texts; this examination provides an understanding of the contribution of texts themselves to literacy.

The need of citizens for literacy and of educators for an understanding of the nature of readable text are urgent, not only for the population Mike Rose describes, but also for the changing shape of our society, our economy, and the nature of work (see also DePalma). *Workforce 2000*, a United States Labor Department study conducted by the Hudson Institute, provides projections concerning both workers and work as we approach the turn of the century. A strong majority of those entering the work force by then will be nonwhite, female, or immigrant Americans, all groups who may be members of Rose's "underprepared" population (*Workforce* 95). Moreover, the work they do will require much higher levels of skill and education than are currently needed, such that postsecondary education will be prerequisite to many jobs, in many sectors of the economy (*Workforce* xxvii and 97). Indeed, the report makes clear that

> job prospects for professional and technical, managerial, sales and service jobs will far outstrip the opportunities in other fields. In contrast to the average gain of about 25 percent across all occupational categories, the fastest growing fields—lawyers, scientists, and health professionals—will grow two to three times as fast. On the other hand, jobs as machine tenders, assemblers, miners, and farmers actually decline (*Workforce* 97).

Needless to say, the educational needs of the work force will reflect these changes in the types and distributions of work. While it is clear that citizens will need other kinds of abilities, there will be need for the specific literacy skills that can be addressed and enhanced by the basic research discussed below, as the report notes that

> If every child who reaches the age of seventeen between now and the year 2000 could read sophisticated materials, write clearly, speak articulately, and solve complex problems requiring algebra and statistics, the American economy could easily approach or exceed the 4 percent growth. . . . [I]mproving the educational preparation of workers (is) not the only item on the nation's agenda between now and the year 2000. But . . . certainly among the most important (*Workforce* 116-117).

Readable writing, by which I mean specifically expository prose and not fiction of any sort, provides the foundation for all kinds of educational preparation, including that in mathematics; therefore, understanding expository written text is fundamental to the success of the "underprepared" and everyone else entering the changing work force.

This perspective is supported by other scholars concerned with the same issue of critical literacy. Commenting on Paulo Friere's work on literacy as a means of empowerment, linguist Noam Chomsky points out that

> writing is an indispensable method for interpersonal communication in a complicated society. . . .[I]ntellectual progress and cultural progress and moral progress for that matter require forms of interaction and communicative exchange that go well beyond that of speaking situations. . . .That's a form of empowerment. . . .Doing things that will stimulate critical analysis, self-analysis, and analysis of culture and society is very crucial. In fact, it seems to me that part of the core of all education ought to be the development of systems of intellectual self-defense and also stimulation of the capacity for inquiry, which also means collective inquiry (Chomsky 16).

The need for critical literacy, in the view of all the scholars noted here, is one of the central means of creating a work force and citizenry that will be able to function as we move into the next century. In my earlier work, I have discussed the acquisition processes by which underprepared students among others develop some aspects of literacy (Horning, *Teaching*). In this book, I will make clear that full participation in our complicated society depends upon literacy for all citizens; this requisite critical literacy can be understood through the research I will discuss.

The nature of literacy and how texts are produced and understood has recently been the subject of intense theoretical discussion and research. In literary studies, the proposals of deconstructionists and reader-response theorists address a few of the same issues that are the focus of this book. Several readers of this manuscript have proposed that my findings either support deconstructionist views or refute these views. My own understanding of current theory is that both sides may be right: My proposals support the deconstructionists' view of text as transactional in nature (Winterowd, "Introduction" xi), i.e., not exclusively text centered or writer centered, but rather, as occupying a middle position between the reader and writer. On the other hand, my view is that readers and writers meet in the text, and the focus of my analysis lies in the text itself. My research is perhaps a step away from a "pure" deconstructionist view of the "complicity of readers and writers in all acts of composing" (Crowley 36). This step seems necessary to me, though, as the need to understand the fundamental nature of literacy is so pressing and the sheer quantity of expository prose with which citizens must work is so large.

Despite the urgency of the need to understand the nature of comprehensible prose, readable writing is a highly complex matter. Although there has been much basic research, the processes of reading and writing are not yet fully understood. Partly, this is because they both require several different kinds of interaction between the writer and the reader. Neither process can be studied in isolation, and both must be studied within the context of shared cultural knowledge and expectations about texts. For this reason, studies of second language learners' responses to texts are pertinent, as are studies in contrastive rhetoric which reveal the impact of cultural and ethnic constraints on text. In the developing multicultural academic community and work force, the varied perceptions of readers and writers of different backgrounds contribute to an understanding of features of text that can enhance communication between readers and writers (DePalma, D'Souza).

The interwoven aspects of text processing meet in the text itself. In my research, my focus is on meaning: How do writers and readers come to a shared understanding in a text? Psycholinguistic evidence suggests that writers can write in specific ways to enhance their comprehensibility to readers by using two text features: psycholinguistic redundancy and cohesion. *Redundancy* is the necessary information overlap in a text that helps ensure that the writer's meaning reaches the reader. The overlap comes from specific linguistic features of the text and from the information readers bring to the text, including cultural knowledge and expectations about discourse. *Cohesion* is the feature of paragraphs and longer texts that makes them texts rather than disconnected sentences. Both redundancy and cohesion can be enhanced by writers, and there is evidence that doing so improves comprehension for readers (Chapman, Irwin, F. Smith *Understanding*).

One cautionary note is in order before the discussion begins. At the beginning of the work on this manuscript, an interesting problem developed. I was going to give a talk about my research and was creating overhead transparencies trying to describe the issues involved in readable writing: factors in readers like interest and motivation, factors in writers like having a clear point to make, and finally, factors in the text, the psycholinguistic issues to be addressed in this book. I wanted to create Venn diagrams, overlapping circles, to show that these factors were all interrelated and overlapped one another. But the computer software I was working with would not allow the circles to merge into each other.

The more I have thought about this problem, the more it has seemed to me to be a good metaphor for the difficulty in defining and describing readable writing. It never seems possible or preferable to set aside readers' concerns or writers' strategies. Thus, the software provides just the right metaphor, in that it precludes merging these issues visually and suggests the impossibility of dealing with the text as a disembodied product, dissociated from the people who produce it and those who are trying to understand it. On the other hand, literacy draws on numerous fields and highly complex issues, and factors in the text are reasonably accessible, tangible, and thus measurable in various ways.

For this reason, this book focuses on text factors primarily and exclusively, and, with the exception of some speculative consideration of personality factors in responses to text, treats readers and writers only insofar as they are reflected in the text itself. There are a number of different factors involved, and they do overlap. I intend to make a case for merging them in order to show that, insofar as these diverse factors merge in a text, text factors are central to readable writing. Moreover, they can be analyzed and separated into specifics that can be taught to and learned by anyone interested in producing or understanding a readable text.

In what follows, I begin with a thorough explication of the phrase *readable writing* and its relationship to a number of related concepts such as *readability* and *comprehension*. Once my terms have been set forth, I review the varied perspectives from which critical literacy must be studied: linguistics, including cohesion and functional-systemic grammar on which cohesion analysis is based; psychology, including our understanding of how people process text in both production and comprehension as well as the role of personality preferences in literacy; reading theory, including the nature of the process in mature readers and second language learners; and studies in rhetoric and composition, including investigations of the writing process and multicultural contrastive analyses of the structure of text.

I will then present research data and evidence from four studies demonstrating the central role that redundancy and cohesion play in reading and writing. Finally, I address the relevance of the findings for our theoretical understanding of the nature of reading and writing, and for the practical matter of developing and enhancing literacy in our current and future educational environment. Members of the academic community who work with students developing critical literacy, as well as others concerned with encouraging broader participation in higher education and in our increasingly diverse society, will profit from this wide-ranging inquiry into the nature of text.

Some further thoughts before the exploration begins. Topics like literacy, readability, discourse processing, and comprehension have been much studied. Any library search of books or educational documents will turn up dozens of references to these topics. The complexity of literacy is such that it requires considerable detailed study, almost like an artist who reworks the same subject repeatedly, using different media, approaching the work from different angles. Claude Monet, for instance, the French Impressionist, is well-known for having painted his famous water lilies many times. Monet attempted, over many paintings, to capture the qualities of the lilies, the water, the interaction of light, shadow, and reflections. Similarly, the role of the text itself in the nature of literacy warrants repeated examination from many angles.

My experience suggests an additional metaphor for the multidisciplinary nature of this exploration. Literacy is more like a puzzle consisting of many small pieces to be fitted together. While the number of pieces may be finite, it is still a very large number, and we lack a clear picture on the box which can sometimes be helpful to solution. As I worked on this manuscript, I also did jigsaw puzzles as a way of at once distracting myself from the rigors of book writing and thinking about the intricacy of literacy in a different and especially nonverbal context. *The Psycholinguistics of Readable Writing* begins, then, with an overall picture, albeit somewhat fuzzy, of readable writing and the text factors of which it is composed.

CHAPTER 1

Readable Writing

It's always good to start with humor. Here are two jokes that help illustrate the differing perspectives of readers and writers, in a somewhat different, though related realm than adult literacy: language acquisition. There is a stage of language acquisition in which children understand some features of jokes, but, at least in my daughter's case, are missing a key element. Consider these jokes, for example, particularly if you can't summon a polite laugh or mild smile:

> Why did the turtle cross the road?
>   To get to the shell station.
> Why did the hamburger go away from the bun?
>   Because it wanted to be on the tray.

The first riddle is funny in a way that the second one is not, and the humor in it has to do with the play on the meanings of turtle, shell, and a brand of gasoline—a play that is missing in the second riddle. When my 4-year-old made up the second riddle, she was in a stage of children's language development at which she had learned the proper format for riddles, but she had not yet developed an awareness of language as language, an ability to shift from her own perspective to that of another, and an appreciation of variation and play in meaning (deVilliers and deVilliers 171-2). This metalinguistic awareness comes somewhat later in language development.

VARIED PERSPECTIVES ON READABLE WRITING

Readers' and Writers' Perspectives

For students learning to write, the ability to write readable prose requires a similar ability to shift from the perspective of the writer to that of the reader. The interwoven and interlocking features of text require a merger of readers' and writers' perspectives. Some writing texts try to help students develop the ability to shift from writer to reader (Flower, Kiefer). Beginning writers, however, often are unable to make this shift, and may claim, for instance, that, if they state their point at the beginning of an essay, the reader will have no motivation to read the rest. Despite this claim, when students read essays in which the point is clearly stated at the outset, they judge the essays to be "good." Unlike children engaged in language acquisition, an internally motivated process largely immune to direct teaching, writers can be taught to shift from a writer's to a reader's perspective. Doing so can help writers understand the key factors that make writing readable.

Multicultural and Individual Perspectives

A further kind of understanding is needed by readers and writers to make a connection in readable writing, and this understanding is cross-cultural and incorporates an awareness of individual variation. The cross-cultural variables have to do with how members of different cultural backgrounds create and understand texts, and studies in contrastive rhetoric have contributed much to clarifying the diverse angles from which people might view text as readers or writers. The individual variables have to do with personality preferences that influence the shapes of the texts writers create and responses these texts evoke in readers. These issues have been studied especially carefully in the disciplines that bear on readable writing, and also play a role among the subjects in my studies and their responses to the passages I used. My research demonstrates that, while various cultural and individual constraints influence its shape, the two essential psycholinguistic features of *cohesion* and *redundancy* cross all cultural and individual boundaries in a way that permits a deep understanding and appreciation of readable writing.

Disciplinary Perspectives

Recently, much of the research published in the major professional journals that touch on literacy has concentrated on the need for readers and writers to be able to shift perspective, each to the view of the other, and to be able to cross cultural and psychological boundaries. Research in several academic disciplines has examined the issues with which I am concerned: linguistics, psychology, reading, and writing research all claim to have "good" writing as their central focus, though research questions are phrased differently depending on the discipline involved. In fact, none of these disciplines alone can address the nature of "good writing" or "readable text" or "comprehensibility" or "reader-writer-text-interaction," since a full understanding of readable writing requires cross-disciplinary, cross-cultural study. My argument hinges on this point, that given the complexity of readable writing, only a multifaceted examination can account for and explain its key characteristics.

Methodological Perspectives

Moreover, this examination must be specifically varied in terms of methodological approaches. The problem is somewhat akin to those blind people trying to describe an elephant: legs, trunk, tusks, and so forth do not give a full picture. Not only each discipline, but also each methodology, has something to contribute. Language analysis deals with the "stuff" of readable writing: the elements of language and their connections, bound as they are to what Halliday has called "context of situation" and cultural preferences for the presentation of ideas in text. These elements make some texts hard and others easy, exclusive of focus on production or comprehension. Psychological studies help with an understanding of how language is processed by readers, revealing the ways in which writers produce and readers understand, permitting a meeting in the text. Psychological approaches are also helpful in looking at the preferences and predispositions of writers generating readable writing and readers responding to it.

The disciplines more directly focused on reading and writing also offer alternative research strategies. Reading research has grappled with readability for years, and contributes models of reading in progress as done by both first and second language readers, and studies of the elements of text that are countable and measurable. These quantitative studies and counts tell us some but not the whole story. Writing research also looks at process, brings in prior knowledge and cultural constraints, particularly when the work in contrastive rhetoric of different cultures is included. Writing research also offers models of writing in progress, writers' personae, and what they may or must be doing in the course of generating a text.

Readable writing is best understood from all these perspectives, and taken together, these diverse approaches incorporate a range of methods of study, too. Some of the research to be discussed in the first few chapters of this book consists of formal experiments. Some of it consists of less formal studies of individual readers and writers under various conditions. Some of it involves studies of texts as texts, excluding the writers and readers on either side. Some of it is case studies of individual readers and writers. Again, each approach has something to offer to the understanding of readable writing. I will argue that only by using a comprehensive set of approaches, encompassing a wide range of methods, can we arrive at a full understanding of the nature of readable writing. I have used a variety of strategies in the research studies I will report in the second half of the book, both formal empirical studies that provide numerical results and statistical

analyses, as well as text-based studies, individualized methods, and case studies, and taken together, all of these provide evidence to support my proposals about the nature of readable writing.

DEFINING READABLE WRITING

The *readable writing* to which I have been referring can only be defined generally here. First, readable writing as I am discussing it pertains only to expository prose, not to literary forms. The research of scholars in the disciplines I have noted, and my own studies, indicate that this readable writing of nonfiction prose involves what has been called *readability* (countable, objective features of texts per se), *comprehensibility* (those qualitative characteristics of prose such as discourse conventions, reader aptitude, interest, motivation, and prior knowledge of the topic of the text), and *difficulty* (the relative ease of a particular text for a particular reader at a particular time). Drawing on all these concepts, my major thesis is that readers and writers meet in readable writing when the text itself incorporates the psycholinguistic features of cohesion and redundancy, the major characteristics that make possible the connection of reader expectation and writer intention. In the remaining portions of this chapter, I will define and describe the nature of cohesion and redundancy, to set the basic terms of my discussion.

COHESION IN READING

Cohesion, the first of the two key features of readable writing, plays a central role in reading as the process of getting meaning from print. Cohesion connects a string of sentences to form a text rather than a series of unrelated statements. *Cohesion in English*, Halliday and Hasan's seminal work, presents a detailed system for analyzing cohesive relationships in text. The unit of analysis for cohesion is the cohesive tie. One simple example of a cohesive tie is a pronoun and its antecedent. Pronoun/antecedent ties and other cohesive ties may occur within a single sentence, but also occur across sentences. These cohesive ties among sentences contribute most strongly to creating a text. Halliday and Hasan discuss five major types of cohesive ties that occur in text: reference, substitution, ellipsis, conjunction, and lexical cohesion (13). These are found in texts as

> particular features—repetitions, omissions, occurrences of certain words and constructions— which have in common the property of signalling that the interpretation of the passage in question depends on something else. If that "something else" is verbally explicit, then there is cohesion (13).

Cohesive elements can be words or sentence structures and may or may not be adjacent to one another in the text. Cohesive ties can be categorized and counted.

Studies on cohesion in reading show that it makes a substantial contribution to readable writing, and this is the reason cohesion studies are of interest (Irwin, "Cohesion" 38). Two studies make clear the relevance of cohesion to reading and comprehending. The findings suggest, first, that the perception of cohesive relations in text develops over time as students mature as readers. Moreover, a second study reveals that increasing the level of cohesion in text improves reading comprehension as measured by reading time and recall of content.

In the developmental study, readers show growth in their abilities to perceive cohesion in text and to use it to support comprehension as they get older. The study, done by British scholar L. John Chapman, involved 1,500 children between the ages of 8 and 15 (*Reading: From 5 to 11*). Chapman used a specialized version of the Cloze procedure (wherein a text is prepared with every nth word deleted, and readers fill in the resulting blanks) called the GAP technique. With GAP, only a few words are deleted, with selection determined by their key role in the major cohesive ties of the passage. The subjects in Chapman's research showed a clear developmental pattern: beginning readers were unable to fill in the blanks, mid-level readers could produce fill-ins somewhat acceptable in the passage, and fluent readers could fill in the blanks with the same words the author used or very close synonyms. Chapman concludes that readers develop an awareness of cohesion over time and make essential use of it to get meaning from print.

The second study shows how mature readers make use of cohesion in text, and shows that increasing the numbers of cohesive ties can improve readers' comprehension. In this study, Judith Irwin designed two versions of a passage differing in the number of cohesive ties, and then used reading time and recall as measures of comprehension (Irwin, "Effect"). In terms of both measures, the version with more cohesive ties produced significantly better comprehension. Cohesion plays a central role in reading, these studies suggest, so that, when writers increase the number of ties, readers will understand a text more fully and more easily.

COHESION, WRITING, AND COHERENCE

Studies on cohesion by scholars interested in writing are less clear on its virtues (Haswell). Some of the disagreement stems from diverse views of what cohesion is, and how it differs from *coherence*. Again, though much has been written on these topics, I want to give basic definitions here because of their relationship to my thesis that cohesion and redundancy are central to readable writing.

Coherence refers to the ways in which the parts of a piece of writing are linked together to form a whole. It is often confused with cohesion, but the difference is essentially one of scale. While cohesion pertains chiefly to links among sentences and within them, coherence is the broader characteristic of unity of the text as a whole. Both cohesion and redundancy contribute to coherence in texts.

These terms require some further explication. Reading scholars disagree less than writing scholars on the terminology, as indicated by Moe and Irwin in their discussion of "Cohesion, Coherence and Comprehension:"

> Cohesion is only one component of coherence. In addition to cohesion, at least one other factor must be present for a text to have coherence; that factor is organization. Other factors like situational consistency add coherence to text. . . .Cohesion exists within text and adds to the coherence of text. It may be useful to think of coherence as something the reader establishes—or hopes to establish—in the process of reading connected discourse. . .coherence is both a text related and a reader related phenomenon. (5)

Larson, who provides a fine summary of major studies on cohesion in composition research (66-72), agrees with this definition, and goes on to say that

> the determination of coherence is fundamentally an interpretation by a reader. It is part of a transaction between text and reader—between the reader's world and the writer's language. (72)

Coherence comes from cohesion and redundancy. Both come from the writer's language, cohesion specifically from the ties the writer builds in, while redundancy comes from both the writer's language and the "reader's world" in a particular linguistic and psycholinguistic sense.

Writing research on cohesion is still in a fairly basic stage, despite the number of studies that have appeared since Witte and Faigley's early research in this area. Larson's recent summary indicates disagreements over terminology and disparities in the findings of researchers. For example, Neuner found, like Witte and Faigley, that ties do not define good writing, but when he examined cohesive chains (sets of ties semantically related to one another), he found that good student writing has longer chains, more diverse vocabulary, and more mature word choices. Other research supports Neuner's findings (Yang). Haswell complains that writing research on cohesion is "a mess" (314) even though he intuitively supports the idea that cohesion is central to good writing. Diverse studies from different points of view will eventually illustrate the ways in which writers use cohesion as a tool to help readers link up with their text.

Reading research on cohesion, as discussed above, provides strong evidence of its key role in the process of getting meaning from print. In due course, writing research will be likely to support and show clearly the nature and role of cohesion in good writing. While this basic research in the composition area continues, the evidence from reading suggests that cohesion is one of two key factors contributing to readable writing. The second is psycholinguistic redundancy.

REDUNDANCY IN READING

The best definition and most careful exposition of the role of *redundancy* in reading comes from the work of Frank Smith. Smith says that redundancy consists of

> Information that is available from more than one source. In reading, [it] may be present in the visual information of print, in the orthography, the syntax, the meaning or in combinations of these sources. . . .Redundancy must always reflect non-visual information; prior knowledge on the part of the reader permits redundancy to be used. (*Understanding* 311)

Redundancy is the characteristic of written language that helps ensure that the reader gets the message, so it is another means by which readers and writers can connect in text. Redundancy has several complex features when considered together with cohesion. It resembles cohesion in that readers usually are not conscious of its presence and importance. However, it differs from cohesion in that some forms of it do not appear in a text but come from the reader's contribution to the meaning, drawn from prior knowledge of both the language and the substance of the text.

The nature of these redundant reader contributions is explained in the work of psychologists Ralph and Lyn Haber. They note that readers make use of three overlapping kinds of knowledge to tap the redundancy that makes reading possible (171-88). First is knowledge of visual input, including letter and word shapes and printing conventions. A second kind is knowledge of language rules, including letter co-occurrence and syntactic and semantic co-occurrence rules and restrictions. Finally, knowledge of the world incorporates experience with real-world events, as well as broader knowledge of text types and styles.

According to the Habers, all of this knowledge is mobilized in the process of getting meaning from print. Their research has looked carefully at the interaction of what readers see on the printed page and information they already have. Redundancy makes reading possible because it helps enhance our vision:

> With higher redundancy, greater amounts of text are perceptually accessible for processing. It is this relationship of redundancy to the size of the field of view that

> provides the mechanism by which expectancies operate in and facilitate the reading process (Haber and Haber 188).

While psycholinguistic studies show that our visual and memory capacities are limited, this research demonstrates that redundancy helps us overcome our physical and mental limitations in reading and comprehending text (F. Smith, *Understanding* 64-86).

Some of the evidence of the importance of redundancy in reading lies in common-sense experience. Language can be condensed substantially for a classified ad or telegram with little loss of meaning. Yet another example is the speed of reading novels or newspaper articles, compared to a text in theoretical physics, and the likely difference in levels of comprehension. In part, this difference is the result of the relative amounts of redundancy in these texts. Novels often are highly redundant, drawing heavily on readers' prior knowledge of human behavior as well as their general knowledge of language. The more readers know about a text, the less they have to look, and the less they have to see, as the Habers point out. Best-sellers, for most readers, are considerably more redundant than a theoretical physics text.

My empirical research supports this position as well. One of my studies demonstrated that increasing redundancy improves readers' comprehension of text, as measured by Cloze scores. I increased redundancy syntactically and semantically in three passages of text on different topics, but at approximately the same formula readability level and length. Increasing both syntactic and semantic redundancy significantly improved comprehensibility of two out of three passages. In the third passage, the increased redundancy made no significant difference to comprehensibility. Further studies showed that the third passage was anomalous in ways that precluded the impact of the increased redundancy (for details on the original study and its follow-up, as well as operational definitions, see Horning, "On Defining," and chapters 7 and 8 of this volume). This study and the rest of my research, discussed in detail in the second half of this book, provide an integrated examination of cohesion and redundancy; the findings support my contention that increasing redundancy improves the writing quality of a text insofar as it becomes easier for readers to understand.

REDUNDANCY IN WRITING

Several pieces of evidence in the research on writing make clear the importance of redundancy to good writing. Some of this evidence, like that from reading research, draws on common-sense advice. Writing texts generally advise students to begin by stating a clear thesis or point at the outset, then supporting this point with evidence in the body, and restating the point at the end. Such a structure creates the simplest form of redundancy, through repetition.

Other standard advice to writers suggests that they tie their explanation of an especially complex point to something in the reader's personal experience, creating redundancy between the text and the reader's nonvisual, experiential prior knowledge. In a way, I created this type of redundancy above when I mentioned reading experiences with novels and theoretical physics texts. When writers are advised to define specialized terms in their texts, they are creating a kind of semantic redundancy. These kinds of common-sense strategies for student writers are good examples of redundancy, and of the ways in which redundancy contributes to the coherence of a text, the ways its parts "hang together."

Additional evidence for the role of redundancy in writing comes from studies of writing quality. Some of this research, like the work on cohesion, is based on Halliday's analyses of language (Halliday). Barbara Couture, seeking a way to describe "good writing," discusses its "thematic unity" ("Systemic Network" 2: 68), which arises from the interaction of elements in the semantic system. In Halliday's scheme, meaning comes from three functions of language: the *ideational* (the argument or point of a text), the *interpersonal* (the relationship of writer and audience), and the *textual* function (the choices of language, including word choice, sentence structure, and so on). The thematic unity of a text derives from the "interdependent realizations of ideational, interpersonal and textual functions" (Couture, "Systemic Network" 2: 74). In part, Couture's view supports the concept of redundancy, which lies in the interaction of the point, audience, and language choices.

Yet another aspect of redundancy demonstrating its relationship to writing quality appears in William Vande Kopple's work on the functional sentence perspective. This work, as Vande Kopple makes clear, also draws on Halliday's theory of language. Vande Kopple looks at given-new structure in sentences and discourse. The given information taps redundancy, drawing on the readers' prior knowledge and on the development of the text. Vande Kopple has found in several studies that a given-new arrangement of information in substantial paragraphs produced "significantly more readable and memorable" (86) passages than those arranged in other ways. Findings from reading research already discussed are consistent with Vande Kopple's results.

Writing research, then, indicates the importance of redundancy to readable writing, and while the research discussed pertains to passages of a paragraph or more, redundancy also pertains to individual sentences and to relations between and among sentences, and in this way, redundancy and cohesion are more closely related than the discussion thus far might suggest. In fact, they are related in ways essential to the nature of good writing, because each contributes to the coherence at the center of a piece of good writing. Cohesion and redundancy are related to one another in various ways.

RELATING COHESION AND REDUNDANCY

First, cohesive ties support and enhance redundancy within the text. Where a pronoun refers back to a noun in a preceding sentence or sentences, information overlap or redundancy is created. Indeed, each cohesive tie contributes to the redundancy of the text as a whole. Referential ties of pronouns and antecedents are the simplest example. Ties of substitution, where synonyms are substituted for particular nouns, again provide more than one source for the same information. Similarly, lexical cohesion, achieved through repetition or the use of synonyms, presents the concept behind an idea more than once. Even ellipses, because readers are expected to fill in the missing information, contribute to the redundancy that derives from the reader's prior knowledge. Finally, conjunctions, the fifth category of cohesive tie, make explicit meaning relations in the text. These connections in meaning are a form of cohesion that contributes to readers' ability to receive the author's full message. Insofar as conjunctions help connect the writer's ideas, they enhance information overlap, and so derive from redundancy. The various forms of cohesion either provide tangible types of redundancy like repetition, or support the relations among ideas in the text, enhancing the readers' ability to get the major points.

Halliday and Hasan, writing about cohesion, mention the concept of *texture*, which distinguishes texts from nontexts. Texture consists of cohesion and two other features of text:

> One is textual structure that is internal to the sentence: the organization of the sentence and its parts in a way which relates it to its environment. The other is the "macrostructure" of the text, that establishes it as a text of a particular kind—conversation, narrative, lyric, commercial correspondence and so on. (Halliday and Hasan, *Cohesion* 324)

It should be clear that the first of these features is a kind of syntactic redundancy, and the second relates to the redundancy that comes from the readers' prior knowledge of types of texts, such as story grammars (F. Smith, *Understanding* 238) and other general information. It also should be clear that these concepts are remarkably similar and have overlapping elements. But they are not the same thing. Both elements are contributors to texts where writer and reader come together, that is, to readable writing.

PLAN OF THE BOOK

Thus far, I have set forth the main definitions of the terms that are central to my exploration. The two text factors, cohesion and redundancy, are the characteristics of text that allow readers and writers to understand one another. An understanding of these factors and their roles in text is fundamental to literacy, the most basic and essential need for students in postsecondary education in this and the next century. This book is primarily about literacy, about students' ability to read effectively and critically as it is related to their ability to write for themselves and others. And let there be no mistake: In the United States, we are experiencing a literacy crisis among vast portions of our citizens. Students' abilities to read and write derive from qualities of expository text; it is on these qualities that this book concentrates.

What follows immediately here is the overall context for the research I have done, situating it in the work of four academic disciplines that contribute to understanding literacy: linguistics, psychology, reading, and writing. Texts can be studied from the vantage point of each of these disciplines, and each has a contribution to make to the overall picture. These four anchoring points work like the corners of a jigsaw puzzle, locating the end points of the sides, framing a traditional, four-sided picture.

With the frame in place, the studies reported in Chapters 7-10 provide placement for the major pieces in the middle. The study mentioned above, in which I showed that increasing redundancy improves understanding of text, had generally consistent results such that in two of the three passages, increasing syntactic and semantic redundancy improved the Cloze scores. The results of this study are reported in Chapter 7. A further study of the original passages with redundancy enhanced showed that this anomalous passage was, in its original form, much less cohesive than either of the other two. It had substantially fewer cohesive ties. And there were other linguistic and psychological factors in this passage that precluded better Cloze scores with the enhancement of redundancy (see Chapter 8). In addition, I have examined cohesion's contribution to the passages and have explored the interaction of cohesion and redundancy. To get a picture of how readers respond to this interaction, I have looked at first-year college students' responses to the passages in an oral reading study (Chapter 9) and at professional reader-writers' responses to these texts (Chapter 10). The studies, moreover, employ a range of methodologies, because, as I have indicated, diverse approaches are crucial to the investigation of the complex phenomenon of readable writing.

As we begin to get a picture of readable writing, the findings overall suggest strongly that cohesion and redundancy are essential to the linkage between readers and writers in readable text. The pieces of the readable writing puzzle are intertwined in the ways I have begun to describe and have pictured in figure 1-1.

Cohesion pertains to specific relationships among and across elements in the text, and strong empirical evidence suggests that it contributes directly to readable writing. Redundancy plays a broader role, encompassing Halliday and Hasan's notion of texture and some reader factors because of the role of readers' prior knowledge. There is common-sense evidence to support the role of redundancy in reading as well as empirical support. By incorporating research in

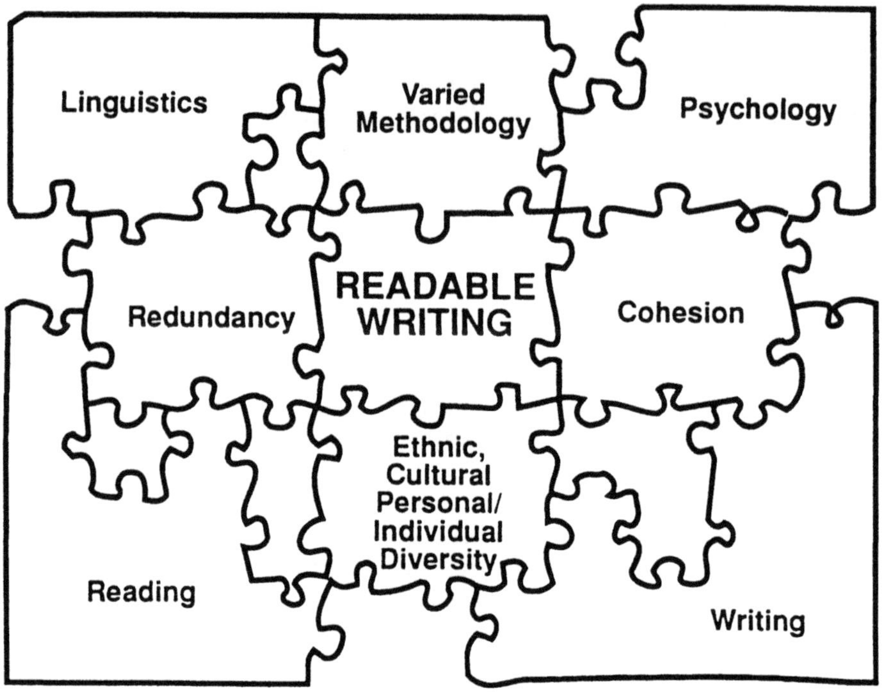

FIGURE 1-1

linguistics and psychology, as well as studies done in reading and writing, my findings, using varied methodologies and taking into account cross-cultural and individual variables, demonstrate the importance of cohesion and redundancy to readable writing that contributes to the critical literacy needed by all citizens.

CHAPTER 2

Relevant Research I: Linguistics

My research review begins with a book which appeared in its first edition in 1971. When I read the first edition of Frank Smith's *Understanding Reading*, I was a young graduate student interested in various aspects of applied linguistics. I had been teaching English as a second language and studying both theoretical and applied linguistics. As a pragmatically oriented person, I was much more interested in the applied areas than in theories of syntax, phonology, and semantics. But I was especially interested in reading, and Smith's work was to me a wonderful concatenation of linguistics, psychology, information theory, and practical matters.

My interest in cross-disciplinary work is quite pertinent to the studies to be discussed here, because the nature of readable writing requires much crossing of disciplines usually kept separate in an academic context. In my earliest work, I did not see the outlines of the puzzle I am assembling in this book, but I knew from the beginning of my studies that research in several areas was pertinent to my interests. The various disciplines discussed by Smith apply to the reading aspect of readable writing, and also to the writing aspect, at least to some degree. However, Smith does not deal with varied approaches to linguistic analysis, nor did he detail the writing theorists' strategies for analyzing meaning and evaluating the "quality" of a text in the early editions of *Understanding Reading*. These divergent approaches, while sometimes mutually hostile in an academic context, yield a thorough explanation of the nature of readable writing.

Initially, I was interested in Smith's discussion of redundancy, and in his claims that redundancy underlies the ability to read fluently despite our not being conscious of it. My first research study (as described briefly above and discussed in detail in Chapter 7) pursued the nature of redundancy, creating operational definitions of it in both syntactic and semantic terms and experimenting to see if increasing redundancy in texts improved readers' comprehension. The results of this research suggested the pertinence of redundancy, but raised many more questions. Some of these led me to my present focus on the text itself.

Actually, some of my results in that initial study were quite confusing to me and to others who examined my study. The more I have looked at readable writing, the more my work has come to resemble a jigsaw puzzle in a number of ways. It has become clear over time that the puzzle has four definite corners in academic disciplines containing research that bears on readable text: linguistics, psychology, reading, and writing. It seems to me that each of these corners has a number of pieces in it, each of which contributes to the picture. I don't have the picture on the puzzle box top to go by, and that raises the difficulty factor substantially; I am quite sure that while I have major sections of this puzzle, there are still missing pieces.

The pieces that go in the linguistics corner generally come from a view of human language ability different from the widely accepted model of transformational-generative grammar proposed by Noam Chomsky and more recent modifications of it. However, this differing approach is consistent with one point I am trying to make, that readable writing requires divergent approaches to understanding at any depth. Cohesion analysis, drawn mainly from the work of M.A.K. Halliday, clarifies qualities of text that facilitate the meeting of reader and writer.

THE LINGUISTICS CORNER

When I began looking closely at individual text factors, very nearly the first problem I ran into was the additional problem of complexity and a related problem, measurement. At issue is what to measure and how to measure it. Few linguistic studies involve experiments with subjects generating numerical data suitable for statistical analysis. Linguists are more likely to study individual sentences or sets of sentences generated by real speakers, and to propose theoretical explanations based on them concerning human language capabilities. Keeping the methodology issue in mind, I heard and began reading about work in linguistic theories other than the transformational-generative grammar in which I had been trained. As I learned more about text analysis, and looked at computer-based systems for analyzing texts, I heard more and more about cohesion as a factor in text, and a factor that contributed to readable writing. Thus, linguistic analysis from varied theoretical and methodological perspectives comprises a first corner in the puzzle of readable writing.

Although I was still strongly interested in redundancy, I began to have a sense that cohesion was relevant to the issues I was studying. Then I chanced upon another book, *Reading Development and Cohesion*, by L. John Chapman. I began Chapman's book the way I started every book on reading, checking the index for references to redundancy. To my pleasant surprise, I found discussion of redundancy, and reference to my own work as well as to Smith's. Finding that another scholar had combined these ideas in this way convinced me that cohesion was quite pertinent to my questions.

Ultimately, by this winding path, I came to read Halliday and Hasan's *Cohesion in English*. The analysis of cohesive ties, and my studies of the role of cohesion in readable writing, draw from this text and other work in the area known as systemic-functional linguistics, developed by Halliday. Halliday's work, like that of other linguists, consists of analyses focusing on text per se, without particular consideration for whether large numbers of speakers will generate a particular utterance. However, a chief advantage of Halliday's work is his analysis above the level of the sentence and his consideration of the context in which language occurs. I turned to Halliday's work, then, for this examination of discourse, which I needed to analyze the passages on which I was working. For Halliday, text analysis is a central focus (*Introduction* xvi), and for this reason, some theoretical background is pertinent to the following discussion.

HALLIDAY'S SYSTEMIC-FUNCTIONAL LINGUISTICS

M.A.K. Halliday is a British linguist whose work draws from that of J.R. Firth. Firth, also British, believed that language had centrally a social function, and that analysis of language had to include an examination of the social context in which it occurred. Firth has been described as the first British linguist, in the sense that he was the first person to hold an academic title in linguistics in Great Britain. R.H. Robins, discussing Firth's place in the history of the discipline, writes:

> Like American linguists, Firth drew on the work and thought of anthropologists, in his case particularly that of B. Malinowski, who . . . developed his theory of context of situation, whereby the meanings of utterances (taken as the primary data) and their component words and phrases, were referred to their various functions in the particular situational contexts in which they were used. (Robins 213)

Firth also made a specific connection between formal analysis of linguistic elements (sounds, meanings) and "context of situation," looking toward the analysis of meaning as being contingent on function (Robins 214). Firth's interests were strongly pursued by Halliday, leading to the work on cohesion which contributes to an understanding of readable writing.

Trying to summarize all of Halliday's theory is a massive task, but an overview of the major ideas will put the concept of cohesion in a theoretical context. Some of the challenge of this material results from the interwoven use of several sets of nested terms. Several key ideas are explained well in a recent volume:

> Grammatical systems were organized by Halliday in two ways, reflecting the degree and nature of their interdependence. Most basically they are organized by rank, with clause, group/phrase, and word acting as the points of origin of distinct networks of choice. . . .The second major organizing principle is metafunction. . . .Functional components in the grammar . . . reflect the more general metafunctions: ideational, interpersonal and textual. (Hasan and Martin 4-5)

These metafunctions are explained by Halliday when he says that the ideational metafunction is "reflective" and is used "to understand the environment," while the active or interpersonal metafunction is used "to act on the others" in the environment (Halliday, *Introduction* xiii). The textual metafunction is "a resource for ensuring that what is said is relevant and relates to its context" (Halliday and Hasan, *Language* 45).

For Halliday, then, language must always be considered within its context of situation. That context can be analyzed in terms of three components that relate to these metafunctions: *field*, "what is happening, . . .the nature of the social action that is taking place"; *tenor*, "who is taking part, . . .the nature of the participants, their statuses and roles"; and *mode*, "what part the language is playing, what it is that the participants are expecting the language to do for them in that situation. . .including channel (spoken or written. . .) and . . . rhetorical mode" (Halliday and Hasan, *Language* 12).

COHERENCE AND COHESION

Looking at the language mode, Halliday claims that all texts have coherence, by virtue of which they are perceived as a whole rather than as a string of unrelated sentences. Other scholars have expanded this idea, discussing various features of texts that unify them into wholes (see deBeaugrande 16-17, for example, the scholars mentioned in Chapter 1, and see Mosenthal and Tierney for a review of Halliday and Hasan's work on this point). Each text has its own internal context or coherence, which is essential to understanding it. One element contributing to this coherence is cohesion, an aspect of *texture* in texts, which Halliday and Hasan define as

> the set of linguistic resources that every language has (as part of the textual metafunction) for linking one part of a text to another. . . .: reference, substitution, ellipsis, conjunction and lexical cohesion. (Halliday and Hasan, *Language* 48-49)

Cohesion is not grammatical in nature and lies beyond the level of the sentence (Halliday, *Introduction* 288). But cohesion is only one element in Halliday's analysis of text or the language mode.

TEXTURE IN TEXTS: COHESION, SENTENCE STRUCTURE, DISCOURSE TYPE

All texts also have texture. This term has a special meaning within Halliday's systemic-functional linguistics. Texture in a text has three components, *cohesion*, *structure within sentences*, and *overall structure*. As Halliday and Hasan say, "Neither cohesion alone, nor internal textual structure alone, suffices to make of a set of sentences a text. Texture is a product of the interaction between the two" (*Cohesion* 326).

In addition to cohesion, the second element of texture is structure within sentences. This structure generally divides into two parts, *given* and *new*. The given part of the sentence is optional, so it may or may not appear. The given component expresses "what the speaker is presenting as information that is recoverable to the hearer from some source or other in the environment—the situation or the preceding text" (*Cohesion* 326). That is, given information is redundant. New information is quite different, since it must be present, and since it expresses "what the speaker is presenting as information that is not recoverable to the hearer from other sources" (*Cohesion* 326).

The given-new structure within sentences contributes to texture, and it should be clear that it provides a different view of the redundancy of text. Given information is, as noted, redundant syntactically and semantically, whereas new information may be redundant syntactically, but is not redundant semantically. The relationship of redundancy and cohesion will be addressed in greater detail in Chapters 3 and 6 below. From a linguistic point of view, in Halliday and Hasan's theory, the given-new structure lies within sentences, contributing to texture, whereas cohesion fosters connections across sentences.

Hasan defines the *structure of a text*, the third component of texture, as "the global structure of the message form" (Halliday and Hasan, *Language* 53) and goes on to give examples drawn from Japanese Kabuki plays and Greek drama. Narratives and sonnets provide other examples of structure (*Cohesion* 327). But she also says that ordinary conversation possesses a structure in this same generalized sense (Halliday and Hasan, *Language* 53-54). Structure is tied specifically to the context of the situation in which the text occurs, as analyzed by its field, tenor, and mode. Each of the genres has a structure. (From a psychological point of view, these structures are significant, since psychologists view them as part of a set of expectations needed for the interpretation of text called a schema. This concept will be discussed in Chapter 3.)

Cohesion, then, is one of the three factors contributing to the texture of a text, making it a coherent whole. But it is a very important factor, because it is available to analysis and can be altered specifically in a text to produce different effects. The relevance of cohesion to describing readable writing is explicated clearly by Halliday and Hasan:

> The analysis of cohesion, together with other aspects of texture, will not in general add anything new to the interpretation of a text. What it will do is to show why the text is interpreted in a certain way; including why it is ambiguous in interpretation wherever it is so. . . .(T)he analysis of cohesion will not tell you that this or that is a good text or a bad text or an effective or ineffective one in the context. But it will tell you something of WHY YOU THINK it is a good text or a bad text. . . (*Cohesion* 328)

Cohesion, though only one aspect of texture, helps explain why people respond as they do to a text, and helps evaluate text quality; for this reason, it must be explicated in detail. Each instance of cohesion in a text is called a cohesive tie, and ties are the basis of Halliday and Hasan's analytic system. In a simple form of cohesion, say a pronoun and its antecedent, the relationship between them is called a *cohesive tie*. The number of cohesive ties can be analyzed and counted in a passage of text, and doing so does help to account for some aspects of how readers respond to a text (see Chapters 8 and 9 for a discussion of the cohesion levels in the passages I have been studying).

TYPES OF COHESION

As noted in Chapter 1, there are five types of cohesive relationships in texts (*reference*, *substitution*, *ellipsis*, *conjunction*, and *lexical cohesion*); these are discussed in detail in Halliday and Hasan's *Cohesion in English*. Reference is the first of the five types of cohesion discussed—it is probably the one we think of most easily when thinking of the forms that cohesion might take in language. The simplest example of referential cohesion is a pronoun and its antecedent. In a text "John and Laurie did homework. Then they went outside to play." the word *they* refers back to John and Laurie in the first sentence. The connection of pronoun and antecedent creates cohesion between the two sentences in the text.

Reference actually occurs in two different kinds of settings in language: *exophoric reference*, where the reference is to the situation in which the language occurs, as distinct from *endophoric reference*, which is reference within the text. In endophoric reference, there are three types: *personal*, *demonstrative*, and *comparative* (*Cohesion* 31-37). Generally, pronouns are used for reference, either personal pronouns or demonstrative pronouns and adverbs, except in the case of comparative reference, where comparative adjectives or adverbs are usually used (*same*, *additional*, *identically*, *differently*, *equally*, and the like).

A second type of cohesion comes from substitution. Substitution is similar to reference in that both involve reference to the same thing, but the difference is that "substitution is a relation in the wording rather than in the meaning" (*Cohesion* 88). Halliday and Hasan say that

> A substitute is a sort of counter which is used in place of the repetition of a particular item. . . . [and] the substitute item has the same structural function as that for which it substitutes. . . . (T)he three types [are]: nominal, verbal and clausal. (*Cohesion* 89-90)

There are only a few substitutions possible: *one*, *ones*, and *same* work as nominal substitutes; *do* is the lone verbal substitute; and *so* and *not* function as substitutes at the clausal level (*Cohesion* 91).

Ellipsis, a third kind of cohesion, is also like substitution. Actually, Halliday and Hasan would readily agree, I think, that their distinctions among the different forms of cohesion are very fine ones and are sometimes hard to distinguish. However, for the purposes of actually analyzing text, the distinctions are useful. Ellipsis might be seen as a special kind of substitution, where the substitute is zero or nothing, but ellipsis is still a distinct form of cohesion:

> We are referring specifically to sentences, clauses, etc. whose structure is such as to presuppose some preceding item, which then serves as the source of the missing information. An elliptical item is one which, as it were, leaves specific structural slots to be filled from elsewhere. This is exactly the same as presupposition by substitution, except that in substitution an explicit 'counter' is used, eg: *one* or *do*, as a place-marker for what is presupposed, whereas in ellipsis nothing is inserted into the slot. (*Cohesion* 143)

Because ellipsis does not involve specific parts of speech, it is harder to give examples, but in a text like "Which hat will you wear? This is the best." the word *hat* is omitted from the second sentence, and deletion is an instance of ellipsis (*Cohesion* 149).

The fourth of the five types of cohesion in text is conjunction. Conjunction is especially useful in discourse, because most cohesive conjunctions help to relate various parts. Conjunction is usually achieved through the use of conjunctive adverbs (including simple coordinating conjunctions like *and*, *but*, *then*, *next*, -ly forms like *subsequently*, compound adverbs like *nevertheless*, and prepositional phrases like *in addition* and *in spite of*). Halliday and Hasan sort the conjunctive relations into four major categories: *additive*, *adversative*, *causal*, and *temporal*, and then add *intonation* as a kind of conjunction for spoken language (*Cohesion* 242-273).

Conjunction is somewhat different from the other kinds of cohesion. As Halliday and Hasan say:

> Conjunction . . . is not simply an anaphoric relation. Conjunctive elements are cohesive not in themselves but indirectly, by virtue of their specific meanings; they are not primarily devices for reaching out into the preceding (or following) text, but they express certain meanings which presuppose the presence of other components in the discourse. (*Cohesion* 226)

While conjunction is somewhat different from the first three kinds of cohesion, it is a distinct form, and one to which readers and writers must attend closely. Also, conjunction is one particular way of easily enhancing the cohesion of a text, and is part of some fairly common advice given to writers.

The fifth and final type of cohesion analyzed by Halliday and Hasan is lexical cohesion. Lexical cohesion is quite complex, because it centers on word choice. This kind of cohesion can be achieved in a number of different ways, including repetition of the same word, use of synonyms, use of a superordinate term (like using *animal* in place of *dog*), or more generally through the use of general nouns (like *people*, *thing*, *matter* or *place*). In addition, lexical cohesion is sometimes achieved through collocation, the tendency of a group of words to occur together. As an example of collocation, Halliday and Hasan quote a lengthy passage from John Muir on Yosemite, and list a set of collocational cohesive words: *mountaineering*, *peaks*, *climb*, *ridge*, *ride*, *travel* (*Cohesion* 274-287). Lexical cohesion has much to do with the vocabulary of a text, and makes a contribution to the overall cohesion of a passage.

ANALYZING COHESION: COHESIVE HARMONY

The various forms of cohesion are taken together and analyzed in a specific strategy for text analysis proposed by Ruqaiya Hasan, called *cohesive harmony*. Cohesive harmony calls for study of the cohesive ties in a text and produces a measure of the overall coherence. Although it has some subjective components that weaken its quality, cohesive harmony analysis yields an appraisal of some qualities of a text that contribute to my analyses of the passages I have been studying.

There are three parts to a cohesive harmony analysis. This analysis consists of both a study of the content words and other words that establish cohesion in a text (like pronouns and conjunctions), and a study of the relationships among groups of these key words, called *tokens* in the analysis. The analysis itself, even on a short passage, is quite complex (a detailed example appears in Halliday and Hasan's *Language, Context and Text* 89-94).

Generally, cohesive harmony analysis has several steps, involving a careful look at the cohesive ties that appear in a text. The first step is to produce a lexical rendering of the text, which is simply a listing of content words. From this lexical rendering, lists or chains of related words (*tokens*) are grouped together into one of two kinds of chains: *identity* chains and *similarity* chains. For an identity chain, "every member of the chain refers to the same thing, event, or whatever. . ." (Halliday and Hasan, *Language* 84), while in similarity chains, items "refer to non-identical members of the same class of things, events, etc., or to members of non-identical but related classes of things, events, etc." (Halliday and Hasan, *Language* 84). The measurement of cohesive harmony is obtained in part by calculating the total number of tokens involved in cohesive chains.

The second step in the analysis is to examine the chain interaction in the text. *Chain interaction* deals with the ways in which the main ideas are related to each other grammatically in the passage, and is defined operationally by Hasan:

> A minimum requirement for chain interaction is that at least two members of one chain should stand in the same relation to two members of another chain. . . .The relations that lead to chain interaction are the very ones that exist between the constituents of a clause or of a group, for example, does, doing; sayer, saying; doing, done-to. . . . (Halliday and Hasan, *Language* 91)

Unfortunately, in the work published thus far, Halliday and Hasan do not give a complete explication of these rather subjective categories of chain interaction. As a result, a full analysis of cohesive harmony is not possible without making highly subjective judgements concerning the relationships among elements in chains.

Several concepts contribute to the next component of cohesive harmony:

> 1. *Relevant tokens*: All tokens that enter into identity or similarity chains; these divide into: (a)*central tokens*: those relevant tokens that interact; (b)*noncentral tokens*: those relevant tokens that do not interact;
> 2. *Peripheral tokens*: All those tokens that do not enter into any kind of chain. . . . (Halliday and Hasan, *Language* 93)

Finally, using these various categories, several calculations can be made. The first is the one described above, which provides a measure of the number of tokens in chains as opposed to those not involved in some chain. The more tokens involved in chains, the more coherent the text. Second, the more central tokens there are, the more coherent the text. And finally, the more interaction there is among the chains, the more coherent the text. All three elements give a picture of the overall cohesive harmony of the text (Halliday and Hasan, *Language* 93-94). Despite the subjective nature of chain interaction, the rest of the analysis *is* useful, as will be shown in the analysis of the passages provided in Chapter 8.

Cohesive harmony, and the analysis of cohesive ties in text that underlies it, taken together give a good understanding of how the ideas in a text are presented and related to each other. This helps to account for why readers find some texts more readable than others, and why, as I hope to show below, I got very different results from treating three passages in very similar ways. In any case, this kind of analysis, detailed and exhaustive though it seems, is not the whole story. It only places some pieces in the linguistics corner of the jigsaw puzzle of readable writing. Some other pertinent linguistic work will provide support for propositional analysis, to be discussed in the next chapter.

REVIEW AND PREVIEW

The discussion thus far has been an examination of the major theoretical points of systemic-functional grammar that pertain to reading and writing and the analysis of text factors in those processes. Cohesion and analytical approaches to it relate to several of the strategies for text analysis used by reading and writing researchers, and these are approaches I have applied to the passages I have been studying. These analyses of cohesion in the text itself focus both on the language elements and also on the context in which the language occurs, given Halliday's discussion of the relevance of field, tenor, and mode of discourse. Because of the pertinence of context of situation and language elements, findings across languages, particularly from second language acquisition, and across individuals, contribute to the understanding and appreciation of what constitutes readable writing. Moreover, cohesion-related studies support varied methods of investigating the nature of readable writing. Ultimately, the diversities yield an understanding of the role of the text itself in literacy and the contributions of readers and writers to readable texts.

However, before we can examine the passages, the other three corners of the puzzle, psychology, reading theory, and writing theory, which provide background, need to be explored. Much work that is pertinent to text factors has been done from a psychological perspective, where researchers have been studying text processing. We turn to the psychological research on text processing and analysis, mental representations of meaning, schema theory, personality preferences in text, and to redundancy as a psychological and linguistic phenomenon, in the next chapter. Each of these pieces in the psychology corner contribute to the picture of the nature of readable text.

CHAPTER 3

Relevant Research II: Psychology and Psycholinguistics

As I have said, my first study on redundancy raised a great many more questions than it answered. I was curious to know why my results had turned out as they had. It seemed to me, and to others who reviewed what I had done, that, since I had treated three passages of text identically by enhancing redundancy, a factor known to improve readers' understanding, the results should have reflected this enhancement consistently, and yet they did not. Thus, I had some pieces for the readable-writing puzzle, but I also had many more that seemed like they should fit somewhere but did not. Often, in solving a jigsaw puzzle, pieces that seem as though they should go in one place really belong someplace else; I turned to the psychological research to see if I could find a more appropriate place to put some of the pieces I had.

As noted above, one of my questions concerned what to measure and how to measure it, and in addition to my explorations of linguistic theories that might help to account for how text is arranged, I was also in need of a means to analyze content and in need of research that examined redundancy. Where I found help on these matters was in psycholinguistic research on text and the human mind. Although some research that bears on the things I am interested in has been done by reading researchers (to be discussed in Chapter 4), and some in discourse analysis and/or writing research (to be covered in Chapter 5), it is chiefly in the psycholinguistic research that I found what I needed.

The psycholinguistic research provided useful understanding of the components of readable writing through application of several alternative research methods, and a theory and an instrument through which to understand and appreciate individual variation. The psycholinguistic studies yield insights into the nature of text and how meaning can be analyzed and represented through psycholinguistic analysis of text processing and propositional analyses of content; in the studies from the information processing perspective, psycholinguists have developed the concept of redundancy that underlies a substantial portion of my work; and other work on personality gives a framework for considering how writers and readers exchange meaning in text, based on personality preferences analyzed by the Myers-Briggs Type Indicator. Psycholinguistic research also offers an array of methods: Some of the work has focused exclusively on text itself, and some of it is specifically experimental in nature. Again, the diversity of approaches is important to addressing the complexity of readable writing. The psycholinguistic corner of the puzzle, then, incorporates varied methodologies and helps reveal how the psychological characteristics of readers and writers interlock with the linguistic features of text to produce readable writing.

PSYCHOLINGUISTIC RESEARCH ON TEXT PROCESSING

Psycholinguistics is an odd sort of field. It is a cross-disciplinary area where the shared territory is not exactly solid ground for either. Michael Tanenhaus supports this view in his overview of the field and historical analysis of the development of psycholinguistics (Tanenhaus 1). His historical perspective helps to clarify why psycholinguistic findings are pertinent to the questions I am studying. Tanenhaus points out that, by the mid-1970s, psycholinguistics had largely given up research on sentence processing because of the lack of support for a transformational-generative model of language. Attention turned to meaning and to "higher level processes such as the comprehension and memory of discourse or text" (11). In conjunction with this focus, propositional models of text were developed by cognitive psychologists (12). In addition, discourse studies led researchers to look at anaphora (pronouns and antecedents) and uses of inference in the interpretation of text, and relied to some degree on the work of Halliday and Hasan, which I have already discussed in Chapter 2 (Tanenhaus 12).

Psycholinguistics developed numerous approaches to the problem of representing meaning in memory. The issue of the organization of meaning or knowledge is quite complex, and psycholinguists don't even agree on what the competing theories are. For instance, a first proposal suggests that there are two systems that we use, a verbal one and an image one.

> The imaginal system is specialized for the encoding, storage and retrieval of nonverbal information that is sensory or spatial in nature. . . .The verbal system is specialized for the processing of information that is linguistic and nonspatial in nature. (Donahoe and Wessells 483)

The two systems function separately, perhaps in the two hemispheres of the brain, but are related. There is some evidence supporting this approach, particularly in research on hemispheric specialization. But a number of questions have been raised about constructing images as distinct from storing them, and these have not been resolved (Donahoe and Wessells 484-85).

A second view is that memory is active and constructive, drawing heavily on prior knowledge. In this view, information is stored in an abstract form separate from its linguistic representation (Donahoe and Wessells 486f.). A third alternative suggests that sentences are stored as sets of procedures, seeking answers if the sentence is a question, or appraising truth value if the sentence is a statement (Foss and Hakes 149-50).

PROPOSITIONAL ANALYSIS OF TEXTS

The fourth alternative analysis of memory, which has been the one most useful in my research, is a view I will call *propositional/schema* theory. In this view, knowledge or meaning is encoded in memory as a series of propositions.

> Each proposition is made up of word concepts, which are also abstract, and which are different, in a variety of ways, from words. A word concept in a proposition may appear in a real sentence as a word or a phrase. The word concepts may serve one or two functions within the proposition: they may be predicator/relational terms (often verbs), or they may be arguments. (Horning, "Propositional Analysis" 50)

Propositional analysis is a system used to analyze the main idea content of a passage, and is helpful for psycholinguistic research in comprehension and recall.

Propositional analysis has linguistic support for centering its sentence-level focus on verbs as predicators in several recently proposed models of human language ability. These analyses of language are some of the large number of competing transformational, posttransformational, and nontransformational proposals. One interesting feature of a number of these proposals, however, is their general agreement that verbs are quite central to language. This observation is supported by a review of government-binding theory, generalized phrase structure grammar, and lexical-functional grammar (Wasow 203), and by another alternative proposal, Peter Binkert's theory of residential grammar (Binkert, *Cognitive Basis* 73). The consensus among these alternatives about the importance of verbs provides good support for the different view of analyzing content in text offered by propositional analysis and proposed by psychologists and researchers in psycholinguistics (Kintsch; Kieras, "Good and Bad Structure").

Perhaps because the propositional analysis system has been worked out fairly specifically and stays close to the actual sentences of the passage, it has attracted a lot of attention and has been used extensively in research (Bovair and Kieras; Turner and Greene; Kintsch). Propositional analysis provides a method of studying the meaning of a text initially at the sentence level, but in this approach, text meaning can also be studied at the discourse level. Moreover, because psycholinguists have used this system, not only to approach discourse level analysis, but also to look at text-reader interaction, it is particularly helpful to understanding readable writing.

At the discourse level of analysis, a second level of propositional analysis, the propositions form an ordered list in which they are categorized as subordinate or superordinate, and some propositions are embedded in others. The whole ordered list of propositions for a passage is called its *text base*, and the text base is particularly useful for analytic purposes. The text base reveals the macrostructure or overall outline of the passage, and can be tested for coherence among other things.

The third level of analysis of meaning in this system addresses text-reader interaction. Here, the system looks specifically at written text read by a reader, and again, this is why this approach to the representation of meaning in memory has particular value for my research questions. The focus here is: How do the text and the reader interact? Schema theory provides the answer.

The text base derived from propositional analysis can be organized in terms of a *schema*, which is defined as

> a representation of a situation or of an event; it is a prototype or norm and specifies the usual sequence of events that is to be expected. Just like other concepts, schemata are fuzzy and imprecise. (Kintsch "Comprehension" 78)

Kintsch and other propositional researchers give several examples of schemata: a birthday party schema suggests such substantive elements as presents, guests, balloons, and so forth; a restaurant schema involves seating, ordering, service, payment, and the like; and a psychological research article typically has formal elements, which include, predictably, an introduction, review of the literature, methods, results, and discussion. The schema is proposed as a set of substantive and/or formal expectations the reader brings to any reading task, and fills in with the particular propositions provided by the text. This concept is closely related to the proposals about texture of texts given by Halliday and Hasan, as described in Chapter 2.

Research findings using propositional analysis provide support for this model for the meaning of a text. Walter Kintsch's empirical findings, for instance, suggest that more propositions make a passage harder to read and recall (as measured by reading time and numbers of propositions recalled). Also, the kinds of propositions, subordinate as opposed to superordinate, also have an impact on difficulty, with superordinate propositions being recalled more easily (Kintsch 150). These findings are based on experiments in which the length of the passages was controlled and the reading time was either controlled or measured carefully. Thus, propositional analysis provides a model of text analysis for which there is some empirical verification.

Kintsch has done additional work that supports the claim that readers construct a text base that gives some measure of their comprehension, and the coherence of the text base affects readers' ability to do this. In examining the nature of different texts in terms of readers' comprehension and learning, Kintsch found that more coherent texts allow readers to comprehend better (as measured by their recall of the text). According to Kintsch, coherence consists of the numbers of shared arguments and connections among sentences in the text. These would presumably be indicated in part with cohesive devices of the kind under study here. Comparing texts with differing levels of coherence thus defined, Kintsch found empirical support for a common-sense notion that recall was much stronger in more coherent texts (Kintsch, "Learning From Text" 100). A propositionally based analysis of reading recall shows that cohesion and other elements of coherence have an impact on readable text. These findings draw on, and are consistent with, the linguistic analysis proposed by Halliday, as reviewed in Chapter 2; I will present a propositional analysis of the passages I have studied in Chapter 8.

CONNECTING PROPOSITIONAL ANALYSIS TO COHESION

The relevance of cohesion to comprehension is also supported by research that has used the propositional system to look at the specific impact of cohesion. Judith Irwin's 1980 report on an empirical study of the effect of cohesion on comprehension makes clear that adding cohesion to a text improves comprehension as measured by reading time and propositions recalled (Irwin, "Effect" 325). Irwin looked at both reading time and content recall, using propositional analysis of the text and of the readers' recalls. On both measures, she obtained statistically significant results showing that adding cohesive ties helped readers read more quickly and recall more (Irwin, "Effect" 331). Irwin's work provides additional empirical confirmation for the theoretical claims of the linguists and psycholinguists.

An early piece of research that focuses specifically on writing conventions, using propositions as a basis of the study, reveals one aspect of the writer's contribution to a readable text. Kieras compared paragraphs in which a conventional structure of a topic sentence followed by cohesive supporting sentences was followed by paragraphs lacking this predictable pattern (Kieras, "Good and Bad Structure" 13-28). He found, by measuring readers' notion of the topic of the paragraph, their reading times, and their recall, that unconventional paragraph structure made for much more difficult reading. Readers' topic responses and recalls were analyzed using propositional analysis, and this sort of data gives one indication of why this system of analysis has been so widely used. It helps to provide insights into several aspects of readable text, and will be useful to the examination of features of the passages to be presented in Chapter 8.

The research done on propositions and schemata gives a workable approach to text analysis, and while the propositions are subject to a technical and specific analysis, the analysis of schemata is less precise. Despite the lack of precision, readers and writers bring to a text their preconceived ideas about the topic, their interest level, and so forth, and notion of a schema captures these issues. Thus, psycholinguistic research on memory and the shape of meaning offers a strategy for text analysis that permits further exploration of the nature of readable writing. In addition, the evidence psycholinguists provide comes from both empirical and text-based studies. Next we can turn to other psycholinguistic research that focuses on one of the two features of readable writing, redundancy.

PSYCHOLINGUISTIC RESEARCH ON THE ROLE OF REDUNDANCY

Propositional analysis taps some features of readers' and writers' encounters in text that also pertain to redundancy. Propositional analysis may make possible a clear picture of when writers repeat ideas or key word concepts, as defined by the theory. At the level of discourse, propositional analysis addresses a different aspect of redundancy, as it analyzes readers' prior knowledge as represented by a schema. A detailed psycholinguistic description of redundancy comes from research based on information processing. The concept of redundancy derives from information theory, an area related to psycholinguistics and also to theoretical analyses of communication. The relevance of redundancy to readable writing became clear to me when I began reading Frank Smith's work.

Smith defines *redundancy*, as I noted in Chapter 1, most simply as

> information that is available from more than one source. In reading, [it] may be present in the visual information of print, in the orthography, the syntax, the meaning, or in combinations of these sources. (Smith 311)

The simplest kind of redundancy comes from repetition, but as Smith points out, redundancy is not usually so obvious or simple. The letters, word order, and presentation of examples, and so forth, are all more subtle forms of redundancy. In addition, some redundancy is created by the reader's prior knowledge of the text. The more redundancy there is, the quicker and easier the reading of it, since

> the reader makes use of nonvisual information, using something that is already known to eliminate some alternatives and thus reduce the amount of visual information that is required. Redundancy represents information you do not need because you have it already. (Smith 58)

The less visual information needed, the faster reading becomes, and the easier it is.

A straightforward example of this phenomenon has to do with most people's everyday reading experiences. All of us read the newspaper fairly rapidly, since it draws heavily on our knowledge of the previous day's events. It takes longer to read the paper when there is a major news event concerning matters about which we do not have as much prior knowledge. A similar situation occurs if we compare our reading speed and comprehension in a new subject, say, at the beginning of a college course, compared to our speed and comprehension at the end of the term. Usually, if we have understood the course material, the reading is much more efficient (i.e., faster and with better comprehension) by the end of the term. Perhaps redundancy accounts for why college students frequently read text material following a lecture on the topic rather than beforehand. Once they have had the lecture, the reading may become somewhat redundant. Finally, think about the difference between reading a best seller and reading a text on theoretical physics, as discussed in Chapter 1. For most people, the best seller will be considerably more redundant.

REDUNDANCY AND PRIOR KNOWLEDGE

The role of the redundancy created by the reader's prior knowledge has been explored in some detail by Smith and also by other researchers. Clearly, part of people's prior knowledge may include their preference for certain kinds of texts. In addition, though, there is an nice fit between the information available from the source (written text in this case) and what readers already know. H.J. Hsia calls this *input-memory* redundancy:

> IMR is neither the redundancy among various kinds of information stored in the memory, nor the redundancy between memory and external information, which is infinite; IMR is simply the redundancy between input and memory. . . .High IMR . . . decreases the difficulty and increases the comprehensibility of a communication. (Hsia 73)

While Hsia does not report empirical research to support the importance of the concept or its relationship to reading, a study by Janice Keenan shows the complexity of the relationship between the printed page and readers' prior knowledge. Keenan and her colleagues designed a study of reading time for two-sentence paragraphs in which the two sentences were referentially coherent but differed in their degree of causal relatedness. The findings reveal that readers attempt to make sense of the text based on their own knowledge of relationships of ideas, that is, Hsia's input-memory redundancy (Keenan et al. 115-126). Prior knowledge from memory contributes to redundancy beyond the sentence-level redundancy I defined, and the discourse level redundancy that is enhanced through the use of cohesion. It enhances a reader's ability to get meaning from print. My studies suggest that the various types of redundancy play a central role in reading and comprehending.

PSYCHOLOGISTS' VIEW OF REDUNDANCY

Some support for redundancy viewed from a slightly different angle appears in the work of Haber and Haber. The Habers review a substantial body of psychological research that taps several categories of redundancy and their interaction:

> We have sorted redundancies into categories of: (a)those available from the visual input; (b)those based on the reader's language system, independent of the text; and (c)those pertaining to experience, or to world knowledge. These redundancies, of course, interact. The reader not only sees the text, but uses his [sic] linguistic and experiential knowledge at each instant in processing. Visual features and these other knowledges combine to limit the possible alternatives, thus increasing predictability down the line. (Haber and Haber 183)

Their review of various studies of reader knowledge of redundancy and use of it in reading shows that

> a growing body of experimental literature demonstrates that readers know and use a number of the redundancies we have described, ranging from redundancies based on visual features on the printed page to those based on knowledge—both linguistic and experiential—in the reader's head independent of the text at hand. (Haber and Haber 188)

Exactly how redundancy helps in reading is also discussed by the Habers. They note that normal readers can see, not only the letters or the word they are focused on at any particular moment, but also some surrounding letters or words. How much more text the reader can perceive is a function of the redundancy: More redundancy allows readers to perceive a wider span of the text in each reading fixation (Haber and Haber 194-5). A further point is that this widened viewing area creates "successive overlap" (196) in what the reader sees, so that each patch of text is actually available for viewing more than once, either peripherally or when looked at directly. Thus, readers can process more text more efficiently if there is redundancy.

A full understanding of the types of redundancy and their impact on the physical act of reading shows how redundancy helps readers:

> knowledge of the structure of the language, of the spelling conventions, of the individual letter features, and of the topic being read all have direct perceptual implications for the reading process. Redundancies improve effective acuity; they enlarge the effective field of view; they create successive overlap: all of which are direct aids in extracting meaning from text. (Haber and Haber 198)

The Habers's work shows that redundancy is an essential aid to reading, needed to allow readers to get meaning. However, redundancy is subtle, and generally speaking readers are not aware of it or of their use of it. I will give operational definitions of the syntactic and semantic redundancy I used in the passages I studied in Chapter 7. My research demonstrates that specific types of redundancy can be made conscious for readers and for writers, that redundancy interacts with cohesion, and that the two factors together play a central role in the nature of readable text. The psycholinguistic findings considered thus far, then, contribute a specific approach to the analysis of content and a detailed examination of the nature of redundancy and its function in readable writing. Psycholinguistics has an additional contribution to make to the puzzle of readable writing, in recent analyses of personality preferences as they affect literacy.

PERSONALITY TYPE AND TEXT PROCESSING

In addition to the study of technical features of text discussed thus far, there are a number of other personal, individual factors that play a part in composing and comprehending. Most of these, like interest, motivation, fatigue, distractions, and such, prove extremely difficult to analyze, measure, or in some cases, even define. Recently, however, some new research has been published on personality and writing that sheds light on the more individualized aspects of readable writing. This analysis of personality derives from the work of Carl Jung; it looks at writers' preferences for producing certain kinds of texts. The concept of preferences in writing, and its expansion to readers and their reactions to texts, adds some key pieces to the puzzle of readable writing.

Jung's theory has provided the basis for a psychological instrument called the *Myers-Briggs Type Indicator* (hereafter MBTI). The MBTI consists of short multiple-choice questions that ask for preferences on activities, or responses to pairs of words. The profile from the instrument is presented in terms of four areas of behavior and response to the world: where people focus their attention, how they acquire information, how they make decisions, and how they orient themselves to the outer world (Myers 5-6). The Type Indicator offers a way of looking at why writers choose to present information in certain ways, and, perhaps by extrapolation, why some texts are more accessible for some readers and less accessible for others. Personality preferences interlock with propositional/schema theory and with the concept of redundancy, which we will consider below, and play a role in the responses of readers to the passages, as discussed in Chapters 9 and 10. Among the positive features of the MBTI are that it presents preferences as strengths, so that interpretations of an individual's type stress positive capabilities; moreover, a person's preferences are apparently unrelated to culture or ethnicity.

The notion of preference is easy to understand, and is basic to the ideas of the MBTI. Handedness is an easy example of preference: Most people prefer to use one hand rather than the other, although most can do the same task (not necessarily equally well) with either hand (Myers 4). As with handedness, each end of these bipolar dimensions has its own virtues and gifts. The MBTI is thus an assessment of potential strengths, not of pathology. In an analysis of personality preference, one kind of preference has to do with where people prefer to focus their attention, internally on their inner world, or externally, on other people, things, and the world around them. This yields the first of four results from the MBTI, a letter representing *introversion* (I) or *extraversion* (E).

A second result from the MBTI reveals how people prefer to acquire information. If one's chief preference is for obtaining information through the senses, this translates into a preference for here-and-now, practical, realistic information gathering. The opposite preference on this scale is to look at connections in a 'big picture' framework. Information is gathered with an eye toward the future, centering on inspiration and imagination. The preference for sense-based information gives a *sensing* (S) result on the indicator, while a preference for intuitive possibility gives an *intuitive* (N) result (Myers 5).

The third area explored by the MBTI relates to decision- making preferences. Using the information gathered by either sensing or intuitive strategies, people make decisions generally in one of two ways. The first of these is by logical, objective reasoning, and analysis. A second strategy is to make decisions based on person-centered responses that hinge on caring and personal investment. A preference for logical analysis gives a *thinking* (T) preference on the MBTI, while a preference for person-centered decisions gives a *feeling* (F) preference (Myers 6).

The final area of preference has to do with how people deal with the outer world. One preference is for structure, organization, and a planned way of life. People at this end of this continuum are easily able to move toward closure, and tend to like finite endings. The opposite preference on this dimension is for more spontaneity, for an adaptable approach that makes use of available possibilities at any moment. The preference for order and closure produces a *judging* (J) result on the MBTI, whereas the more spontaneous point of view produces a *perceiving* (P) result (Myers 6).

The analysis of personality preferences is somewhat more complex than this description of the Type Indicator suggests. First, beyond the results of the MBTI on the four dimensions, each type has a dominant process, a reflection of an individual's most often used and most highly developed preference. The concept of dominant process is quite complex and not well understood in terms of how it might affect readers and writers in readable writing. In addition to the role of dominant process in understanding individual preferences, several researchers have looked at the influence of personality type on learning styles and at the role of type in management, mating, and other areas (Kroeger and Thuesen; Keirsey and Bates; Lawrence; Lowen). These are also complex areas of investigation. I will, for the most part, confine my discussion to the four dimensions here. It appears that temperament, an analysis of the interactions of certain dimensions, may contribute to our understanding of people's responses to text. For this reason, I will speculate about the implications of temperament as discussed by Keirsey and Bates for responses to texts in the case studies reported in Chapter 10.

PREFERENCES, READING, AND WRITING

The results of the MBTI are given as a four letter code, indicating a person's preference in each of these four areas: ENFP, INTJ, ESTJ, and so forth, producing a total of 16 possible combinations. These preferences have an impact on learning processes generally (Keirsey and Bates 121-128), and on language learning in particular, as second language acquisition research has acknowledged (H. Brown, *Principles* 110-114). With regard to written language, a writer's production of text and a reader's reception of it will be influenced by the natural preferences of each.

Introverts and extroverts approach writing differently, as pointed out by Jensen and DiTiberio (the following discussion summarizes Appendix 3 of *Personality and the Teaching of Composition*). Introverts tend to follow many writing process texts' recommendations, generally writing by prewriting, writing, and rewriting. They plan ahead, outlining before writing, typically work alone and pause a lot at the start of a writing task until the overall direction is clear. They write best about ideas, but usually leave out examples drawn from their own experience, and may get bored with writing because they have planned ahead in great detail. An extroverted reader of the manuscript of this book, for instance, complained that I, a strong introvert, did not give enough examples that he could relate to, a complaint that arises from differences in our preferences.

Extroverts, in contrast, like to talk before they write or to have some real experience to go on. They do little advance planning and tend to write very quickly, as their ideas develop as they write. Outlining works best for them after rather than before writing, and revision for extroverts is most successful if they can talk to readers before they attempt to revise. They write best about experience, though it may be a superficial account if they don't have enough real contact with an audience. Extroverts really prefer to talk out a writing task.

In evaluating writing, introverts prefer writing that shows insight and reflection (Jensen and DiTiberio 134). Extroverts generally prefer writing that shows initiative and less analysis, especially if they are extroverted feeling types (EF). I want to extrapolate from this to readers' responses more generally. Such extrapolation is supported by some work in second language acquisition research on the impact of personality on language learning. In particular, John Schafer looked at reader responses to text and found that a particular language background may give readers a particular set of expectations. Contrastive rhetoric (to be discussed in Chapter 5 on writing research) shows how these expectations are built into a text when it is written. Schafer found a particularly clear example in Vietnamese coupling (the juxtaposing of opposites) that is linguistically and culturally based (Schafer 119). Perhaps the introverts among the Vietnamese are particularly good at coupling, which probably requires a highly reflective preference.

This example suggests that readable writing is subject to both personality preferences and cultural predispositions, and that when these are understood and appreciated, the text can be shaped accordingly by writers and/or processed more effectively by readers. Approaching this matter from a different direction, John Schumann presents a similar view of the importance of personality in language matters. He discusses the concept of social and psychological distance in second language learning, focusing on a subject who had particular difficulty in learning English as a second language. When Schumann talks about ego permeability and other psychological constraints, he reports results of experiments using other psychological instruments, but since he is concerned about feelings, empathy and related issues, I believe he is talking about personality preferences. Ego permeability and other psychological constraints, Schumann has claimed, play a role in success or failure in second language learning (Schumann 69-100). Perhaps greater ego permeability is found among extraverts, making them more successful at second language learning.

Other researchers present a similar approach in discussing the concept of a *filter* operating during language learning (Dulay, Burt and Krashen 46 and Krashen 3). In particular,

> this filter is that part of the internal processing system that subconsciously screens incoming language based on what psychologists call "affect": the learner's motives, needs, attitudes, and emotional states. The filter appears to be the first main hurdle that incoming language data must encounter before it is processed further. It determines (1) which target language models the learner will select; (2) which parts of the language will be attended to first; (3) when language acquisition efforts

> should cease; and (4) how fast a learner can acquire the language. (Dulay, Burt and Krashen 46)

Clearly, the filter is controlled by personality preferences at a very basic level, and in the present discussion, these preferences play themselves out in the production and comprehension of text. The more highly social, extraverted learner may be able to lower the filter more easily and thus have an easier time with second language learning. There are other ramifications for personality preferences particular to readable writing.

IMPLICATIONS OF TYPE FOR COMPOSING AND COMPREHENDING

Jensen and DiTiberio were looking specifically at teachers evaluating student writing. However, it seems clear that "Whether extraverted or introverted, . . . raters' basic orientation to life can affect how they evaluate a text" (134), and the same can be said of readers more generally. I speculate that introverts generally have a style preference for texts with a fair amount of introspection, with clear presentation of ideas (especially if also thinkers), and with order (especially if also judging). Extroverts, in contrast, are more likely to prefer, and find more readable, texts that deal with experience, that may not necessarily have a strong order, and that use many examples. While there is no strong empirical evidence for these speculations, and while the implications of preferences are more complicated due to the interactions of the dimensions, some of the case studies discussed below (in Chapter 10) will allow more detailed consideration of these speculations.

The sensing-intuitive continuum also has direct connections to writing preferences. Writers with a sensing preference tend to like specific and detailed directions for a writing task, and tend to focus on grammar and mechanics in revising. They present facts effectively, but may lack an overview or context in which to place the facts and can get stuck if they are overly focused on the pattern or the technical aspects of writing. Intuitive writers, on the other hand, prefer general directions and a lot of latitude in a writing task. They write quickly, generating ideas and creating organization as they go. They are best at discussing theory and unique approaches to problems, but leave out examples and sometimes don't follow the directions given. They like to leave the technical details of writing until the very end (Jensen and DiTiberio 173-4).

As graders or evaluators, sensing and intuitive types respond quite differently to texts:

> the sensing types tend to evaluate the concrete text, the words on paper, while intuitive types tend to evaluate the concrete text in light of the inferences they may make from it. (Jensen and DiTiberio 135)

As a result of these differing responses, sensing teachers tend to appraise grammar and mechanics, and to look for structure and texts that state the point explicitly. Intuitive teachers are less concerned about specifics and appraise a text based on the inferences they make from it and the possibilities that follow from those. It seems likely that, as readers, sensing types will like more explicit texts, whereas intuitives won't mind a lack of explicitness and will be willing to follow an author through a more speculative or exploratory kind of discussion. Given the distribution of MBTI types in the population, where studies show that people with the S preference outnumber those with the N preference by about three to one, these varying preferences may help to explain some of the responses to my texts to be discussed in Chapters 7-10 (Jensen and DiTiberio 165).

The third continuum in the MBTI scheme deals with a preference for thinking or feeling. As writers, thinkers like to set themselves some distance from a topic, and follow a clear structure in their discussion of it. They can make good use of feedback when the respondent gives a rationale, and often need to add more examples to their logical, analytic style. It is often hard for writers with a preference for thinking to handle topics calling for feelings or personal experience. Feeling types prefer those topics in which they have or can develop a personal investment and can appraise their writing in terms of its effect on the reader. They can make good use of feedback that focuses their attention on the audience response, and like to make contact with readers, but their writing is often organized by narrative structure and can be sentimental. They struggle with writing tasks that require logic or a particular pattern and like to make their writing "interesting" (Jensen and DiTiberio 175-6).

Thinking and feeling types evaluate writing differently, and, as Jensen and DiTiberio point out, this is the dimension that has to do with making judgments and decisions. Thinkers "value good content and organization over good style," while feeling types "value the more personal qualities of writing" (137). As readers, more generally, similar preferences probably appear. So readers who are thinking types are likely to prefer to read content-oriented texts with clear organization and little personal information, while feeling types are more likely to respond well to a text with ideas made personal and/or discussed in terms of feelings. These thoughts about the implications of thinking and feeling types in reading are, of course, only speculations about how readers might respond to ordinary expository text, such as I have used in my studies, and not comments on what kinds of texts various types of readers might choose in a library or other open choice situation. This discussion of personality type and preferences in reading and writing texts does not address questions of interest, motivation, self-concept of the learner, and the like, which are quite subjective and very difficult to measure effectively.

The final dimension of the MBTI is judging/perceiving. As writers, judgers handle writing expediently: They divide the work and get started fairly quickly, working on the paper section by section, but sometimes not developing their ideas fully. They are good at meeting deadlines, because they tend to plan, but sometimes are hemmed in by the planning. Sometimes, judging types start before they have really thought their topic through, and often need to take more time before they start writing.

The perceiving type, in contrast, can do very well with a broad topic but may have problems focusing and narrowing the topic enough to get the writing done to meet a deadline. Perceivers need long periods of time to devote to writing and often do excessive research before they can start to write. Their drafts are often too long, incorporating considerable information not strictly relevant to the topic, and they often lack a clear and specific thesis. Although their writing tends to provide a very thorough discussion, they can be overwhelmed by the topic or present it in a disorganized way.

When evaluating writing, judgers evaluate more quickly and are more comfortable using holistic evaluation techniques than are perceivers. "Perceiving types, who value thoroughness over decisiveness, usually feel that rating an essay without a comprehensive reading borders on malpractice" (Jensen and DiTiberio 138). While the judging type looks for resolution of an issue, perceiving types seek a thorough discussion of the topic at hand. Perceivers usually rate a longer essay above a short one regardless of its content (139). When reading more generally, I speculate, judgers will prefer a text that has closure, a clear-cut ending, while perceivers want depth of exploration and postponement of closure. I will explore the implications of the MBTI's relationship to text preferences in detail below (Chapter 10).

Thus, my explorations in psycholinguistics gave me more pieces for my puzzle about the nature of readable text. One piece, marked text analysis, offered propositional analysis and schema theory, to help with the analysis of the content of the text and how readers approach a text in terms of their prior knowledge. In the area of information processing, investigations of redundancy and explanations of why it plays a crucial role in reading gave me a key piece of my puzzling picture. Finally, in work on the influence of personality type on writing, I found pieces of evidence of the nature of readable text concerning how people with particular preferences look at and respond to passages that might help to account for the array of results that I have obtained in my various studies. Text processing and studies of redundancy in texts, and as furnished by the readers' prior knowledge, provide additional strategies for scrutiny of the text itself, while an understanding of personality preferences provides a means of addressing writers' and readers' preferences that shape the meeting ground they share in readable writing. These pieces interlock to explicate the concept of readable writing, and assist toward the goals of understanding its nature and how readers and writers can best make use of it.

CHAPTER 4

Relevant Research III: Reading

The next corner of the puzzle I want to put into place is the reading corner. In this corner are a wide variety of theoretical and practical pieces of explanation of the process of getting meaning from print. This is also a substantial corner, containing both concepts and models for reading in one's native language and an array of views of reading in a second language. The nature of the reading process, and the methods of measuring how texts can be made maximally accessible for readers, keeping in mind their linguistic, psychological, ethnic, and cultural preferences, are key issues for the passages in my studies to be discussed below. Here, I want to review the current models of reading in both first and second language, and various proposals about the nature and measurement of readability, examining the contribution of these models and methods to understanding the nature of readable writing.

Reading is a remarkably complex process, and the richness of the activities involved in getting meaning from print has only recently approached detailed description. *Reading*, for my purposes, is defined as getting meaning from print. Some other key terms, discussed previously in Chapter 1, appear frequently in this chapter, so a bit of restatement is in order. *Readability* is a term that captures one component of readable writing, those tangible, measurable features of text that are now often appraised by computer programs. Readability plays a role in *difficulty*, a term I have been using in this book to refer to the ease of understanding of a text for a particular reader. However, readability is only one aspect of the readable writing that allows reader expectation and writer intention to coincide through the use of redundancy and cohesion. Another aspect of readable writing is *comprehensibility*, those qualitative features of discourse, organization, and so on that facilitate the meeting of readers and writers in a text. Reading for understanding or comprehension, then, is a multifaceted activity.

Studies based on this appreciation of the sophisticated nature of reading examine the process from the diverse perspectives of text, readers, and related issues. Similarly, approaches to difficulty, when seen as simple ease of text per se, also fall short of tapping the complexity of reading. In terms of methodological and measurement issues I have raised, strategies are needed that not only address countable elements but also permit varied strategies for the examination of a much wider range of factors that figure into the way readers and writers connect in a text. By including a discussion of several kinds of research and an analysis of proposals that include different languages, cultures, and individual variations, I intend to demonstrate that, from the reading perspective, readable writing draws upon redundancy and cohesion. We turn first to the emerging description of the nature of reading.

MODELS OF THE READING PROCESS: PRINT VS. MEANING

There have been a great many proposals about the nature of the reading process, and each has been discussed in detail from both theoretical and practical perspectives; scholars have also given careful consideration to both empirical research issues and to how a model might be applied to teaching reading. Generally, the models fall into three broad categories: *print-based models*, proposing that readers move from letters and words to sentences and paragraphs, and then to meaning; *meaning-based models*, that focus first on hypotheses that readers bring to text, and then suggest that readers draw only minimal information from the visual display to create meaning; and *combined views*, those that suggest that reading requires both ongoing analysis of the printed page and the forming and testing of hypotheses about meaning.

To some extent, these models show the historical development of reading research, as the earliest proposals were mostly of the first type, usually called *bottom-up processes*, while the second type, *hypothesis-based* or *top-down processes*, are a kind of middle stage, and many current models incorporate both views, usually referred to as *interactive proposals*. The latter two views, top-down and interactive, are the ones that provide the strongest basis for the research I have conducted. These need to be sketched in greater detail.

The top-down view of reading is the one usually credited chiefly to Kenneth Goodman, whose extensive individualized research with oral reading and reading miscues (mismatches between what readers say aloud and what actually appears on the page) strongly supports a view of reading as a hypothesis-testing process. Goodman has claimed that reading is a "psycholinguistic guessing game" (K. Goodman "Reading") in which readers make reasonable guesses about the content of the text, and use the page to confirm their guesses. The chief strength of Goodman's view is that it has a

> procedural preference for allowing the reader to rely on existing syntactic and semantic knowledge structures, so that reliance on the graphic display and existing knowledge about the sounds associated with graphemes (graphophonemic knowledge) can be minimized. . . .his model always prefers the cognitive economy of reliance on well-developed linguistic (syntactic and semantic) rather than graphic information. (Samuels and Kamil 23)

Often, Goodman's work is discussed together with Frank Smith's proposals. Smith agrees with Goodman that immediate meaning identification (F. Smith, *Understanding* 148f.) is the chief goal of reading, and so also takes a top-down view. But, as noted earlier in the present exploration, Smith's

> greatest contribution. . .is to explain how the redundancy inherent at all levels of language (letter features, within letters, within words, within sentences, within discourses) provides the reader with enormous flexibility in marshaling resources to create a meaning for the text at hand. (Samuels and Kamil 24)

Because, from the top-down point of view, *reading* is defined as the process of getting meaning from print, readers are thought to rely most centrally on what they already know and to create meaning based on minimal information from the text.

More recently, scholars have raised questions about the top-down view based on both earlier views of reading as bottom-up and thus more linear, and current views of reading from the practical side of the classroom/how-to-teach-it perspective. It is fine to believe that reading chiefly involves meaning created by the reader, and that readers approach texts with hypotheses about meaning already in place, but how do people learn to do this in the first place? Some other questions have been raised as well: what if readers know little about the topic and are not able to make hypotheses about the text; and, even if they can do so, sometimes it may be a longer process than relying more directly on the text display. Thus, there are both pedagogical questions and efficiency questions about the top-down view.

THE INTERACTIVE ALTERNATIVE

These valid questions have moved the field along to what might be described as a more balanced view, the interactive model of reading. Two proponents of the interactive view are Rumelhart and Stanovich, and they agree on key features of this model. Generally, the interactive view proposes that reading is both bottom-up and top-down, such that the top-down hypothesis-testing processes are supported by bottom-up text analysis processes, and vice versa. In Stanovich's interactive-compensatory model, a weakness in the reader or the text in any one area can be compensated for by reliance on another area. From the interactive perspective, not only letters, words, sentences, and other visual features, but also readers' prior knowledge and ability to establish and test hypotheses, play a key role in how reading goes on.

The interactive model is pertinent to my studies in several ways. First, the interactive view incorporates propositions and schemata, suggesting that readers draw, not only on the visual display of the text wherein lie the propositions, but also on background knowledge and information the psychologists propose in the schema concept. Second, the interactive view draws on several types of research methodology: individualized research with readers, larger empirical studies of groups of subjects responding to texts, and studies of the nature of text as text. Finally, this view draws in the concept of redundancy (a feature of texts and readers) from the psychological research discussed above and also incorporates linguistic work on cohesion (a feature of texts) discussed in Chapter 2. Because schemata have been shown to be part of what readers bring to text, and because they play a central role in reading in an interactive view, this view seems most helpful to understanding the nature of readable writing. Scholars analyzing the role of prior knowledge in reading comprehension discuss this point:

> According to schema theory, comprehension is a matter of activating or constructing a schema that provides a coherent explanation of the relations between the objects and events mentioned in a discourse. In contrast, the conventional view has been that comprehension proceeds by aggregating the meanings of words to form the meanings of clauses, aggregating clauses to form sentences, sentences to form paragraphs and so on. In this view, comprehension is a linear, text-driven process. . . .The meanings of the words in a text cannot be 'added up' to give the meaning of the text as a whole. The click of comprehension occurs only when the reader is able to evolve a schema that explains the whole message.
>
> According to schema theory, reading involves more or less simultaneous analysis at many different levels—from the textual levels of graphophonemic, morphemic, semantic and syntactic features, to the experience-based levels of knowledge of specific content, pragmatics, and interpretive things. Reading is conceived to be an interactive process. . . . (Wilson and Anderson 34-35)

Thus, the model of reading I am proposing, incorporating both the receptive part of the process, reading, and the productive part, writing, argues that reading must be interactive and constructive, involving both top-down and bottom-up processing. Considering reading in a writing context (see the next chapter), it will be clear that reading must be interactive during writing even if no model provides a complete, thorough, utterly satisfactory explanation.

COMPLEXITY OF READING

Indeed, some other work on the relationship of reading and writing takes up this rather complex view of reading as involving readers' interactive reliance on both text and their own constructed understanding of meaning, and the inadequacy of even this complicated description. Most researchers who are interested in the connections between reading and writing processes find them even more complex than I have thus far suggested. Indeed, some have proposed that *all* models fall short because they are not complex enough (Grant-Davie 1-2 and 4).

Some of the trouble with models of reading and/or writing lies in the fact that the models are often proposed outside of the context in which these activities occur, but as Halliday's work suggests, the context of situation is always relevant and crucial to any proposal about language and language use. Grant-Davie's work reviews various models of reading and writing considered together, and he notes the importance of and lack of consideration for the social context of these activities (Grant-Davie 3). In *The Presence of Thought: Introspective Accounts of Reading and Writing*, a very different approach to the study of reading and writing that considers context very thoroughly and carefully, and that draws again on individual cases as the data base, Marilyn Sternglass comes to the same conclusion (202-04). In her critique of protocol analysis as an approach to reading and writing, Sternglass notes that

> reading and writing are activities so intrinsically bound up with the entire life experience of individuals that it becomes clear that such controlled descriptions can account for only a small part of the composing process. . . . (Sternglass 202)

and similarly, studies of reading are only a specimen of the range of activities involved in the process. Neither protocol analysis nor stimulated recall approaches to writing research allow, according to Sternglass, for sufficient consideration of

> how the circumstances of a particular reading and writing episode affect its shape or how this specific episode fits into the larger experiences and goals of the writer. It is clear from the descriptions of the reading and writing activities of our students that complex individual interpretation is involved in the decisions made in relation to each aspect of each task. (Sternglass 203)

Like Grant-Davie, Sternglass sees these as extremely complex and highly individualized processes.

Context of situation as Halliday has proposed, and schema theory, as the psychologists have proposed, taken together with the influence of personality preferences, and all these holding while reading goes forward, with top-down/bottom-up reliance on text factors like redundancy and cohesion, might all together provide a fairly accurate picture of reading. Only when all of these factors are considered can we begin to fill in the reading corner of the puzzle frame, getting an adequate analysis of what makes for readable text. And there is more theory to consider, because reading scholars have also considered the nature of the reading process as it occurs for those reading in a second language. This additional view provides support for this complex analysis of the nature of reading, and will shed further light on what constitutes a readable text.

READING IN A SECOND LANGUAGE

Findings in *second language acquisition* (hereafter SLA) research support several aspects of the nature of the reading process as we have discussed it thus far. Specifically, SLA work helps provide a synthesis of the various models of reading that accounts for the development of reading ability among both first and second language learners, and thus the synthesis gives a more global picture of reading. Moreover, this research demonstrates the relevance of redundancy and cohesion to reading, in not only a first but also a second language. It furthermore suggests that the claims I am making have broad, multicultural implications, in that they are not bound to a particular language or to the cultural or ethnic background of individuals. Instead, the diverse support for redundancy and cohesion provides a means of understanding and appreciating alternative approaches to the ways readers and writers connect in readable writing.

Second language studies provide this help for two reasons. First, more generally, research in SLA suggests that it resembles first language acquisition insofar as it draws on the principles of *universal grammar*, "innate principles. . . which define the class of possible human languages and therefore constrain the range of hypotheses that a child can entertain about the structure of its language" (Broselow 201). Although some scholars have proposed that these innate principles might be unavailable in SLA, especially for adults, research suggests that it is more likely that both first and second language acquisition draw on knowledge of universal grammar (Broselow 203).

Second, reading, as one activity in SLA, also seems to resemble reading in a first language in general terms, but to be different from it in various ways. In particular, it is not at all clear that SLA readers fit well with the top-down models that are widely popular in reading theory and practice for native speakers. Several books have been devoted to interactive proposals concerning second language readers, and the interactive models seem more appropriate (see Carrell, Devine and Eskey and Devine, Carrell and Eskey). Part of the reason for this is that there are a number of ways in which second language readers differ from those reading in their native language:

> (1)They may or may not read in the first language; there is, in fact, surprisingly little current information on how, why, and what students read in other cultures. (2)If second language students do have literacy training, we still do not know how they approach reading in their first language as a social phenomenon; that is, do they view reading as a major academic, professional, and entertainment activity, or do they read much less, for far fewer purposes? (3)Second language readers are often assumed to transfer readily their first language reading abilities to the second language context; however. . . there is no adequate empirical evidence for assuming such a strong position. (4)Second language students coming from different orthographic traditions do appear to be affected by differing orthographic conventions, depending on their stage of reading skills acquisition. (5)Second language readers do not begin reading . . . with the same . . . language knowledge. . . . (Grabe, "Reassessing" 58)

as those learning to read in their first language. Thus, there are salient differences in second language reading. However, while these differences make exclusive support for the "top-down" view of reading difficult, they lead logically and substantively to a consideration of the interactive proposals, because interactive analyses of reading propose that readers draw on both text resources and their own resources, making it possible for them to carry out reading in a second language. Indeed, Grabe's work reviewing the relevance of interactive views of reading suggests that he strongly supports application of interactive models to the second language reading situation (Grabe, "Reassessing" 56, "Current Developments. . .Reading").

A second review of reading by second language learners reaches the same conclusion after a comprehensive review of both first and second language reading research (Swaffar). This review supports an interactive analysis of reading in second language as well as first, and also supports the relevance of schema theory and context of situation in a complete picture of reading. When these findings are applied to the practical issue of teaching second language reading, Swaffar points out that, in addition to interest level, motivation, and other affective factors, second language reading must also consider key text factors. These factors include content and logical organization (schema theory), coherence, and cohesion (Swaffar 140).

The relevance of schema theory in particular has been examined and reexamined in second language reading, and at least some research shows that schemata are equally pertinent in second language as they are in first language reading (Carrell, "Schema Theory" and Wolff). Patricia Carrell has done a substantial amount of research on this point, and has a fairly consistent set of findings supporting the claim that familiar schemata in terms of both the content of reading and familiar rhetorical organization contribute significantly to writing that is readable for ESL students (Carrell "Content and Formal Schemata," "Facilitating ESL Reading," "Schema Theory and ESL"). Thus, the text factors I have been looking at are pertinent for second language reading as well as for those reading in their first language.

Interactive views of reading seem to provide particular support for students learning to read English as a second language, the focus of Grabe's review. Interactive views are helpful, according to Grabe, for a number of reasons: They remind us that reading is not exclusively a top-down enterprise; they suggest that bottom-up skills are equal to top-down skills in successful reading; they show that a lack of a large recognition vocabulary in the second language can seriously impede reading; they account for some students' difficulties with reading through an overreliance on guessing about a needed schema or too much word-by-word reading; and they propose that second language reading abilities may develop in a staged fashion, including development of higher and lower level processes (Grabe, "Reassessing" 63).

The work in SLA on reading supports an interactive view of reading, and in addition supports the relevance of the propositional/schema theory of comprehension proposed in the psychological research (Carrell, "SLA. . .Reading" 225-6). Second language reading also points up the relevance of context, as proposed by Halliday (Grabe, "Reassessing" 64-65). Moreover, there is pertinent research showing that second language readers, at least those learning to read English as a second language, are sensitive to both cohesion and redundancy in English texts.

A number of interesting studies have been done in this connection with adult Hebrew speakers learning English as a second language. Marsha Bensoussan, who has studied the effect of both redundancy and cohesion on reading in this situation, has found, using a special form of *Cloze procedure* (a reading test where a passage is prepared with every n-th word deleted and readers fill in the resulting blanks), that redundancy and cohesion both can enhance reading comprehension (Bensoussan). This research contributes to my findings for several reasons: It demonstrates that redundancy and cohesion are as important in second language reading as they are in first language reading, and it shows that Cloze procedure is useful as a means of measuring the effect of these text factors on comprehension. Cloze can be used in large scale empirical studies and so complements the research perspective of individualized case reports offered by other scholars. Though Cloze is not the only or most useful tool for examining comprehension, or the only one I have used with my texts, it has been used extensively and has yielded useful findings in my studies and in other work on reading.

READING MODELS IN L1 AND L2: SUMMARY

To summarize the discussion of reading thus far: Reading researchers, drawing on diverse methodological approaches, have proposed various models of the nature of the reading process. In general, reading theorists have moved from a bottom-up view of reading as mostly a matter of letter, word, and sentence recognition to a top-down view of reading as mostly a matter of large scale comprehension created by the reader with minimal support from the text. Most recently, theorists have proposed a view of reading that incorporates both of these positions, usually called an interactive view, wherein reading involves not only text-based but also reader-based activities.

The interactive view fits well with pertinent research from linguistics that considers context as well as text structure in the matter of cohesion. It fits well with psychological research that considers context in the idea of schemata and considers redundancy insofar as redundancy taps both text features and features drawn from the readers' prior knowledge. It also fits well with psychological research on personality preferences, allowing for differences in how readers respond to various text factors based on how they view the world and prefer to take in and analyze information for decision making (F. Smith, *Understanding* 53-60).

Viewed from yet another angle, the interactive view is supported by research in second language acquisition and second language reading. Although people acquiring a second language apparently draw on universal grammatical principles, suggesting that, in dealing with key text factors (such as redundancy and cohesion), they have access to their knowledge of general linguistic principles, there are also salient differences in reading in a second language. But these differences lend support to the broadly based interactive view of reading. In addition, second language reading research demonstrates that both redundancy and cohesion can enhance reading for nonnatives.

READABILITY RESEARCH

For both first and second language readers, the shape of the text itself is one of the essential elements of reading, though not the only one. A large number of attempts to describe, measure, and evaluate text per se derive from research on readability in the sense that I have been using it here, to refer to features in the text itself that are part of readable writing. With the background of reading models directing our focus to the textual component of reading, we can turn to the research in readability. Readability usually means the ease of understanding a particular text for particular readers, based on how the text is written (Klare 681). Readability research has focused generally on countable, tangible features of texts. These aspects of text must be considered even though they don't provide a complete picture of readable writing. All factors that play some role in reading must be examined, because reading is so central to education and is increasingly required of people in our society, even though ability, as developed by students in public school, is diminishing (Klare 681-2). These are concerns raised by Mike Rose in *Lives on the Boundary* and by Frank Smith in his proposal that children learning to read must be invited to join what he calls the "literacy club" (*Understanding* 215). These concerns figure in the concept of critical literacy or what has been called a "literacy of thoughtfulness," thinking, reasoning, evaluating the substance of texts and the ability to convey the results of such activities in other texts (R. Brown, *Schools* xiii).

The central problem in readability, as I suggested initially in Chapter 1, is that attempts to examine key factors contributing to readability give only a partial view of the nature of readable writing. Just to review the use of this term, I am considering *readability* to include only those tangible, countable features of texts per se that seem to influence their difficulty for a particular group of readers. Readability defined in this way fails to tap discourse-based and reader-based features of text like redundancy and cohesion. These features are central to readable writing and thus to the literacy needed across the population.

Until recently, most attempts to appraise readability have made use of formulas that incorporate counts of words, sentences, syllables, or other features of text thought to contribute to difficulty. These provide from the reader's point of view what Klare calls *predictions of readability* (703). In addition, at the writer's end of the readability continuum, there are concerns with production of readability, attempts to answer the question "How can I write readably (or more readably) for intended readers?" (Klare 703). The many formulas now in use do a limited number of things very well: They count word frequency as an indicator of word difficulty, they appraise some syntactic factors like sentence length, they give a rough idea of grade level appropriateness of reading material, they incorporate use of Cloze procedure to avoid use of multiple-choice questions as measures of comprehension, and they have become highly efficient when run by computer (Klare 687-88).

With regard to the matter of producing readable writing, readability research in general and the formulas in particular have been less successful. In production research, scholars have attempted to use a small number of passages of limited length and have looked at small numbers of variables, usually holding content constant (Klare 709). The effect of the formulas on the readability of school textbooks has been disappointing. In college texts on writing, there is no widespread agreement on which factors contribute to good writing—one study found 156 variables in 15 books (Klare 715). In addition, the task of writing is sufficiently complex that it is not clear whether writers can keep the features of readability in mind while generating text. For this reason, as Klare asserts, online computer-based text analysis systems that evaluate and comment on various text features can be helpful to the writer concerned with readability.

Klare's review of readability research makes a distinction between research on predictions of readability and research on production factors. This distinction is useful because it leads to new ways of analyzing the problem. George Klare says that there are certain measurable factors known to be useful for predicting readability (683 and 703-4). Among these are counts of content words, syllables, and the like—all things countable by various readability formulas. There are also certain features of text production that figure prominently in comprehensibility, like propositional density, which are either already measurable or soon to be measurable by computer. Thus, while neither prediction variables alone nor production variables alone provide a complete picture, taken together the two provide a much improved analysis of readability.

FORMULA MEASURES OF READABILITY

Perhaps the most complex issue in readability studies concerns the instruments used to measure it. Various measures have been tried: the formulas use counts of words, syllables, sentences, and so forth; other studies use Cloze procedure or a modified Cloze called GAP *analysis*, and still others use reading time and recall as measures. Readability measurement usually begins with text features known to be helpful for predicting the difficulty of material for a certain group of readers. Readability formulas have been analyzed, criticized, reformulated, and reviewed entirely too often (cf. Klare and Davison and Kantor). However, the formulas do work, in a limited and specific way.

Certain features counted in readability formulas are helpful. For instance, some formulas count numbers of concrete words and numbers of syllables, and use these in an equation that produces a readability score. Melissa Holland notes that "more concrete words are easier to understand and remember independently of length and frequency" (6), and the ratio of content words to function words also has an impact on comprehensibility of text (9). Various formulas tap these factors and do make useful predictions. For example, there are specific counts of content words, counts of syllables in relation to overall words, and counts of sentence length.

These counts are now available by computer in Michael Schuyler's "Readability" program, among other places. Schuyler provides a summary of nine of the most popular formulas. Several of these derive a count of content words, using different strategies. In the Dale-Chall formula, a list of 3,000 words is provided, words found to be familiar to fourth graders in a test done by Dale and Chall (Schulyer 564). The Fog formula makes use of a count of three-syllable words, and the Automated Readability Index counts word length in characters. All of these are attempts to get a numerical measure of the content words in a passage. The reason for this approach is that research shows that content word counts have something to do with the readability of a passage. However, content level is one, but not the best or only, measure of readability.

Many of the formulas make use of syllable counts. The Flesch formula uses a count of syllables per hundred words (Schuyler 567), and Kincaid's revision of the Flesch formula uses a ratio of syllables to total number of words. One of the flaws in the formulas, as is often pointed out, is that the classic formula counts numbers of words and numbers of sentences, and the number of syllables may not correlate with either of the other two factors. That is, some formulas differ from one another in terms of what they count and in terms of the readability levels they assign to a given passage.

There are a number of major problems with them, whether they are used to judge the suitability of a text for a third grade class or whether they are used as guidelines for writing (Bruce and Rubin 7). In a thorough critique of formulas, scholars have made clear why their use is "misguided" (Bruce and Rubin 5):

> readability formulas do not measure all the factors that influence the comprehensibility of a text. Because most of the formulas include only sentence length and word difficulty as factors, they can account only indirectly for factors which may make a particular text difficult, such as syntactic complexity, discourse cohesion characteristics, the number of inferences required, the number of items to remember, the complexity of ideas, rhetorical structure and dialect. Further, because the formulas are measurements based on a text isolated from the context of its use, they can not reflect such reader-specific factors as motivation, interest, values, or purpose. Nor can they reflect different readers' cultural backgrounds or the effect of the circumstances in which a passage is read. (Bruce and Rubin 7-8)

For all these reasons, having to do with text factors, reader factors, and the context in which the reading occurs, the use of readability formulas often leads to problems. These writers conclude that the formulas at best give only the most general sort of estimate of the readability level of a text (Bruce and Rubin 21). This recent conclusion is consistent with the lengthy analysis of Klare, who is the leading scholar on readability and who reviewed virtually all the formulas in use once in the early '60s and a second time more recently as part of a comprehensive review of reading research. Moreover, as Baker, Atwood and Duffy point out, formulas are mostly based on a bottom-up view of reading, and not on the more recent and more sophisticated top-down or interactive analyses. Finally, as I have already noted, the problem of what to measure and how to measure has been a central issue in my research and that of others in the field (see Chall for some discussion).

Overall, then, formula-based strategies for the analysis of readability leave many central aspects of reader-writer interaction in text untapped. Davison and Green's fairly recent book entitled *Linguistic Complexity and Text Comprehension: Readability Issues Reconsidered*, an edited collection of essays on research in cognitive psychology and in linguistic and educational theory, attempts to consider readability from more diverse perspectives. Despite the interesting range of approaches provided in the collection, the anthology includes only one reference to redundancy (in a discussion of phonological redundancy rules) and no references to cohesion at all. The editors freely concede that readability is an extremely complex problem.

Several pieces in the Davison and Green book consider factors that are part of the analysis provided by readability formulas, and explain why these factors do not account for readability at all or only in a limited way. Studies of what happens to technical texts, when revised following formula-based guidelines, do not show improved comprehension for readers (Baker et al. and Charrow). Some of the studies involve reading by adult proficient readers, and some by children learning to read (Kemper; Green and Olsen). Generally, these studies find that discourse-based factors like cohesion and context play a much more central role in determining difficulty (Frazier) than do measures of sentence complexity (Crain and Shankweiler), word complexity (Randall) or sentence length (Carlota Smith).

Because readability formulas can give one approximate estimate of difficulty, I have used them in the studies reported below, along with a number of other measures. Readability research has gone on from formula-based studies to the kind of work summarized in the Davison and Green anthology. There are also discourse-based processes, cohesion-based processes, and various other strategies which warrant discussion. I will attempt to make clear why some of these strategies strike me as being more pertinent to my work than others, and why they seem to have the greatest relevance for readable writing. First, however, some discussion of other attempts to address readability is in order.

READABILITY ANALYSIS BY COMPUTER

Klare provides an interesting overview of the Writer's Workbench system, a different kind of computerized analysis of text. Writer's Workbench is a text analysis system developed by Bell Laboratories that I used in working with my passages (see Chapter 8). I used Writer's Workbench along with a number of other formulas and counts of text elements because these tap the readability component of readable writing. Writer's Workbench will analyze a passage of text and give feedback on a number of different scales or issues: spelling, punctuation, repetition of words, faulty phrasing, split infinitives, readability indexes, length of words and sentences, distribution of sentence lengths, simple and complex sentences, passives, nominalizations, style standards, abstraction level, and several other factors (Klare 716). Recently, a number of other similar systems have been developed that perform similar kinds of analyses (HBJ Writer, Grammatik, and the like).

Most of these systems, like other approaches to readability, suffer from various weaknesses. Klare notes that

> word and sentence variables (or style variables) are not the only contributors to readability. Among the more obvious missing candidates are organization, format, and illustrations. . .another [is] variables in subjects serving as readers. . . . Still

> another thing concerns the conditions of experimentation and their inevitable effects. . . . (717)

In the terms I have been using throughout this book, the countable elements of readability are part of the larger picture of readable writing, but not all of it. My analysis of the passages I have been studying and testing includes these factors, and I will report many counts of text elements in Chapter 8. Though Klare does not mention measures of cohesion or redundancy specifically, he suggests that there are additional factors that text analysis systems do not address. Thus, other less strictly empirical or nonquantitative means of examining texts, and how readers respond to them, need to be considered, including Cloze and some variants of it, propositional analysis, and miscue analysis.

ALTERNATIVE STRATEGIES

Cloze and Other Measures

Readable writing is more complex, as I have argued, than counts of sentences or syllables can suggest. One approach to readability mentioned in passing by Klare but not considered in detail is the use of Cloze procedure, as advocated by John Bormuth. In this procedure, mentioned briefly earlier, a sample passage of text is prepared with words deleted, usually following some standard formula, such as every fifth word. The deletions are replaced by a blank of standard length, and readers are then asked to fill in these blanks with the words they believe the author used in the original version of the passage.

The fill-ins are then scored using either an exact-match or synonyms-acceptable scoring system, and the scores are thought to give an appraisal of the difficulty of the passage for that particular group of readers. There has been considerable research supporting the use of Cloze procedure since it was originally proposed in the 1950s (Taylor, Bormuth, Chall). Bailey and Harrison's study is a follow-up to Bormuth's work, showing that Cloze procedure taps the redundancy of passages; in addition, the procedure is reasonably efficient to use, and it taps both top-down and bottom-up factors in reading.

In the last 10 years or so, partly as a by-product of work on cohesion in text, a different type of Cloze procedure has been developed by John Chapman and other scholars. In this approach, instead of deleting every nth word in the passage, just a few items are deleted, and they are chosen at points where the major ideas in the passage intersect. These points are discerned through an analysis of the cohesive patterns of the passages and cohesive chains, using Halliday and Hasan's system discussed in Chapter 2. Chapman argues that this measure, called *GAP technique*, yields information about readers' sensitivity to cohesion in texts, a factor shown to be pertinent to comprehension (Chapman, *Reading: 5 to 11*; Irwin, "Effect"). Cloze procedure, and the variation on it provided by GAP technique, offer one means by which to look at texts and readers' responses. Another way of addressing the issues pertinent to readable writing comes from propositional analysis.

Propositional Analysis as a Measure of Comprehensibility

Discourse analysis, one area known to be pertinent to readable writing, has made great progress in the last 10 years or so, in the development of systems of text analysis that examine factors in the text and also certain aspects of reader activity during the process of getting meaning from print. Of these, propositional analysis currently provides some useful insights. Tierney and Mosenthal ("Discourse") have done a meticulous review of propositional analysis as a system for the study of texts. They explain how it works and provide a critique as well.

Tierney and Mosenthal review propositional analysis drawing chiefly from the work of Walter Kintsch as discussed in Chapter 3. Kintsch's system involves breaking down each sentence of a passage into its idea units, called propositions. These propositions reflect the knowledge of the writer. They are built around verbs, a feature supported by the newer nontransformational analyses of linguistic knowledge such as that proposed by the theory of residential grammar (Binkert, *Generative*). Comprehension occurs as the reader processes the content of the passage in the form of propositions, and fits them into the overall meaning of the text, or its macrostructure. The system works well on all types of texts, and can work on passages longer than one sentence. However, this system is also extremely difficult to use, despite the creation of a manual of procedures for propositional analysis written by Turner and Greene, and an easier, simplified version of propositional analysis worked out by Susan Bovair and David Kieras. Moreover, Tierney and Mosenthal point out that the rules for creating a macrostructure are not strongly supported empirically and require much further study.

Still, Kintsch has turned up some interesting findings. Kintsch takes reading time and recall as the two salient measures of readers' understanding. Even his earliest studies showed that more propositions require more reading time (with length held constant), and that certain types of propositions were easier to recall than others (Kintsch, *Representation*). Also, repetition of arguments (elements within propositions) has an impact on difficulty, as does the number of different arguments found in the propositional analysis of a passage. Although arguments in propositional analysis and content words counted by formulas are not necessarily the same thing, both examine the substance of the passage.

A useful development in propositional analysis for the issues of interest here is the availability of a computer program which counts propositions and can compare lists of them. One such program has been written by David Kieras, and he describes it in Britton and Black's *Understanding Expository Text* ("Thematic Processes"). The program does not do the basic propositional analysis, but can take a list of propositions prepared by a researcher and compare them to another list. In Kieras's studies, he has used a list of propositions drawn from a text he asked readers to read. After reading, subjects write down a brief summary of what they recall from the passage, and this summary is similarly broken down into its propositional components. The program will compare the two proposition lists and provide information about them. Since empirical data shows that propositions have a clear relationship to comprehension as measured by reading time and recall, the work of Kintsch, supplemented by Bovair and Kieras, provides an analysis of this propositional component. On the other hand, propositional analysis stays quite close to the surface form of a text and requires considerable subjective judgment by the analyst, so it, too, has weaknesses. A third alternative is offered by studies of readers' oral renditions of text through miscue analysis.

Miscue Research

Miscue analysis provides a different approach to readers' responses to text. This analysis was originally developed for use in the diagnosis of individual reading performance and reading problems. It involves the use of a taped oral reading of a passage followed by a partially prompted recall of the content of the text. Miscue analysis provides a way of examining the extent to which readers comprehend text given their oral deviations from the printed page, as well as a system for studying readers' use of grammatical information; therefore, it offers an individualized methodology for studying how readers respond to a passage of text.

Miscue research among both adults and children reading in a first language or a second language supports this use of miscue analysis. As Mark Clarke has pointed out, miscue research generally has been demonstrated to be an effective tool for examining reading and has been useful for studying both adults and children because it involves some universal features, no matter who is doing the reading and no matter whether the text is in the reader's first or second language (Clarke 79). Although some methodology and measurement issues have been raised about miscue research having to do with how well it taps silent reading and with use of recall data (Clarke 79), it offers the advantage of permitting close examination of reader responses in the course of one kind of text processing. Clarke also notes a consistency between Cloze results and miscue results, finding that his data demonstrate that both Cloze and miscue analysis provide similar measures of reading comprehension (Clarke 76).

With regard to readability research, then, we have available both direct counts of Klare's prediction factors especially through computerized application of readability formulas, and counts from analyses of production factors in computer-based writer's helper programs like Writer's Workbench. All these systems (formulas, Cloze, discourse analysis, and miscue analysis) give some information about texts and readers' responses, about readability and comprehensibility. However, all have weaknesses, and neither individually nor collectively do they take into account the full complexity of reading as discussed in the first section of the chapter. Most importantly, however, none of the approaches considered thus far permits a complete look at the two features central to readable text, cohesion and redundancy. So we turn to further studies which do address these two major pieces in the puzzle of readable writing.

DIFFERENT ALTERNATIVES FOR MEASURING READABLE WRITING

Cohesion Research

Studies discussed in Chapters 2 and 3 have established the significance of cohesion to readable writing. For example, to study the effect of cohesion on comprehension of text, Irwin did a study using rewritten passages of text ("Effect"). Irwin designed two versions of a passage differing in the number of cohesive ties, and then used reading time and recall as measures of comprehension. In terms of both reading time and recall when measured by the numbers of propositions recalled (using the system proposed by Kintsch, *Representation*), the version with more cohesive ties produced significantly better comprehension. These results suggest that cohesion plays a key role in readable text.

Additional developmental evidence supports this view. Chapman's research on 1,500 British children between the ages of 8 and 15 shows that children move along a reading development continuum which reflects their ability to get meaning from print (Chapman, *Reading: 5 to 11*). Chapman used the specialized version of the Cloze procedure called the GAP technique as described above, in which only a few words are deleted from a text, and those chosen play a key role in cohesive ties in the text. The subjects in his research show a clear developmental pattern such that beginning readers were unable to fill in the blanks, those in the middle stages could produce a fill-in with a somewhat acceptable response, while fluent readers could fill in the blank with the same word the author used or a very close synonym. Readers develop an awareness of cohesion over time and make substantial use of it to get meaning from print. Thus, the developmental research also shows that cohesion plays a role in how readers respond to readable text, and readers' ability level determines how much use they can make of cohesion in their effort to get meaning from print.

Other studies of cohesion's impact on reading support Chapman's developmental findings. A study on the effect of cohesive ties on listening and reading comprehension found that there are age-related differences in readers' ability to make use of cohesive ties, and this is a particularly salient finding, since the study looked specifically at cohesive conjunctions among other kinds of ties (Bingham 55-56). (Cohesive conjunctions figure importantly in the studies reported in Chapters 9 and 10.) Moreover, the study suggests a developmental sequence for different types of ties (causal ties are acquired prior to adversative ties according to Bingham (57)). Finally, the same study found a relationship between the ability to understand and use cohesive ties and reading ability as measured by standardized tests (Bingham 58). Some of Judith Irwin's more recent research supports this connection, and Irwin has demonstrated the importance of teaching readers about the nature of cohesion and its importance to comprehension (Irwin, "Linguistic Cohesion" 14-23).

Cohesion's significance is clear beyond the developmental level as well. Cohesion, as Tierney and Mosenthal point out, is not a system of content analysis ("Discourse"). Instead, cohesion is the feature of text that relates sentences and allows us to judge that a string of sentences (paragraph, chapter, book) form a unified text. Cohesion analysis, as described in the linguistics chapter, examines a passage for five types of cohesive ties: reference, substitution, ellipsis, conjunction, and lexical cohesion. As with propositional analysis, cohesive ties have been found empirically to be related to difficulty. More cohesive ties increase reading speed and improve recall in at least one study (Irwin, "Effect"). For writers, cohesive ties are relatively easy to add and can make a real difference to a text. The data on the passages in the studies discussed below in Chapters 9 and 10 reveal the difference cohesion can make.

Halliday and Hasan have added to their claims about cohesion through the analysis of cohesive chains, another way of looking at content. Hasan discusses cohesive chains in *Language, Context and Text.* Her research shows that the content words or tokens in a passage (its lexical rendering) fall into two different types of cohesive chains, *identity chains* and *similarity chains.* Hasan defines a *cohesive chain*, first, as "a set of items each of which is related to the others by the semantic relation of co-reference, co-classification, and/or co-extension" (84). From this basic definition, Hasan says that the relationship among the items determines which of the two different types of cohesive chains a particular chain might be. Thus, an identity chain occurs where "every member of the chain refers to the same thing, event, or whatever" (84), that is, a relationship of co-reference. In contrast, similarity chains have their members

> related to each other either by co-classification or co-extension. Each such chain is made up of items that refer to non-identical members of the same class of things, events, etc., or to members of non-identical but related classes of things, events, etc. (84)

From an analysis of chains, several reasonably objective counts can be derived. Hasan's first of two key claims that are helpful here is that the more tokens in a passage that fall into chains, the more coherent the text is (*Language* 90). The second claim Hasan makes pertains to two different types of tokens, *peripheral tokens*, which are not in chains, and *relevant tokens*, which are in either an identity chain or a similarity chain. Hasan says that the lower the proportion of peripheral to relevant tokens, the more coherent the text (*Language* 93). The resulting counts are presented below help to account for the special features of the 200-series passage I have studied, in which the addition of redundancy did not improve Cloze scores measuring readers' comprehension of the text.

Cohesion analysis is helpful to the study of readable writing, both because it is somewhat more objective than propositional analysis, and because it has been fully explicated by Halliday and Hasan. But even so, it is difficult to feel confident about the data generated in such an analysis, and even more difficult to verify an analysis by using a second scorer, because the systems of analysis are complex and not easily learned. With propositional analysis, even using the Bovair and Kieras simplified system, judgements are highly subjective and again, difficult to verify. Still, Tierney and Mosenthal rightly point out that cohesion provides a useful descriptive analysis of text. Moreover, cohesion analysis provides some numerical data, albeit subjective in nature, that can be fitted together with the more objective, if superficial, counts of syllables, content words and so on, producing a more complete analysis of a text. Still, cohesion alone does not capture as much about the complex nature of reading and writing readable text as possible.

Discourse Research and Redundancy

One study demonstrates the usefulness of a discourse-based approach to difficulty, and ties together some of the disparate views discussed in this chapter. Moreover, this study points the way to the upcoming discussion of writing in Chapter 5, the production side of readable writing. Olsen and Johnson undertook to reevaluate a prior study of readability and revisions to text. The prior study had shown that, despite manipulation of texts on standard readability criteria (sentence length, vocabulary level, and the like), readers did not find the passages more readable (Olsen and Johnson 209). But these results, Olsen and

Johnson argue, can be explained if "key concepts in the analysis of discourse: reference, cohesion, givenness, topicality. . ." (209) are taken into account.

When the authors of the original study simplified the vocabulary and syntax, they also made the texts more difficult by inadvertently removing markers of cohesion. In particular, the cohesion of repeated subjects or subject pronouns was lost (Olsen and Johnson 220) and many inferences were required in the revised versions, making them more challenging, especially for poor readers (Olsen and Johnson 224). In addition, there are various within-sentence problems resulting from the attempts to simplify the vocabulary and to shorten the sentences (Olsen and Johnson 225). The discourse-based analysis shows that the simplifications had additional effects on the texts which were not considered. The result of the reanalysis leads Olsen and Johnson to conclude that

> Any realistic model of language comprehension must take into account at least the nature of the language processing faculty itself, the reader's knowledge of the language and of the 'world' (the domain of discourse), and the structure of the text itself. Unfortunately, modeling the reader's knowledge of the language and of the world is extremely difficult to do and is an area where individual differences may be, probably will be, strongly significant. Thus, most researchers have tended to place relatively little emphasis on those factors related to individual differences and to focus on the nature of the language processing faculty and the structure of the text, aspects that seem to be better understood and easier to represent. (Olsen and Johnson 226)

Moreover, they go on to say that use of "common patterns of text structure" (227) is relevant to reading for both those learning to read and for those using reading in the course of day-to-day activity. In sum, these scholars suggest that redundancy (i.e., those "common patterns"), cohesion, and other discourse elements play a key role in readable writing. The results of my studies, to be discussed in the second half of the book, address the full range factors that pertain to readability, comprehensibility, and difficulty, and to readable writing. We can make use of the elements that are countable by a computer, and combine them with discourse and other factors known to make a difference.

We have now seen that there are three corners to the puzzle of the nature of readable text, each with its varied but interlocking pieces—linguistics, psychology, and reading. The writing corner, to be taken up in the next chapter, will help to complete the frame of the puzzle. This chapter has reviewed research in reading from several different angles: models of reading in both first and second language, and studies on readability and aspects of comprehensibility, using both formula-based analysis, and discourse and comprehension approaches. This work demonstrates the central role of the text factors redundancy and cohesion in reading and in the nature of readable text. The reading research looks at readable writing from the perception side, i.e., from the standpoint of how text is processed by readers, and does so using varied methodologies. In the next chapter, we approach readable writing from the production side, in a review of studies in writing and rhetoric that show the necessity for redundancy and cohesion in readable writing.

CHAPTER 5

Relevant Research IV: Writing

Writing researchers have paid a fair amount of attention to findings in linguistics and psychology about cohesion and redundancy, and generally, rhetoricians and composition theorists have always had a strong interest in making writing readable. Texts on writing abound, full of advice on "good writing" and "readable writing," making the writing corner quite varied and interesting. However, the writing portion of the puzzle is also complicated by the fact that there is considerable disagreement about terms like *good* and *readable* among writing scholars. Moreover, researchers who are studying writing hold widely disparate views about the importance of process versus product, of text versus the writer. My exploration of this field draws together the work of those who have investigated the nature of text as it provides insights into readable writing.

Some scholars provide rhetorically based discussions of discourse and related issues, drawing mostly from focused studies of text (Larson; Winterowd, "Grammar"; Witte and Faigley). Others offer linguistically based discussions of the analysis of text and the variations in the writing task for second language learners, offering diverse cross-cultural and cross-individual alternative methodologies including cases of individual writers, text analysis, or empirical studies (Smith, *Writing*; Vande Kopple; Markels; Grabe and Kaplan; Coe; Couture; Neuner and Yang). Still another group has carried out empirical studies, think-aloud protocols, and case studies in the form of psychological investigations of writing processes and writer/reader interactions (Kintsch and Yarbrough; Jensen and DiTiberio; Haas and Flower; Tierney and Pearson; Tierney and Mosenthal, "Cohesion"; Brand and Brandt). Various other approaches have also been tried.

A portion of this work provides the basis for the kinds of treatments I have used in the passages I have been studying, and at least some of it coincides with the work reviewed above. As is true in a jigsaw puzzle, this research may seem to fit in the other corners we have already pieced together, but it also fits into this corner for writing research. Ultimately, it is important to keep in mind that like a jigsaw, all these pieces interlock. Grabe has pointed out the connections among the different approaches to discourse:

> In the last 5 years, the study of written discourse by means of co-occurring linguistic structures, cohesion and information structures and orderings have been the most productive areas of research. . . .While to some extent coherence represents a semantic interpretation of a text in terms of macrostructure, logical relations among clauses, and information structuring, it is reasonable to suggest that cohesion relations and co-occurring lexico-syntactic features also must play a role. The fact that linguistic features, cohesion features and information structuring often appear to overlap in interesting ways only reinforces this larger view of the factors involved in perceived textual coherence. (Grabe, "Current Developments. . .Discourse" 50)

Through their varied approaches, some writing researchers share with reading researchers the view that redundancy and cohesion play key roles in readable writing and lend assistance to this central claim, as well as support for the need for varied methods and a cross-cultural understanding of the impact of redundancy and cohesion.

In this chapter, I will review the segment of writing research that lends support to my view of the nature of readable writing. In the generic definition that has been the basis of the discussion so far, readable writing comes about when reader expectation and writer intention coincide in a text, expressed through use of cohesion and redundancy. Examining the writer intention portion of this working definition requires, first, a general model of writing, paralleling the models of reading reviewed in the preceding chapter. Positioning the diverse pieces of writing research, I take up those rhetoricians' views that address the key features of readable writing, concentrating mainly on the discussion of cohesion from the writing side.

There are useful insights about writing, like those from reading research, that derive from studies across languages, particularly from contrastive rhetoric, functional linguistic analysis and other second language studies. I will also draw on psychological studies of writing to round out the overview of writing research that pertains to readable writing. As has been true in the other chapters from the various disciplines, selected work in rhetoric and composition studies related to the questions I am investigating provides substantial support for my major claim that readable writing relies on redundancy and cohesion, as well as for the view that these complex processes require varied research methodologies and a multicultural appreciation of the nature of text.

A PSYCHOLINGUISTIC MODEL OF WRITING

The general state of rhetoric and composition studies is that of a new field, with scholars involved in energetic, basic research. If there is a generally shared view of the nature of writing and how it is best taught and learned, it is probably the "process" view. From this perspective, writing is thought to be a process or a series of processes, sometimes linearly described as *prewriting* (brainstorming, planning, nutshelling, applying heuristics, etc.), *writing* (or composing, creating, transcribing ideas into words, etc.), and *rewriting* (also called revising, reconsidering, editing, reviewing, transforming writer-based to reader-based prose, and so on). Most practicing teachers and researchers agree, however, that the complexity of writing exceeds any simple model of this kind. The point made earlier with regard to models of the reading process, that their inadequacy lies in the fact that most are not complex enough (Sternglass, Grant-Davie) applies equally to models of writing.

A scholar who would agree with this view of the complexity of models is Frank Smith, who has written a careful analysis of the nature of writing that effectively frames the work I want to review here. Smith provides a fairly sophisticated view of writing and takes into consideration the impact of both factors of interest here. In *Writing and the Writer*, Smith discusses redundancy in terms of writing conventions, and cohesion as one kind of convention used by writers to create readable text. While Smith's discussion in its entirety provides a substantial description of writing and of the complexities of trying to describe various aspects of the process, his comments on "writing episodes" (Smith, *Writing* 105-6) are a useful starting point for the present discussion.

These episodes are the moments during which the text is created, using, in Smith's terms, *composing* (the invention of the text as strings of words in phrases and sentences) and *transcribing* (visible production of the text). These acts of writing, separated from prewriting and revising, are complex and often involve prewriting and revising going on simultaneously, but can nonetheless be considered separately. Writing activity draws on redundancy and cohesion in three of its elements.

In Smith's view, writing occurs when words actually appear on paper, and when this occurs, the writer is not in control of what is happening. Under these conditions, redundancy figures prominently as part of our unconscious knowledge of language. As Smith says:

> Whether the words are created as they are put onto paper or whether they are first heard in the writer's mind does not change the basic fact that the writer has no control over their arrival, except for the ultimate control of not putting them on paper or of erasing them from the paper. We can make decisions about words when they are manifest, when they are accessible to conscious inspection in the

> imagination or on paper, but we cannot control what arrives in the first place. (*Writing* 106)

As these writing episodes take place, a piece of text is constructed and the writer's thinking continues to unfold. Writers control the text once it has appeared, of course, in revising and editing, adding and deleting, and so forth. Smith's point that writing episodes tap unconscious thought processes is quite central to my argument; one key feature of redundancy is that awareness of it, as Smith suggests here, is unconscious for both readers and writers. Writing episodes, thus, are one part of writing that draws on text factors.

What shapes the product of writing episodes is the specification of the writer's intentions, and these are also not necessarily conscious or expressed in words. The specification of the writer's intentions draws on writers' and readers' prior knowledge, a second part of writing where redundancy appears. Smith's view is that this specification differs from an outline or other overt planning, and is more subtle in nature:

> the intentions are not the same as the text; they will probably never at any one time have the same form or detail as the text. Nevertheless, intentions are the basis upon which the text is formed. I want to employ a special term for all of these intentions, which at one time or another are relevant to a potential or developing text; I shall refer to them as the specification for the text. It is with reference to this specification of intentions, this specification for a text, that we think about when we think about writing, when we write and when we decide whether we have written what we wanted to write. And to the extent that we can put the specification into words at any time, so can we talk about what we want to write (or would like to write). (*Writing* 111-12)

How the composing and specifications come together in a description of composition is as follows:

> . . .composition is not a matter of putting down one word after another, or of translating successive ideas into words, but rather of building a structure (the text) from materials (the conventions) according to an incomplete and constantly changing plan (the specification of intentions). (*Writing* 118)

Here, Smith mentions the third element that picks up the text factors I have been examining in my research: conventions. These are both global and focal in nature: global conventions include schemata (such as a story schema, a research article and the like) and other more general agreements that we have about texts, while focal intentions take into consideration the construction of sentences, paragraphs, spelling of individual words, and other similar factors, including cohesive devices.

When writers and readers meet in a readable text, the writer's intentions and the reader's expectations coincide, so that the reader's predictions are confirmed by the writer's text. The writer uses conventions and schemata, as well as the reader's prior knowledge developed within the text and from the reader's knowledge outside the text, to enable the reader to predict what will appear in the text. When he talks about reader expectations (*Writing* 95) Smith is really talking about redundancy, both within the text and between the text and the reader's prior knowledge. Cohesion he describes as one of many conventions in writing. Research in other areas of writing, including the work in contrastive rhetoric that reveals the differences in conventions in writers' first and second languages to be discussed below, provides support for Smith's discussion of the importance of conventions (Atkinson; McKay; Purves; Reid). With this description of the overall shape of writing and the role of redundancy and cohesion in it, we can turn to the research from the writing perspective that explicates the relevance of redundancy and especially cohesion.

THE RHETORICIANS' VIEW OF WRITING

The rhetorically based analyses of writing have looked at issues of cohesion and coherence for some time now, but as I noted in the opening chapter, the definitions of the terms are somewhat befuddled in writing theory (see Larson for comments on this point). One of the earliest discussions of cohesion and coherence is Ross Winterowd's 1970 essay "The Grammar of Coherence," in which he generally suggests that coherence has to do with relationships in texts longer than a single sentence. The relationships he enumerates are "coordinate, obversative, causative, conclusive, alternative, inclusive and sequential" (831) and may be expressed or implied. In his exploration of these relationships, Winterowd suggests the kinds of relationships captured by Halliday and Hasan's forms of cohesion, especially conjunctive relationships. Despite these scholars' differences over terminology, Winterowd, like Halliday and Hasan, was interested in the question of what makes a text a text rather than disconnected sentences; that is, he was interested in discourse.

This question has been pursued by other writing researchers over the past 15 years, and as Richard Larson observes, was really spurred by appearance of *Cohesion in English*. Numerous attempts to define *cohesion*, *coherence*, and other related terms have followed, but, as Larson says, ultimately

> the determination of coherence is fundamentally an interpretation by a reader. It is part of a transaction between text and reader—between the reader's world and the writer's language. (Larson 72)

Though I agree generally with Larson's comment, the text factors I have been studying are crucial to the transaction, and can be identified and dealt with practically for the purpose of analyzing prose and helping readers and writers meet in readable texts.

Other discourse-based discussions support this view as well. Witte and Faigley's research study is one early example of work done from the writing perspective that points up the significance of cohesion for writing. They agree that the research support for the concept of cohesion comes from diverse fields, but their own study examined assessments of writing quality in student essays by University of Texas freshmen. Although their findings do not support the claim that more cohesive ties make better writing based on a simple quantitative analysis, they agree that

> cohesion is an important property of writing quality. To some extent the types and frequencies of cohesive ties seem to reflect the invention skills of student writers and to influence the stylistic and organizational properties of the texts they write. . . .All discourse is context bound—to the demands of the subject matter, occasion, medium and audience of the text. Cohesion defines those mechanisms that hold a text together, while coherence defines those underlying semantic relations that allow a text to be understood and used. (Witte and Faigley 202)

This passage further clarifies the difference between cohesion and coherence, but raises the question of what constitutes good writing. The quality of the writing in the student essays studied by Witte and Faigley was based on a holistic appraisal. While holistic scoring has been defended as a useful approach to assessment of writing, it does not have the same flavor as reading time or comprehension or other more objective measures, and may be to some degree a reflection of the readers' personality preferences (see Jensen and DiTiberio). Despite these issues, Witte and Faigley agree that cohesion is pertinent to writing quality. Other evidence from the reading side supports the idea that, in fact, more cohesive ties enhance the readers' understanding of a text, measured by other means (Irwin, "Effect"). Additional discourse-based research supports this view and has addressed the pertinence of cohesion and coherence analysis for helping writers create readable texts (Bamberg; Fahnestock; Stotsky).

Some rhetorically based research is quite focused at the sentence level and examines the particulars of cohesive devices and other features of Halliday's approach to language analysis as they pertain to the problems of analyzing and teaching writing. William Vande Kopple's work with the "functional sentence perspective" is one example of work of this kind. FSP primarily analyzes individual sentences, but does so with an eye toward the presentation of information in the larger text. In this analysis, sentences have two major components, topic and comment, similar to, but not the same as subject and predicate. However, FSP also looks at the content of these components, and it is generally true that the information in the topic component is old or given information, while the information in the comment is new. Vande Kopple studied passages that conformed to these expectations, by comparing them to passages that did not, in terms of comprehension measured by both judgments made by readers and by tests of recall. He found that the passages in which the sentences followed FSP were "significantly more readable and memorable than their variants" (Vande Kopple 54).

There are two points to be made about this finding in the current context. First, FSP gives another way of looking at redundancy. As Vande Kopple says, paragraphs consistent with FSP

> must follow the given-new sequence; given information must be clearly marked by repetition of identical or slightly qualified terms, must match information already in storage, and must be placed in sentence topics, before the new information. On the other hand, it is easy to see that variants frustrate to some extent the reader who expects the given-new sequence. (55)

Given information is thus presented in a highly redundant pattern. Also, when he mentions expectations, Vande Kopple is talking about redundancy, and it seems clear that FSP supports my claims and findings about the nature and importance of redundancy.

A second point with regard to this sentence-level analysis is that it pertains equally well and equally strongly to reading as to writing. Sentence-level analysis of discourse has advantages for nonnative speakers, particularly those trying to learn English whose native languages do not have fixed word order, as English does. Vande Kopple draws on some research done with such languages. The FSP pattern is relatively straightforward to observe and to discuss, and can be helpful whether the texts being examined are to be read or are texts being used to teach and learn writing. Moreover, additional work on sentences, and their interaction in discourse, supports the FSP analysis.

COHESION IN WRITING

Before turning to the work that focuses on the discourse level, several other pieces of research warrant discussion, both dealing with cohesion and particularly with cohesive chains in passages of text. A *cohesive chain* is "a set of items each of which is related to the others by the semantic relation of co- reference, co-classification, and/or co-extension" (Halliday and Hasan, *Language* 83). The chains are established by looking at the cohesive ties among lexical items in the text, but according to some of the research done on these issues, it is the nature of the chains through the whole passage that is crucial.

One study along these lines appears in the work of Jerome Neuner. In his empirical study of freshman writers at the college level, looking at their expository prose, Neuner found that the nature of the chains, rather than the number of ties, made a difference in the quality of the writing. In particular, longer chains were found in expository essays that were judged good using holistic scoring, particularly ones that appear in a single paragraph or ones that tie several paragraphs or the whole essay together (Neuner 100). The implications of this finding pertain to readable writing as follows:

> Understanding chains holds promise for a deepening of insight into the concept of texture as an explanation of how a text attains its meaning. . . .The metaphors used in the cohesion system suggest valuable truths about meaning in discourse. Terms such as chain, distance, tie, coherer, precursor, intersection and network suggest that connectedness is at the core of meaning and that complex meaning is never resolved in a single word or phrase but through longer semantic structures that cross or intertwine with others. (Neuner 101)

Neuner's finding suggests that readable writing does not occur as a by-product of any simple, easily counted or measured factor, but occurs as a result of a number of complex features that intertwine over a passage of text. Not only lexical but also sentence level choices and discourse patterns contribute to readable writing.

Another research study that provides a close analysis of just a few texts supports this view. Agnes Yang's work on "Cohesive Chains and Writing Quality" also examined cohesive chains, this time in the work of a small set of student writers. Yang studied drafts and revised versions, and found longer cohesive chains in the revised texts, and also more instances of chain interaction. Chains are said to *interact* when "at least two members of one chain . . . stand in the same relation to two members of another chain" such as actor-action, quality-qualified and the like (Halliday and Hasan, *Language* 91). Both Neuner and Yang, then, approach text to examine similar issues using different methods, conduct close analyses, and come to a similar conclusion—that it is not only the individual elements, but also their interconnections, that contribute to an appraisal of quality or readable writing. Additional work that focuses on the discourse level clarifies this point further.

Robin Markels's analysis of cohesion examines syntactic and semantic perspectives on it, and draws on the work of psychologists like Kintsch and Kieras. She examines the consistency with which key words are used to draw sentences into a cohesive text in the Halliday and Hasan sense, and has also studied the occurrence of such key words in subject position in sentences, a feature she suggests creates syntactic cohesion, but which from my point of view contributes something to the redundancy of a text, on the syntactic side (Markels, *New Perspective* 41 and 61). This analysis is rather like the given-new strategy proposed by Vande Kopple. Because ultimately Markels discusses the implications of her analyses for teaching and learning writing, it is clear that she believes that cohesion, as she has described it, plays a central role in good writing.

Markels's work shares an bond with other research on cohesion that comes from linguistic analysis. Markels has approached cohesion in writing from both the sentence and discourse levels of analysis. Other scholars, working from a more strictly linguistic base, have addressed cohesion at the level of individual sentences and also at the discourse level. While the previously noted issues of definition of terms and the problem of measurement persist in all of this work, linguistic analyses shed some interesting light on the nature of readable writing.

CONTRIBUTIONS FROM CONTRASTIVE RHETORIC

One set of linguistically based findings has been presented by William Grabe in his work on contrastive rhetoric and its implications for teaching writing in a second language. His careful analyses of text types show that expository prose is a distinct text type, different in several ways from narrative prose, dialogues, letters, and other types of texts. He counts a number of specific linguistic variables and has found subtypes within expository prose as well. These variables, including cohesive devices and redundancy in the form of repetition, may, he suggests, show developmental patterns among language learners and may provide the basis for particular teaching techniques.

Grabe's work is one example of the contribution that contrastive rhetoric makes to our understanding of text types and text processing, and shows, again, that redundancy and cohesion figure prominently in writing, distinguishing among different types and sub-types of texts (Grabe, "Contrastive" 135-36). In addition, contrastive rhetoric's support for cohesion and redundancy ties to my thesis that these features are necessary to readable writing across languages, cultures, and differing ethnic groups. Further support is provided by a recent proposal by Connor and Keller, working on teaching and learning English as a second language ("Directions").

Grabe and Kaplan have found that contrastive rhetoric sheds light on seven areas involved in reading, writing, and readable writing: rhetorical patterns of arrangement, composing conventions, morphosyntax of the language in which the text is written, coherence-creating mechanisms of the target language, conventions of types of texts, audience characteristics and expectations, and prior knowledge (Grabe and Kaplan 271-272). These areas all support the original contention that different languages use fundamentally different approaches to rhetorical organization in expository text, and that these sometimes are carried over or transferred by L2 learners to the new language (Hudelson "Writing" 216; Purves and Hawisher 183 and 185; Hinds 98). More recent work on different types of tasks, given to test writing ability among nonnative speakers, documents the impact of contrastive rhetorical analysis (Reid, "Responding" 191).

The work of Richard Coe also contributes to the cross-linguistic evidence, because, like some other scholars, Coe tries to explain cohesion and its role in the larger discourse, across languages. Coe's work developed in part out of his need to have ways of working on discourse when teaching English to Chinese students. Coe's analysis pertains to English, but he points out that it can be used in any language, and is especially helpful when addressing issues of contrastive rhetoric, comparing discourse patterns in Chinese and English, for example. The analysis also provides an approach to appraising the quality of a text that is yet another means for judging readable writing.

Coe uses the concept of a *discourse matrix*, drawn partly from the work of Francis Christensen and various other scholars. He goes beyond the level of simply analyzing the cohesion between or among the sentences of the passage to look across paragraphs to the whole passage. This kind of analysis solves, he believes, a key problem from the point of view of composition theorists:

> When the study of cohesion is focused on such devices as transition words, there is a clear distinction between the structure of meaning and the transitions which signal that structure. Once we start looking at cohesion created by the repetition of certain words and phrases that name unifying topics. . . the distinction becomes less clear, and it becomes possible to confuse the cues signaling the structure with structure itself. Such confusion is unfortunate because it blurs what ought to be the key question: What is the relationship between cohesion cues and the structure they are presumed to demarcate? (Coe 9)

The study of cohesion alone is not enough; the discourse matrix moves beyond it to the structure of the text overall.

Cohesion cues help to reveal the text structure; they can be found using the discourse matrix. The *matrix* is defined as

> A technique for analyzing and diagramming the patterns of modification (among levels of generality) that constitute a key characteristic of the semantic structure of discursive discourse. Such a drawing is constructed by numbering each T-unit (or sentence or clause) and representing it by a circle. Level of generality is indicated on the drawing by the relation position of the circles. (Coe 108)

There are three basic relationships to be represented in a discourse matrix: *coordination* (including contrasting, contradicting, conjoining, and repeating on the same level of generality), *subordination* (including defining, exemplifying, giving reasons, deducing, explaining, or qualifying), and *superordination* (including drawing conclusions or generalizing and commenting) (Coe 32). The system is complex, but Coe gives many helpful examples of matrices in his book.

The matrix concept has an advantage over some other approaches to discourse, in that it addresses ambiguity and the issue of measurement:

> Ambiguity is thus a necessary and desirable feature of human discourse, which a "grammar of passages" must accommodate, not avoid. For a "grammar of passages,"

> unless it confines itself to surface features, such as cohesion cues, which can be "objectively" catalogued, is ultimately a "grammar" of the cognitive structure represented by the passage. However unsatisfying it may be to those accustomed to the "objective" precision of grammatical analysis, this sort of discourse analysis is by the nature of the case the best that can be done without sacrificing the purpose of doing the analysis in the first place. (Coe 11)

Matrices take into account the complexity of language and the complex relationships among parts of a discourse. What matrix analysis reveals is the patterns in a text, and this in turn provides a basis for judging readable writing, though, as Coe notes in the passage quoted just above, it is not necessarily objective or precise.

Coe goes on to show how matrix analysis can help language learners, both with diagnosis of when writing is readable and when it is not, and with analysis of text in order to get meaning. He notes that writing is easier to read when the discourse follows familiar patterns and uses markers that readers recognize (like paragraphing and cohesive devices) to reveal the structure of the ideas (61). These observations are followed by a sample passage of student writing that has weaknesses that matrix analysis reveals clearly (63). Moreover, on the reading side, Coe claims that similar analyses of passages by professional writers, from textbooks, technical materials, or other sources, can help readers as well.

Such analysis reveals Kintsch's macrostructure or gist of the text and how the ideas are presented (Coe 69). Coe goes on to point out that, when teaching English to nonnative speakers, such an approach moves far beyond vocabulary and speed building to helping such students develop more effective strategies for getting meaning from print (Coe 70). Coe's claims are also supported by Carrell's research on the connections of reading and writing for students of English as a second language. Carrell examined several analyses of rhetorical structure by Meyer and found that knowledge and use of such structures in ESL reading and writing makes a contribution to the literacy of ESL students (Carrell, "Text as Interaction" 47-56).

FUNCTIONAL-GRAMMAR-BASED ANALYSIS

Yet another kind of linguistic analysis relies directly on the functional grammar proposed by Halliday. Functional grammar, with its interest in the context in which language occurs in addition to its concern with relations of ideas in the text, leads to a different way of appraising writing quality and a different sort of approach to teaching writing. Barbara Couture offers several interesting proposals in this connection, in her attempt to appraise "effective ideation" in writing. Once again, the discussion focuses on both sentence and discourse levels, and includes cohesion.

Couture's work picks up the topic-comment analysis of sentences discussed above, but she also picks up concepts that are central to redundancy as discussed here. She summarizes the connection between the two in this way:

> . . .effective ideation is a function of two kinds of meaning systems realized through text: conceptual logic and contextual semiotic. Through systematic lexical and syntactic choices that express logical relationships between topics and comments at the discourse and sentence level, the text promotes the reader's conceptualization of its overall message. Through linguistic choices that comprise registers (conventional ways of saying things in certain contexts) and genres (conventional forms of overall discourse structure), texts present a relevant context for ideational interpretation. (Couture, "Effective Ideation" 88)

The logical relations between topics and comments are established by cohesive devices of various kinds. The concepts of register and genre address redundancy, dealing as they do with conventions of sentences and discourses with which readers are likely to be familiar. These two ideas are described more fully:

> Registers are conventionally adopted ways of speaking or writing that often specify the attitude the reader is to take toward conceptualizing the ideas in the discourse. For instance, they determine the listener/reader's expectations that the discourse will develop hierarchically ordered logical relationships, that it will contain facts to be built upon in succeeding communications, and that it will require reference to some systems of meaning outside the text. These expectations are cued by conventional linguistic features that comprise a given register. (Couture, "Effective Ideation" 80)

About genres, Couture says:

> While registers impose explicitness constraints at the level of vocabulary and syntax, genres impose additional explicitness constraints at the discourse level. They define conventional patterns of linguistic structure of a complete discourse, and they are intertextual—that is, they are defined by their capacity to evoke other texts. . . Unlike register, genre can be projected as complete, for a genre does more than specify kinds of codes extant in a group of related texts; it specifies conditions for beginning, continuing and ending a text. (Couture, "Effective Ideation" 82)

Both register and genre are aspects of redundancy. Conventional linguistic features that constitute a register help create redundancy for that register in a text, while conventional patterns of linguistic structure, which evoke other texts of a similar sort, contribute to the redundancy that makes a research report or fairy tale predictable in terms of form or what Hsia has called *input-memory redundancy*. We have already seen that psychological research further supports such claims (Olson et al., Kintsch; Frank Smith), as does contrastive rhetorical analysis (Grabe, discussed above; Atkinson) and discourse analysis of clauses from a functional perspective, looking at signalling systems within the text (Hoey; Hoey and Winter).

Recent work on features of particular genres provides further support for my claims about cohesion and redundancy. Biber's multifeatural and multidimensional analysis of various genres of spoken and written language shows that there are differences among genres, and these differences deal specifically with cohesive features and other features that contribute to redundancy (Biber 121-169). The findings have implications for the practical matter of teaching writing and for both native and nonnative speakers of English. Biber describes the work along these lines, which he has done with Grabe:

> Grabe and Biber (1987) use the model of textual relations developed here in a pilot study of the linguistic characteristics of good and poor essays written by native and non-native writers of English. That study finds almost no difference between native and non-native essays and only small differences between good and poor essays. The most striking result, however, is that student essays are unlike any of the published genres of English; they use the surface forms of academic writing (e.g., passives), but they are relatively non-informational and involved, and they are extremely persuasive in form. This finding indicates that compositions do not have a well-defined discourse norm in English. (Biber 203-204)

This kind of analysis suggests that specific features of a text help define its genre, and the genre itself, particularly when it is clearly indicated by those features, contributes to redundancy and to making it a readable piece of writing. The results of careful analyses of these elements have practical implications then, in addition to providing support for the relevance of these features to readable writing for which I am trying to argue.

As noted above, when writers choose to use register and genre appropriate to the rhetorical situation (audience, topic and purpose) they find themselves in, good writing is more likely to result. But, as Couture says

> To assert that effective ideation represents a balance between conceptual clarity and contextual exigence is to confirm that neither intellectual logic nor appeal to situational variables alone presumes communicative success. (Couture, "Effective Ideation" 90)

She argues for the need to consider both conceptual clarity and context, both the sentence level need for cohesive devices and the discourse level need for overall redundancy in the chosen genre, to account for what constitutes readable prose.

RHETORICIANS' CONSENSUS ON REDUNDANCY AND COHESION

Reviewing the writing research presented thus far, it is clear that, among specialists in rhetoric and composition who have focused on the nature of text (one of many areas of study in the field) there is agreement to a great extent about the importance of cohesion and redundancy, variously defined, to the creation and appraisal of readable writing. Both the rhetorically based research that examines first and second language student writing/teaching techniques/ rhetorical considerations, and linguistic research on the L1 and L2 processes involved in generating a text and various theoretically based strategies for analyzing it, suggest that cohesion and redundancy are the crucial elements. The text research in rhetoric and composition studies makes clear the intricacy of cohesion, though it is chiefly a feature of the text itself within and across sentences. Redundancy is a bit more complex, since it involves elements in the text at every level (letters, words, and syntactic and semantic structure) and also the prior knowledge of the reader. These elements within the text itself contribute most centrally to how effectively and efficiently people are able to send and receive meaning in written text. Psychologically based work on writing will provide further support for this contention.

PSYCHOLOGICAL STUDIES OF WRITING

Despite mixed results in empirical studies of rhetorical structures and writing quality based on cohesion (Renfrow 86-97 and Horowitz 144-45), basic organizational patterns that contribute redundancy to texts seem pertinent in much other research conducted by psychologists. For instance, Kintsch and Yarbrough found, in their study on the "Role of Rhetorical Structure in Text Comprehension," that the presence or absence of elements in the text which signalled its rhetorical form (often cohesive devices such as conjunctions or ordering elements like first. . .second. . .finally) made a significant difference to readers' comprehension.

Subjects' recall of the topic and main points of the passage was significantly better in passages where words signalling rhetorical structure were present than in altered versions of the same passages with those words deleted. Kintsch and Yarbrough reach several useful conclusions about their findings:

> The present findings imply . . .that the rhetorical cues and canonical ordering that distinguished the good forms of the texts from the bad forms facilitate the macroprocesses in comprehension. . .Rhetorical structure was effective, however, only when a comprehension test sensitive to macroprocesses was used. (Kinstch and Yarbrough 833)

But a further point on measurement

> has to do with the nature of comprehension testing. . . .Comprehension is a common sense term for a whole bundle of psychological processes, each of which must be evaluated separately. Only a collection of different tests, each tuned to some specific aspect of the total process, will provide adequate results. (Kintsch and Yarbrough 834)

Kintsch and Yarbrough's research, like much other material discussed in these opening chapters, seems to show that rhetorical structure, which includes both redundancy and cohesion, has a role in writers' production, and readers' comprehension, of readable writing. However, what is measured and how it is measured determines what we can make of the findings and the claims that result. The research studies to be reported below (Chapters 7 through 10) report results on a "collection of different tests" to examine text comprehension and composition. In the discussion thus far of writing research and in what follows, I intend to demonstrate the relevance of diverse methodologies and to show that varied approaches methodologically and across personalities, languages, and cultures provide support for the intrinsic role of redundancy and cohesion in readable writing.

For example, another approach to writing from the psychological side appears in the work of Jensen and DiTiberio, already discussed (Chapter 3). Their investigations of the array of psychological types and preferences provide a frame in which to put these various approaches to both generating text and responding to it. They propose that people with a particular set of preferences will tend to write a certain way. Though readers' responses to expository prose in terms of personality preferences have yet to be examined in detail by Jensen and DiTiberio or others, they speculate on how writing teachers' evaluations are to some degree based on their preferences. More generally, Jensen and DiTiberio have suggested that readers respond to texts in certain ways because of their personality type, though the nature of the relationship of type and response will require much further study (DiTiberio letter to the author).

Jensen and DiTiberio discuss, in this context, writing variation in different discourse communities. They draw on historians, social scientists, composition theorists, and student writers, four different kinds of discourse communities. The MBTI interactions on the sensing/intuition and thinking/feeling dimensions (see Chapter 3, above, and also Jensen and DiTiberio 18-28, as well as Myers for further discussion) are illustrated in these various discourse communities. The writing students formed a community when they were grouped based on their preferences on these two dimensions and given the assignment to describe time to a Martian.

Across these various discourse communities, personality type clearly influences how people approach the material and how they present their ideas in writing. Those with a sensing-thinking preference are variously described as "analytic scientists. . .or Experimentalists" (19) who prefer empirical knowledge that is "value-free, impersonal, and unambiguous. Data must be collected by a method that is reliable and precise, and they must be analyzed objectively and logically" (19). Student writers with this preference described time objectively in measurable units or parts.

A very different approach comes from those with a sensing- feeling preference. These scholars and writers are "particular humanists" (21) in one scheme, and in another take a personal, ethnographic or case study approach to research. Sensing-feeling writers described time with sensory and concrete language, but use personal particulars to discover general implications.

The intuitive-feeling types, who are in the social science discourse community proposed to be "conceptual humanists" (24) are also practitioners and clinicians. These researchers develop trust and use the strength of their relationship to help motivate others. Student writers with an intuitive-feeling preference use metaphors to describe time to a Martian, providing a somewhat "abstract . . .value-laden . . . [but] holistic" (25) description of time than the other groups.

Finally, there is a group with the intuitive-thinking preference who can also be described as "conceptual theorists" (26), or "formalists"(26). These scholars like to build models but are so deeply committed to theory that they are not concerned about whether the model constructed has connection to reality. The intuitive-thinking student group produced a description of time that reflects little concern with practical aspects, suggesting that time is artificial and arbitrary.

Jensen and DiTiberio reach an interesting conclusion from this analysis:

> . . .we have suggested that personality type—especially once combinations are considered—can explain how historians conceive of and present their content, how scientists, including composition theorists, conduct research, and even how students describe a commonplace concept such as "time." (Jensen and DiTiberio 28)

Thus, personality type appears to play a central role both in how a problem is viewed and studied, and also in how research strategies and results are presented and explored in written form. As I suggested in the psychology discussion earlier, preferences naturally shape responses to written text, both in terms of producing it and in terms of reading it, and will furthermore influence any reader/writer's view of what makes writing readable. As Jensen and DiTiberio show, this influences both what is studied and how it is studied, and what results are found, how they are found and how they are reported. Taking both Kintsch and Yarbrough's suggestion of differing approaches to the problem of comprehension, and Jensen and DiTiberio's description of a range of possible approaches, has helped to yield the multiple approach strategy reported in the chapters that comprise the second half of this book.

VIEWS OF TEXT FACTORS FROM A READING/WRITING PERSPECTIVE

Some additional research on writing from a psychological perspective deals with the junction of reading and writing, a difficult but intriguing angle from which to view the interaction of redundancy and cohesion. Tierney and Pearson have proposed a composing model of reading that takes up this junction. Although they do not see reading and writing as inverse relations of the same process, they contend that readers and writers both are composers of meaning (Tierney and Pearson 64) who engage in essentially similar activities including "planning, drafting, aligning, revising and monitoring" (Tierney and Pearson 64). This claim is supported by a study done by Haas and Flower using a think-aloud protocol to examine what they call "rhetorical reading" and by other research Tierney has done examining readers' and writers' interactions in a text (Haas and Flower 181-2; Tierney, LaZansky, Raphael and Cohen 223).

Readers and writers both plan by setting goals and using prior knowledge of the topic of the text. In drafting, writers attempt to set forth their meaning, while readers create a draft of this meaning in the form of their hypotheses about the text (following a top-down model of reading as hypothesis testing, cf. Frank Smith, Goodman, and others). Altogether, both processes focus on making sense of the text (Tierney and Pearson 68; Haas and Flower 182).

Two activities to be added to the list proposed by Tierney and Pearson occur concurrently in reading and writing: *aligning* and *revising*. Aligning refers to attitude issues—the persona of the writer, and the role the reader takes in response to the text the author presents (Sudol 154-57). Alignment in reading and writing is just one place where the various positions chosen by writers and readers make a key difference to meaning; Tierney and Pearson point out that there are a number of other situations in which adopting a different perspective or alignment can be helpful (69). Though they say that the text can provoke a particular kind of alignment, Jensen and DiTiberio would surely suggest that the writer's presentation and the reader's response each derive at least partly from their respective personality preferences.

Whether and how the text achieves a particular kind of alignment results from the impact of revising. In the process view of writing that underlies most of the research discussed here, writers obviously revise during and after drafting or writing episodes. But Tierney and Pearson propose that readers also revise, fairly continuously, their model of meaning as the text unfolds. Revising, along with planning, drafting and aligning, all go on in the presence of a monitor, an inner voice that serves as "first audience" (75) and reader/responder. The monitor on reading and writing is described as an inside voice that responds to the reading of written text or the writing of it, supervising the construction of meaning.

These processes come together according to Tierney and Pearson as follows:

> . . .we view both reading and writing as acts of composing. We see these acts of composing as involving continuous, recurring and recursive transactions among readers and writers, their respective inner selves and their perceptions of each other's goals and desires. Consider the reader's role as we envision it. At the same time as the reader considers what he perceives to be the author's intentions (or what the reader perceives to be what the author is trying to get the reader to do or think), he negotiates goals with his inner self (or what he would like to achieve). With these goals being continuously negotiated (sometimes embedded within each other) the reader proceeds to take different alignments (critic, coauthor, editor, character, reporter, eye witness, etc.) as he uses features from his own experiential arrays and what he perceives to be arrayed by the author in order to create a model of meaning for the text. These models of meaning must assume a coherent, holistic quality in which everything fits together. (Tierney and Pearson 75)

The process is extremely complex, but essentially reader activity and writer activity are complementary to one another. From another point of view, this composing model of reading considers both the writing side and the reading side of the writing episodes described by Smith and discussed above. The point I want to make about these processes is that the construction of meaning must have redundancy and cohesion built into it in the text.

Tierney and Mosenthal support this claim with their review of text analysis systems. They, like Tierney and Pearson, see reading and writing as related, intertwined activities that incorporate a number of factors:

> discourse comprehension and discourse production involve a complex interaction among the cognitive structures of the author, the text, the cognitive structures of the reader, and the communicative situation. (Tierney and Mosenthal, "Discourse Comprehension" 55)

This view takes in all the factors discussed thus far in this book: the language issues in the text itself, the views from reading and writing, and the situation where psychological factors become relevant. Tierney and Mosenthal believe that the various systems of text analysis they consider can all work together to provide a full picture of discourse comprehension and production, of reading and writing.

In their review of several approaches to text analysis, Tierney and Mosenthal include various proposals for propositional analysis, cohesion as presented by Halliday and Hasan, story grammars, narrative event chain models, prose predicate structural analysis, and mapping. They also raise the nagging question of measurement: what is measured and how it is measured in text analysis, and they remind readers that not every aspect of text can be measured by the systems they review or others, alone or grouped, demonstrating again the need for an assortment of methodologies.

The major finding of Tierney and Mosenthal concerns the uses of text analysis systems, which are these:

> to examine and appreciate the differential responses of readers to text features; . . .to examine and appreciate the text demands placed upon readers; . . .to examine and appreciate the relevance of a reader's text-based inferences; . . .to afford teachers and readers a metacognitive awareness of text demands; . . .to suggest instructional and testing procedures consistent with text demands. (Tierney and Mosenthal, "Discourse Comprehension" 99-101)

Text analysis can yield insights useful from both reading and writing perspectives in terms of how and why readers respond as they do to text. Chiefly, from Tierney and Mosenthal's view, text analysis systems shed light on the way readers and writers interact in a text. A different review from a reading perspective reaches essentially the same conclusion and describes a number of the systems considered by Tierney and Mosenthal (Hoskins 30-40). Although many scholars disagree and much research remains to be done (see Rayner and Pollatsek ch. 8, for example), from the point of view taken here, text analysis then reveals those features in the text itself that make for readable writing.

Deborah Brandt's work on context in writing also focuses on the text itself as a meeting ground for readers and writers. Brandt's main contention is that text features reveal the context in which a writer and reader meet and are a reflection of that context. As she says in an early article:

> . . .three aspects of text—exophoric references, cohesive devices and thematic structure—relate to conditions for meaning in a writer's context of composition. Through exophoric reference, one can glimpse the given world that a writer assumes to share with a reader, the world from which, in a sense, a writer launches a text. Cohesion, although often treated strictly as a textual element, is presented here instead as a context-sensitive strategy. Through patterns of reference and reiteration, for instance, writers reflect their assessment of the need—and leeway—they have for labeling and elaborating in their texts. Choice of theme is also an indication of a writer's attention to what is and can be in reader-writer focus as a discourse unfolds . . . (Brandt, "Text and Context" 105)

With her last point, Brandt suggests that, by doing close textual analysis, we can look inside reader-writer interaction in a text and see what both sides are thinking and where they meet. This is the meeting ground Frank Smith has described between writer intention and reader expectation, a ground revealed in the text features I focus on in the passages I have studied.

Brandt also observes the relationship between her view of context in writing and Smith's psycholinguistic analysis of reading. Context is crucial to the interaction of reading and writing:

> The actual context of any language act are the socially forged conditions of mutual awareness through which our private understandings can be realized with others. To see this shared context as something constituted by shared knowledge is to see how social context can still be at the center of meaning in written discourse even when writer and reader are separated in time and distance. Because this knowledge is socially distributed, intersubjectively assumed, obviously portable, and always at hand, it forges the public link in what are usually thought of as the private experiences of reading and writing. (Brandt, "Message" 152)

From this point, Brandt goes on to discuss the reading that takes place during writing, suggesting that it is like reading more generally, but also that it "serves some sort of important orienting function during composing" (154). This reading involves looking ahead to the next step in developing the meaning of the text, helping the reader set appropriate expectations for what is coming. In these observations, reading and writing meet, again, in the text itself, and both reader and writer work from that base to create a shared meaning.

Brandt's discussion of this point continues in another piece in which she discusses the notion of how readers and writers are involved with one another in text. Cohesion reflects this involvement:

> . . .a repeated phrase or synonym refers not to some retrievable material inscription but to some accomplished experience. Cohesive devices are said to make textual ties but actually they are a result of ties already made between here-and-now participants, writer and reader. . . .What's being made explicit is not a message but the accomplishment of understanding. Collocation and substitution are especially important in this regard in that they indicate a writer's sense of how he or she has just been read . . . These sorts of cohesive devices especially function to maintain a concurrence about what is going on. . . .When cohesion and other lexical devices are taken not as instances of textual self-reference but as indexes to an unfolding writer-reader history, involvement traces in written discourse appear quite high. (Brandt, "Message" 40-41)

Cohesion reflects, in Brandt's view, the way a reader and a writer relate to each other, and to the context in which the text occurs. It is a reflection of this interaction, a way in which meaning emerges from the text as a by-product of the reader-writer meeting. For this reason, cohesion and redundancy are crucial to readable writing.

A PROPOSAL FOR A PSYCHOLOGY OF WRITING

Finally, we come to recent attention focused on the psychology of writing, particularly in the work of Alice Brand. Brand's work, admittedly a beginning, examines the role of emotions in writing. Emotions in this context have been little understood and little studied, as Brand points out, but are the basis of much of our daily lives, including the processes of literacy being studied here. They play a role in what is said in a text and how it is said, and thus, according to Brand

> to be complete, a psychology of writing should include an account of emotional experience . . .to ignore affective experience would be to severely limit our understanding of the human mind in action. (Brand 2)

I contend that the human mind is nowhere in action more clearly than in the production and comprehension of readable writing. Brand's findings, based on her use of an instrument she developed, called the Brand Emotions Scale for Writers, show that writing generally engenders positive emotions across different types of writers and different writing situations. Perhaps this is a function of the kind of involvement Brandt describes as emerging in the text factors under study here. The text itself reveals most clearly the sources of the feelings of satisfaction and relief found by Brand (199).

Perhaps writers' positive emotions are a function of the meeting of readers and writers in text, as suggested by the rhetoricians, linguists, and other psychologists whose work has been reviewed above. The psychological analyses of writing discussed here, including especially these views of reading and writing as they interact, show explicitly the nature of the interaction involved in these activities. The psychologists believe that these interactions are reflected in the text, and, I hope to show, reflected specifically in the text features redundancy and cohesion.

This chapter has reviewed the considerable attention writing researchers have paid to text factors. Writing researchers who have focused their studies on text have studied it from a remarkable range of substantive and methodological directions, incorporating rhetorical analyses, linguistic examinations of sentences and discourses across languages and cultures, reading-based studies of how readers respond to texts, and psychological research on texts from reading, writing, emotional, cognitive, personality, and assorted other perspectives. The writing quadrant of the puzzle, then, extends and interlocks quite closely with all the other areas of the puzzle. In all cases, in the writing research as well as in many of the other areas of inquiry surveyed, scholars who have studied text related issues agree that readable writing is an extremely complex phenomenon incorporating redundancy and cohesion as essential features. However, having framed the puzzle of what it is in the text that makes a piece of writing readable, we can now go on to examine three particular texts, and a diverse series of studies to clarify the role of text factors in them and the responses of readers and writers to them. We begin by again re-sorting the pieces that comprise the middle of the puzzle.

CHAPTER 6

A Fresh Look at the Puzzle of Readable Writing

Jigsaw puzzles provide a challenge because they require visualizing the same thing in a different representation, i.e., the variation between the picture on the top of the box it came in and the scene on the puzzle itself. Puzzles are interesting in part because of this, and also because one can use many different strategies to try to solve them, such as starting with the corners and the edges of the frame, the approach I have been suggesting in the chapters thus far. We have established the four corners of the puzzle of readable writing by reviewing research in linguistics, psychology, reading, and writing. Work on a puzzle can be solitary, but can also be done with help from others, and my work on the present puzzle has certainly benefitted substantially from the contributions of scholars in these diverse areas. But now I propose to sort the various sections of the puzzle and see how additional pieces of research from my empirical studies might be positioned inside the frame.

Thus far, the research on redundancy and cohesion I have discussed investigates their nature and respective roles in discourse. Evidence from linguistics and psychology, as well as from reading and writing, suggests that these two factors play a crucial role in readable text. The work I have drawn together from these four disciplines also provides basic definitions of these features; I will review the definitions again in this chapter. Redundancy and cohesion interlock, as do jigsaw puzzle pieces. Again, in work on a jigsaw, sometimes pieces resemble one another closely, and the similarities can help to position them. But sometimes they differ, and the distinctions can help sort the pieces out for later placement. The points at which redundancy and cohesion meet will be explored below, and the analysis leads to an operational definition of readable writing. As the puzzle pieces are sorted and resorted, my approach and studies will show why redundancy and cohesion are key features of readable writing, and why, despite concerns about research methodology and measurement, they contribute to the critical literacy urgently needed in educational settings and in the population generally.

DEFINITIONS REVISITED

Redundancy, though often thought of as a negative characteristic of language, is defined, as we have seen, as naturally occurring information overlap in language that insures that information is passed accurately from the sender to the receiver of a message. My research began with the formulation of operational definitions of the two types of redundancy that make writing readable.

When *reading* is defined as getting meaning from print, this information overlap provided by redundancy figures in the process. To study the impact of redundancy on fluent reading, I separated it into two types, syntactic and semantic. *Syntactic redundancy* is defined generally as follows:

> Syntactic redundancy is based on predictability. In syntactic terms, redundancy might be increased by making sentence structures conform to the . . . predictable NP-VP (noun phrase-verb phrase) pattern, and by otherwise increasing the predictability of the grammatical structure. (Horning, "On Defining" 318)

And I increased syntactic redundancy in my passages by applying this operational definition of it:

> rearrange highest sentence in an embedded sentence to NP-VP order. . .; replace recoverable subjects and verbs which do not appear at the surface; replace pronouns with their referents; add a referent to any unclear 'this'; replace dummy subjects such as 'it' and 'there' with real subjects in any sentence or clause; and finally, change passives to actives. (Horning, "On Defining" 318-9)

The second type of redundancy, *semantic redundancy*, is defined as

> adding phrases which provide examples, specifications or clarifications to the text. These additions would repeat information by providing the same ideas in several forms, thereby making the meaning more accessible. (Horning, "On Defining" 319)

And operationally, I added semantic redundancy by

> the addition of examples in phrases beginning with 'for example' or 'for instance'; the addition of specifications of particulars, in phrases beginning with 'such as'; or the clarification of a term or concept with a defining phrase set off by parentheses but no verbal marker. (Horning, "On Defining" 319)

I added syntactic redundancy alone to one version of each passage in my research, and semantic redundancy alone to another version of each passage (see Appendix 1 for the passages in their original and altered forms; specific examples of the changes to the texts are presented in Chapters 7 and 9).

The second text factor in readable text is *cohesion*, which works together with redundancy to provide the meeting ground for the reader and the writer. Cohesion contributes to readers' ability to fill in missing information to predict what will appear in the text. Cohesion has been defined and explicated most fully by Halliday and Hasan in *Cohesion in English*, as we have already noted in the linguistics chapter. *Cohesion* is most simply defined as occurring where "the interpretation of some element in the discourse is dependent on that of another" (Halliday and Hasan, *Cohesion* 4). Cohesion operates within sentences but is most influential when it appears across sentence boundaries, so that "Where the interpretation of any item in the discourse requires making reference to some other item in the discourse, there is cohesion" (Halliday and Hasan, *Cohesion* 11).

Halliday and Hasan make clear the importance of cohesion in getting meaning from language, and hence, its resemblance to redundancy:

> One of the major problems in understanding linguistic interaction—it is actually a problem in the understanding of ALL text processes, whether those of dialogue or others, though it is usually posed in the context of dialogue—is that of knowing how the listener fills in the missing information. . . .What makes it possible for him [sic] to go through the process [of filling in missing information and thereby decoding meaning] is the fact that what he [sic] hears is systematically related to its environment—it has 'textual meaning', as we have expressed it; and an essential component in this relationship is its continuity with what has preceded. *The continuity is not merely an interesting feature that is associated with text; it is a necessary element in the interpretation of text. There has to be cohesion if meanings are to be exchanged at all.* (Halliday and Hasan, *Cohesion* 299-300; emphasis added)

That is, cohesion contributes to the information overlap in text, a carefully specified type of redundancy. Like other types of redundancy, cohesion fosters text-reader interaction, enhancing readable writing.

Syntactic and semantic redundancy operate within sentences, while cohesion generally operates most significantly across sentence boundaries. Thus, redundancy and cohesion operate in similar ways at different levels of discourse. In my initial research, all the changes that I made to increase syntactic and semantic redundancy were changes I made in individual sentences. Cohesive ties may be found within sentences, but are particularly significant to readable writing when they connect one sentence to another. My later studies investigate the impact of such changes across sentence boundaries, and explore the interaction of both factors. Halliday and Hasan point out that the most common and general form of cohesion occurs when cohesive ties cross sentence boundaries:

> The simplest form of cohesion is that in which the presupposed element is verbally explicit and is found in the immediately preceding sentence. (Halliday and Hasan, *Cohesion* 14)

Cohesion may be found across several sentences, or the cohesive tie may link to something outside the text altogether (like the reader's knowledge of the world or of text types).

Cohesion alone plays a central role in how well readers understand a passage, as shown by Judith Irwin. Irwin's 1980 study on cohesion and prose comprehension showed that an increase in the number of cohesive ties in a passage significantly improved college students' ability to recall the content of a passage. This finding suggests that cohesion is related to comprehension. But a word of caution is in order here. As Peter Fries, another scholar working on readable writing, points out,

> On the one hand, adding cohesive ties to a text will not increase its comprehensibility if it is already easy to understand. On the other hand, texts which are not well organized are often hard to understand, and if we are to make these poorly organized texts understandable, we must use more signals of the relationships between the ideas expressed. (Fries 12)

Though Irwin's results show that cohesion can be a factor, Fries reminds us that it is but one contributing factor in readable text.

Composition specialists also point up the relationship of redundancy and cohesion. The problem of articulating the connection of the two raises again the concept of coherence and how it interacts with redundancy and cohesion. Some dissatisfaction with current research derives from cohesion scholars' inability to see the relationship of cohesion to other features of the text which contribute to redundancy:

> The number of repeated words or therefores and howevers depends on prior, more global rhetorical decisions. That is, cohesive devices reflect the larger discourse structures they instantiate and so cannot be studied independently of the entire discourse. Thus our epiphenomenal sense of cohesion is entirely a function of our hierarchically prior epiphenomenal sense of coherence. And our sense of textual coherence is a function of our grasp of content. (Colomb and Williams 211)

Our grasp of content, they go on to say, derives from prior knowledge of the topic, and writers must be aware of all of this in readers' responses in order to write readable texts. To see how redundancy and cohesion interlock in text, these two pieces must be placed in the picture of readable writing.

REDUNDANCY, COHESION, AND A DEFINITION OF READABLE WRITING

Readable writing occurs when writers have specific intentions that are realized in conventions of text, including the use of cohesive devices and syntactic, semantic, and discourse-level redundancy, so that readers can set up specific expectations and confirm them through the use of their prior knowledge and the extant redundancy and cohesion of the text.

This definition incorporates the linguistic, psychological, reading, and writing insights discussed in the preceding chapters. To review these, first, from a linguistic point of view, a readable text must have cohesive elements in it, and there is clear evidence that enhancing cohesion increases the comprehensibility (Irwin, "Effect"). Also from a linguistic point of view, my operational definitions of redundancy seem to increase comprehensibility. Moreover, because prior knowledge plays a key role, in the form of input-memory redundancy, the concepts of context of situation from functional linguistics and of schemata from psychological work on text processing help account for the central role of redundancy and cohesion in creating readable text.

Reviewing insights from psychology, we know that, while readers cannot consciously define or describe readable writing, and are not conscious of the presence or functioning of either redundancy or cohesion, they are sensitive to these features. The impact of the presence or absence of redundancy and cohesion is reflected in various reader preferences as described by the MBTI, and in readers' responses to the propositional content of the text.

Reviewing reading theory and work that has been done in rhetoric and composition studies, we know some additional features of readable writing. Reading relies on visual information, the text per se, with its clear markings for enhanced redundancy and enhanced cohesion. Reading also relies on nonvisual information, the readers' prior knowledge, which creates another kind of redundancy with the text. From the writing perspective, readable writing comes about when what Frank Smith has called writer intention and reader expectation match up closely. Writers make their intentions clear through the use of conventions, which writing scholars have explicated and which are predictable in nature (conventions include story grammars, the general plan of a scientific research article, and features of sentence and paragraph structure as well).

Drawing on the four areas of research that bear on readable writing leads me to this definition, which has an admittedly strong focus on the text itself. Although there are other scholars who call for a more reader/writer bound view of text, such as Deborah Brandt, I am trying to argue that readable writing resides chiefly in the text and in the reader and writer to the extent that each appears there. Thus, when Brandt says

> literate knowledge is fundamentally metacommuncative knowledge—knowledge about how people use written-down language to sustain ad hoc involvement in order to arrive at meaning. In the prevailing view, the challenge of becoming literate is learning to fall under the powers of language on its own, to make meaning in the absence of social relationships and social action, to detach oneself in order to deal with abstract language. However, in reality, such language-

> centeredness and psychic separation in reading and writing usually lead to breakdowns in meaning and disruption of the very acts themselves. Effective writers and readers at work see contextual reference in written language. They see how a text relates dynamically and immediately to people, place, time and action—even more specifically, to a me, a you, a here, and a now. *How it relates* is the real challenge in literacy learning—indeed, that is the continual interpretive challenge in any act of reading or writing. (Brandt, *Literacy* 100)

I agree; however, I believe that readers and writers reveal themselves quite fully in the text as they employ redundancy and cohesion to meet in readable writing.

To restate the definition, then, readable writing occurs when writers have specific intentions that are realized in conventions of text, including the use of cohesive devices and syntactic, semantic, and discourse-level redundancy, so that readers can set up specific expectations and confirm them through the use of their prior knowledge and the extant redundancy and cohesion of the text. With this definition, which draws on linguistic, psychological, reading, and writing elements, I want to briefly describe four empirical studies I have conducted that help to account for the ways in which redundancy and cohesion work together in readable text. This discussion will provide an overview of these studies, which are presented in detail in the remaining chapters of the book.

PASSAGES AND STUDIES

The question driving all of my research is this: What is it, specifically in the text as a text, that makes it easy or hard to read? Like other researchers, I have tried a number of hypotheses, testing them empirically and refining them over time, coming to the proposal presented above as an operational definition of readable writing. Turning to the studies, I want to provide a preview of the next four chapters of the book.

As I noted earlier, redundancy alone was the focus of my first study. I took three passages of text on three different topics and altered them by adding operationally defined syntactic redundancy, semantic redundancy and both types. I chose the particular passages used in the study for several reasons (the passages, in their various versions with increased redundancy and increased cohesion, are presented in Appendix 1). First, I knew that the subjects in the first study would be native speakers of English in their first year of college, and I knew that I wanted passages that were appropriate for this group in terms of formula readability level. Second, I chose passages on three different topics, to accommodate a range of possible interests and possible prior knowledge of the topic. Third, I looked for passages that were approximately 300 words long, considering the practical matter of preparing the passages on a single sheet of paper (8 1/2 x 14), as Cloze tests with double spacing to allow room for subjects to fill in the Cloze blanks. Each passage discusses one key idea within the length of the text as presented to the subjects.

The first of the three passages deals with the origins of male dominance in Western society, and is taken from Alfred Adler's *Understanding Human Nature* (this will be referred to in the research reports as the *100 series*, using a simple coding system I have used over all of the studies). The second passage discusses the influence of mass media on the development of sports in America, from the opening of the *New York Times Guide to Spectator Sports* (*200 series*). The third passage takes up the problem of evaluating the performance of governments and is drawn from an undergraduate political science text, Macridis and Ward's *Modern Political Systems: Europe* (*300 series*). A final factor governing my choice of passages was the probability of the students having seen the material before. Since the textbook and Adler passage were both more than 5 years old when I used them, and the sports book was a public library volume, I felt that it was not likely that any or many of the subjects would have seen these passages before.

The first study examined the effect of syntactic and semantic redundancy and of both types of redundancy together. I used four versions of each passage: its original (referred to in the following discussions as 01), a version with syntactic redundancy added as I had operationally defined it (02), a version with semantic redundancy added (03), and a version with both types of redundancy incorporated (04). In the study (see Chapter 7, below), I controlled for length, Dale-Chall readability level, content, and other factors. The passages were prepared as Cloze tests, and each passage was read by 20 first-year college students. In two of the three passages (the 100 series and the 300 series), the addition of redundancy, as I defined it, improved the Cloze scores to a significant degree ($p > .01$). But in the remaining passage (the 200 series, on media/sports), the addition of redundancy made no difference. Because of the degree of control I exercised over the subjects and passages, I concluded that there was something in the third passage for which I had not controlled that must account for why the addition of redundancy did not make any difference there. It is clear from these first results that redundancy has some impact on readable text, so my additional studies have been investigating the anomalous result of the initial study.

In the next phase, I look carefully at the texts themselves, to see what features may have precluded a positive impact for the additional redundancy in the 200 series passage. I have found some interesting measures that suggest that this anomalous passage may have certain features that made the addition of redundancy ineffective. In particular, the cohesion analyses on the original versions of all three passages show that the anomalous passage is somewhat less cohesive than either of the other two. The anomalous series had a mean of 40 cohesive ties, while the other two had 48 ties and 52 ties, respectively. These results make good sense in view of Irwin's finding that more cohesive ties increase prose comprehension ("Effect"). The anomalous passage was less cohesive and less readable for this and other reasons. This finding is consistent with other research of a similar type (Renfrow).

From further analysis of text factors, I have concluded that the anomalous passage was simply different from and harder than the other two passages. This finding derives from reliable computer counts of the numbers of syllables in each passage and the numbers of content words. Logically, one might expect these counts to correlate fairly well, as they do in the two passages where increasing redundancy increased Cloze scores. In these two, there are very strong ($+.8$ and above) and significant ($p < .05$ or better) positive correlations between syllable and content word counts. In the passage where adding redundancy didn't help, the correlation is $-.26$ and is not significant. Moreover, the number of content words is higher in the anomalous passage, as is the number of nominalizations and the number of syllables. Overall, then, although the anomalous passage was equivalent to the other two passages in length, Dale-Chall formula readability level, and in types of redundancy added, it was different from the other two passages in a number of ways that most likely influenced my Cloze results. Although I didn't know it at the time, the anomalous passage was poorly chosen for these reasons and may not invalidate the findings in my other two cases. This second study showed, then, that, while redundancy makes a difference to readable writing, other factors like cohesion contribute to the complex character of readable text as readers respond to it. The results of the text analyses are reported in greater detail in Chapter 8.

The text analysis research included an examination of the cohesion levels in the passages, and this analysis led to the third study. I had gotten extremely interested in cohesion's role in the nature of readable writing. Although I had analyzed the level of cohesion in the original versions of the passages, my next hypothesis called for altering the passages by adding cohesion, to see if, in these passages, as in Irwin's work, the addition of cohesion would increase readers' comprehension. Moreover, because I already knew about the impact of redundancy, I wanted to see how readers would respond to the passages if I increased both redundancy and cohesion. Finally, I was particularly interested in a more individualized picture of reader response than what I was able to see through Cloze procedure.

For the third study, I created a new version of each passage, increasing the number of cohesive ties while still controlling for length, formula readability, and other factors. In this new version (the 05 form for all passages), I added cohesive conjunctions. I chose conjunctions because they were a feature I could count easily and add without invalidating my control on length. There are some other reasons for this choice, and these are detailed in the report of the third study in Chapter 9. In this research, I used four versions of each passage: the 01 version which is the original, unaltered version; the 04, which incorporates both syntactic and semantic redundancy, because this was the version in the first study for which I found the most significant differences in Cloze scores; the newly created 05 version, developed to test the impact of increased cohesion through the addition of cohesive conjunctions; and an 06 version, to examine the impact of both redundancy and cohesion through the addition of cohesive conjunctions to the 04 form.

In this third study, I drew subjects again from a population of first-year college students. Because of my interest in looking more closely at individual reader response, I chose to use reading miscue analysis as the methodology. Each subject read a random version of each of the three passages presented in random order. The subjects read the passages aloud while being audio taped, following standard miscue research procedures, and then wrote a brief summary of each passage after the reading. I hypothesized that increased redundancy and increased cohesion would produce fewer miscues (readers' oral responses that deviate from the printed text) and miscues that would reflect better comprehension. The results of this study, like the Cloze research and text analysis findings, suggest support for the claim that redundancy and cohesion do contribute to more readable writing (see Chapter 9 for details).

In each of these studies, I saw problems with my procedures and with the analysis of the results I obtained, and I had by this time begun to think that perhaps redundancy and cohesion are such subtle features that they cannot be tested through direct empirical measures. As I have been suggesting, the matter of what to measure and how to measure it is a subject of concern and disagreement among scholars in the various fields that pertain to readable writing. As noted below, North and Lauer and Asher look at the nature of research in these areas and come to the conclusion, as does the Conference on College Composition and Communication, that effective study of reading and writing warrants a myriad of research procedures and approaches.

I will come back to this concern in a moment, but with this view of things, I began to think about other ways to find out how readers respond to these texts, and had begun to learn about the usefulness of case study research to focus even more closely on reader responses to text. I had also begun to think differently about how to solve the puzzle of the nature of readable writing as a result of having read Jensen and DiTiberio's book on *Personality and the Teaching of Composition*, and thinking about my own preferences for countable, measurable features of text. The more I thought about these matters, the more clear it became that I needed to conduct a very different kind of study to focus on how skilled readers and writers might respond to these texts. Yet another influence was my reading of Marilyn Sternglass's *The Presence of Thought*, which looks closely at individual responses to reading and writing activity and demonstrates how individual responses to reading and writing tasks can shed light on the issues in readable writing.

These changes in perspective led to the fourth study, which is discussed in detail in Chapter 10. In this study, I used the same set of passages as in the miscue research. My approach was quite different, because this time I wanted to use a multiple case format as described by Robert Yin. In this study, I examined the hypothesis that professional readers and writers would find the passages with increased redundancy and cohesion "better," i.e., more readable writing, and that in revising, they would recommend strategies that would lead to the incorporation of redundancy and/or cohesion in the texts. The case study approach also allowed me to look at the influence of the subjects' Myers-Briggs type, which was available for all of the participants. In Chapter 10, I report the responses of 10 professional reader/writers, who consistently chose forms of the passages with either increased redundancy or increased cohesion, and who recommended revisions that would increase one or both factors in the text.

These four studies represent a variety of "approaches" and all provide different kinds of "evidence" for the centrality of redundancy and cohesion to readable writing. The two words in quotes in the previous sentence are presented this way on purpose, because there are issues of methodology and measurement which must now be considered.

MEASUREMENT AND METHODOLOGY ISSUES

I have attempted to re-sort the results of my studies a number of times. The various studies reported in the material that follows this chapter illustrate my intention to come at the subtle nature of readable writing from varied directions and to pick up evidence in different places. Two interrelated issues arise from this strategy, the problem of what to measure and how to measure it, and in addition to these issues, how to evaluate the results. Often, in this work as in many investigations of human language use, the results are either not in a form suitable for inferential statistical analysis, or even when they are, the results do not often yield clear correlations, statistical significance, or similar evidence that is considered persuasive in other research contexts. What I have compiled here is a variety of suggestive evidence derived from a range of approaches. No one piece of evidence is conclusive, and none of my results are overwhelming in and of themselves. But I hope to show that, taken together, all of the evidence on these very subtle elements makes a clear statement about the nature of readable writing.

I have hinted in much of the preceding discussion that measurement is important to this whole area in my own research and that of the scholars on whose work I rely. Measurement is at issue in reading and writing and in language studies more generally, as is research methodology. Several scholars have pointed this out, including Stephen North in *The Making of Knowledge in Composition*. In his discussion of the development of composition studies, North begins by talking about modes of inquiry and methodological communities in a particular discipline (1-6).

The modes of inquiry North refers to are in part the different subject areas I have reviewed, all of which contribute to our understanding of readable writing.

Discussing research in the social sciences, North finds that a methodological community consists of researchers who share their work among themselves and agree generally on similar procedures, beliefs, and values. Often, individuals belong to more than one methodological community, and indeed, I have drawn all the researchers whose work is reviewed above into a single methodological community. There are a number of communities in composition research, including, in North's analysis, practitioners, historians, philosophers, critics, experimentalists, clinicians, formalists, and ethnographers. He goes on to point out that composition has its origins in both the social sciences and the humanities, and I would add, in the present context, in educational research as well.

These different groups "make knowledge" differently, using differing methods and procedures. I have drawn on several differing approaches to get a full picture of readable writing. These differing approaches deal precisely with the issue of what to measure and how to measure it. Another discussion of the same issue with specific reference to research in composition is Lauer and Asher's *Composition Research: Empirical Designs*, which provides a useful overview of various research strategies that have been used to study writing. Lauer and Asher's goal, like North's, is not to suggest that one kind of research method is superior, but that there are various useful approaches to the questions in the field (Lauer and Asher 3-20).

Because I have used a range of techniques, from true experiments to case studies, I find the claims of both North and Lauer and Asher supportive of my approach. Gordon Anderson, who has also been interested in the nature of reading comprehension, has done a study of a single reader and a single text, applying the sort of multidimensional approach I provide below (Anderson). Anderson found use for schema theory, propositional analysis, cohesion and miscue studies in his analysis of comprehension and text/reader interaction. A similar multidirectional approach is advocated by Irwin Weiser, who has addressed this question from the perspective of teaching writing (Weiser), and is likewise advocated by Lynne Tamor in her work on the subjective nature of text difficulty (Tamor 171-172). Yet another example is provided by Robert Ochsner, who has been examining some of the issues that contribute to readable writing from a physical and biological point of view, and even from this divergent angle, he believes that "readability begins with a text's linguistic form, then develops from this biological source towards a socially constructed meaning" (88). Many scholars who have looked at readable texts from varied angles seem to agree that only by approaching the question of readable text from a range of angles can we derive a complete picture.

METHODOLOGY CHOICES AND RATIONALE

A clear example of the relevance of methodology and measurement issues comes from my first study. I intended to examine redundancy alone there, but later in the text analysis work found that cohesion was also a relevant factor which I had not controlled or even considered. Moreover, the definition of cohesion as one form of redundancy suggests that when I increased redundancy, I ought to have increased the cohesion level as well. But there are two mitigating factors.

First, all the changes I made in rewriting the texts to add redundancy were changes within sentences. Although I did increase the numbers of ties, the ties across sentence boundaries that Halliday and Hasan say are most significant remained basically the same. A second mitigating factor has to do with the use of Cloze scores to examine comprehensibility. A recent study by Shanahan, Kamil, and Tobin suggests that Cloze procedure does not tap intersentence relationships where cohesion matters most. So, even though I added redundancy as operationally defined, and even though there is strong evidence that cohesion is one form of redundancy, my changes did not change the cross-sentence levels of cohesion, and Cloze may be insensitive to these kinds of changes. This is one instance of the what to measure and how to measure it problem discussed above.

Another manifestation of the methods/measurement question concerns using Cloze tests as a measurement device. The Cloze score has been widely used to look at the comprehensibility of text (Taylor, Bormuth) but, as noted above, is the subject of considerable controversy. Despite the fact that Dan Douglas has documented the usefulness of Cloze procedures to evaluate bilingualism and especially bilingual reading ability, other writers have a different view. Douglas describes the clozentropy scoring procedure, and also relates it to redundancy:

> An interesting development in the experimentation with cloze procedure in the measurement of both native and foreign language reading proficiency is the use of a scoring procedure known as clozentropy. This term, first used by Darnell (1968), refers to the application of information theory to the scoring of cloze tests. It has been described in detail elsewhere. . .and was first applied to the analysis of cloze data by Taylor (1954). Briefly, clozentropy involves taking account of all responses to a cloze test provided by a criterion group of subjects, weighting each response according to the probability of its occurrence, then scoring the performance of the test group on this basis. Thus, a test subject who gives responses similar to those of a majority of the criterion group will receive a high score, while one whose responses vary from those of the criterion group will receive a lower score, depending upon how great the deviation is. (Douglas 94)

Cloze tests scored in this way have been used quite regularly with nonnative speakers of English. John Jonz has found that the procedure is sensitive to overall language knowledge and particularly to cohesion and lexical knowledge, two particular areas of interest here (Jonz 61).

Research on native speakers supports the use of Cloze more generally. A careful review of the uses of Cloze procedure and its relationship to redundancy in 1985 suggests that redundancy contributes to a subject's success in completing a Cloze passage (Wardell). This finding is also supported by two studies in Great Britain that looked directly at the relationship of Cloze and redundancy, and that concluded that Cloze, particularly if a synonyms-acceptable scoring system is used, is reflective of comprehension and reveals the impact of redundancy on the comprehensibility of texts (Bailey and Harrison). Moreover, Martin Nystrand has suggested that Cloze, because it measures comprehensibility, is also a useful tool for examining writing and appraising writing quality. Nystrand's view is that writers "constrain" readers in ways that focus precisely on the various types of redundancy in the text (Nystrand 233-34). Thus, Cloze procedure seemed an appropriate task to examine redundancy's effect on comprehensibility as I did in the first study.

In the second study, where I was using various strategies of text analysis, two possibilities presented themselves to me. One was the use of propositional analysis, which I did carry out, and another the use of cohesive harmony and cohesive chains. All of these methods seem to me to be quite arbitrary and subject to the individual judgement of the researcher to an extent that leads to many questions about the results. Although this concern may only be a reflection of my preference for objective, countable, measurable factors in my studies, it is also another reflection of the measurement/methodology question.

The miscue study raises different kinds of methodology questions. Miscue analysis as a research procedure was designed and has been used most effectively as a means of diagnosing individual reading problems of individual students. The developers of miscue research may never have thought of collecting 1,477 miscues from a group of readers and using those to shed light on the features of text that make a difference to reader response. So I have chosen here to apply methodologies in unconventional ways. And it is also true that I have not followed methods precisely. The miscue procedure calls for readers to provide an oral recall of the text they have read, while I asked for a written response and not for a full summary. For all these reasons, I did not treat the reader summaries in the results of the miscue study. I am not convinced that they provide a valid measure of reader comprehension or response.

Finally, there are additional, alternative approaches to the analysis of readable text. Recently, a number of different Cloze-type research strategies have been developed, such as Chapman's GAP analysis and some others. Although I have not used these approaches, and have not pursued all of the strategies available to examine either redundancy or cohesion, my studies represent a variety of techniques. They show suggestively but consistently that redundancy and cohesion are the central features of readable writing, and need to be understood thoroughly in order for readers and writers to meet successfully in text.

The pieces of the puzzle of readable writing have now been re-sorted into separate piles, and the outline of the picture in which the pieces go is clear. Readable writing may be enhanced by increased cohesion and increased redundancy. Redundancy and cohesion interlock in that both are inherent features of language; both access readers' characteristics, knowledge, and activity in reading; and both are essential to the information exchange that occurs in written text. They draw on linguistic characteristics of the text, and on the psychological processing and preferences of readers and writers, and play a central role in reading activity and writing activity. Although the picture of readable writing is still incomplete, these two pieces place the solution to the puzzle close at hand. We turn now to the studies themselves, to place research with texts written in different ways and readers' responses of several types into the frame now set out on the table.

CHAPTER 7

Empirical Studies: Redundancy I—Cloze research

Usually, work on a jigsaw puzzle starts with the frame and the corners. However, sometimes a certain part of the puzzle seems clear and well defined, and so solvers may choose to start with that part. If a puzzle has a small section that is all one color, that is often a good place to start. Our puzzle has its frame and some pieces of the corner areas filled in with previous research. Although it is still hard to see even the outlines of the whole picture, we begin work on the section that focuses on redundancy and its role in readers' responses to texts. In this first study, I examined the effect of redundancy on the comprehensibility of text.

THE PROBLEM: DISTINGUISHING READABILITY AND COMPREHENSIBILITY

One of the most puzzling problems facing those involved with reading is the nature of text difficulty. Difficulty concatenates two issues: readability and comprehensibility. For my purposes, readability factors are tangible features of text that have a limited impact on difficulty. Comprehensibility factors are those more subtle features that have the greatest impact on difficulty. As we have seen in Chapters 2 through 5, readability factors fail to provide a complete explanation, or really much of an explanation at all of precisely what it is that makes a text easy or hard for a particular reader, i.e., its difficulty. Measures of vocabulary level and sentence length used in the classic readability formulas do not really measure difficulty at all, even though, as Klare has pointed out, they are useful predictors of the suitability of a text for readers at a given grade level. The present study examines one feature of readable writing, analyzing difficulty in terms of the amount of redundancy in a text. The results of the study suggest that redundancy has a direct effect on the difficulty level of reading material.

An earlier study suggested a useful format to test the impact of redundancy in text. In it, Ruddell showed that it is possible to improve children's reading comprehension for prose text by increasing syntactic redundancy alone. His finding is explored more fully in my study in two ways: first, both syntactic and semantic redundancy were increased in this investigation, and second, adult native speakers of English were used as subjects. A format similar to Ruddell's was adopted in order to investigate the following hypothesis: Increased redundancy yields increased comprehension of English text for adult native speakers of English.

METHODOLOGY

Design

The independent variable in this study was the redundancy of the text. Increased redundancy was operationally defined in both syntactic and semantic forms in terms of a series of rules applied in the rewriting of text materials. The precise rules are given below in the description of the materials. Following Ruddell's work in examining the impact of redundancy on reading materials for children, the independent variable, redundancy, was increased in each of the three texts in three ways: syntactic redundancy alone was increased, semantic redundancy alone was increased, and both syntactic and semantic redundancy were increased. With the original, unaltered version, this produced four forms for each text: the unaltered form (01), the form with syntactic redundancy increased (02), the form with semantic redundancy increased (03), and the form with both types of redundancy increased (04) (materials may be found in Appendix 1). The dependent variable in the study was the comprehensibility of the text. Comprehensibility was operationally defined as the average Cloze score of a group of subjects on one passage. In the present study, one noun or main verb in every group of six words was chosen for deletion, and replaced by a blank of standard length. The same words were deleted in each version of each passage. In a 300-word passage, this procedure produced about 50 blanks for subjects to fill in. Passages on several different topics were chosen, and were distributed to the subjects at random. All the passages, in both altered and unaltered versions, were of equal length (300 words +/-5) and of equal Dale-Chall readability level (Dale and Chall), grade 12 or 13.

Subjects

The subjects were 240 first-year native English speakers enrolled in freshman composition classes at Wayne State University. The subjects were obtained by asking members of the English department faculty teaching freshman composition to volunteer their classes for the project. Instructors were informed in very general terms about the project, and were asked to administer the passages to their classes. Because these courses enrolled some students who had sophomore standing and some students who indicated on their background forms that English was not their native language, more than 240 subjects participated, but the data used in the study included only eligible subjects, defined as first-year students who were native speakers of English. Myers-Briggs Type Indicator results were not available for the subjects in this study.

Materials

Three passages on three different topics were used in the study: one on the origin and development of male dominance in society (Adler 105), one on the effect of radio and television on sports (Koppett 1-2), and the last on evaluating the performance of government (Macridis and Ward 25-26). Relatively complex material was chosen which had at least one complete idea in the 300-word sample. Finally, the material was taken from sources that were not likely to have been seen by first-year students and that dealt with topics any adult reader might find of interest.

The treatment of the texts to add redundancy draws generally on the work of Frank Smith, the Habers, and other researchers whose work was discussed in the opening chapters, and on some additional research on redundancy from different fields such as second language teaching and technical writing. Steven Darian finds redundancy at all levels of language from phonology and orthography to discourse, and suggests that second language students be taught specifically how to use it (Darian 47). Similarly, David Kieras's work on the comprehensibility of technical prose provides a list of rules for improving comprehensibility, including specific rules on the use of pronouns, on textual coherence, and on avoiding passive voice. These rules add redundancy in several ways and address the use of cohesive devices. Kieras's empirical findings show the importance of redundancy and cohesion (Kieras, "Advanced" 154-56). These strategies support my approach to revising these passages to enhance readable writing.

General Revision Guidelines

In general, the versions of the passages with syntactic and semantic redundancy increased were meant to look and to sound like unadulterated prose, and the traditional factors in readability—sentence length and vocabulary level—were kept relatively constant. On all versions of a passage, the formula readability level (Dale-Chall score) did not vary more than +/- .5 from the original. There were three specific groups of rewriting guidelines that were followed for the versions with increased redundancy. The first group of guidelines was a set of general rules followed closely on all forms:

1. all rewritten forms may not vary more than five words from the original in total length;
2. the last sentence may be edited for length considerations, but the content must remain intact;
3. the readability score may not vary more than .5 from the original;
4. the semantic changes should be spread throughout the passage;
5. changes which would produce awkward or nonsensical sentences should not be made.

Adding Syntactic Redundancy

A second group of guidelines dealt with the following strategies for increasing syntactic redundancy:

1. rearrange the highest sentence (in a sentence with embeddings) to NP VP order (Ruddell);
2. put in understood (recoverable) subjects and verbs;
3. replace pronouns with their referents;
4. add a referent to any unclear *this*;
5. replace dummy subjects such as *it* and *there* with real subjects in any sentence;
6. change passives to actives.

These changes were applied in every case where the criteria for a change existed, except where awkward or nonsense phrasings resulted. The number of changes made was not numerically controlled. I will illustrate these changes with the 100 series.

All of the passages in all versions are presented in Appendix 1, but here I will give specific examples only from the first series. The first sentence of Form 101 (original version) reads as follows:

> So far as the history of the origin of masculine dominance is concerned, we must call attention to the fact that this is a phenomenon which does not occur as a natural thing.

When I altered this sentence to add syntactic redundancy, following the guidelines above, the result is the first sentence of form 102 (added syntactic redundancy):

> We must call attention to the fact that so far as the history of the origin of masculine dominance is concerned, this phenomenon of masculine dominance does not occur as a natural thing.

In the second sentence, I made other changes, so that the 101 version says

> This is indicated by the numerous laws which are necessary to guarantee this domination to men.

while the version with syntactic redundancy enhanced says

> The fact that masculine dominance is not natural is indicated by the numerous laws which are necessary to guarantee this domination to men.

To remove the nominalization and resolve the reference problems in the third sentence, which originally said

> It is also an indication that previous to the legal enforcement of masculine domination there must have been other epochs in which the masculine privilege was not nearly so certain.

I changed it by adding syntactic redundancy, so that form 102's third sentence reads:

> Previous to the legal enforcement of masculine domination there must have been other epochs in which the masculine privilege was not nearly so certain, and this fact also indicates that masculine dominance is not natural.

These few sentences give some sense of the rewriting changes made to the passages to add syntactic redundancy. Similar changes were made to the rest of form 102, and forms 202 and 302 were treated in the same ways.

Adding Semantic Redundancy

The third group of rewriting guidelines was designed to increase semantic redundancy. Since these were additions to the text, a numerical limit of no less than three but not more than five semantic changes was imposed. The limit was imposed because it would have been impossible to control for length otherwise. Again, the general guideline that the text must not sound unnatural was important in selecting the place and nature of the semantic revisions. In general, these additions served one of the following purposes, and each took on its respective form:

1. the addition of an example, marked by a phrase beginning *for example* or *for instance*;
2. the specification of particulars, marked by a phrase beginning with *such as*;
3. the clarification of a term or concept with a defining phrase set off by parentheses but no verbal marker.

From these choices, in general, three different additions were made on the version with increased semantic redundancy, using, again, the general guideline of "normal prose."

I will illustrate these changes using the 100 series passage again as my example, but similar changes were made to all three passages. In form 101, the second sentence was the first place where an addition of semantic redundancy seemed to fit. In form 101, the sentence reads

> This is indicated by the numerous laws which are necessary to guarantee this domination to men.

In form 103, I changed this sentence by adding a specifying phrase, as follows:

> This is indicated by the numerous laws which are necessary to guarantee this domination to men, such as property rights and divorce laws.

Two other changes were made in this passage, of a similar kind, and again, the 203 and 303 versions were treated in about the same fashion.

To create the 04 versions of all passages, I incorporated the semantic changes together with the syntactic changes, keeping in mind the constraints on length and the need for the text to sound natural. Thus, the original version of the 100 series passage (form 101) had its first two sentences this way:

> So far as the history of the origin of masculine dominance is concerned, we must call attention to the fact that this is a phenomenon which does not occur as a natural thing. This is indicated by the numerous laws which are necessary to guarantee this domination to men.

In the 104 version, with both syntactic and semantic redundancy enhanced, the first two sentences read as follows:

> We must call attention to the fact that so far as the history of the origin of masculine dominance is concerned, this phenomenon of masculine dominance does not occur as a natural thing. The fact that masculine dominance is not natural is indicated by the numerous laws which are necessary to guarantee this domination to men, such as property rights and divorce laws.

In the 04 versions of the passages, some changes were needed at the end to make the passage conform to length and readability level constraints, in order to control these variables. In general, though, the 200 series and 300 series passages were all treated in the same way as the 100 series I have discussed in these examples.

Procedures

Members of the English department faculty teaching freshman composition volunteered their classes for the project. Those who participated were given a set of directions and a packet of tests. The students received the test passages and uniform directions from their instructors. Passages were randomly assigned. The students first answered a series of background questions, dealing with class level, native language, citizenship, age, sex, and so on. They then had 20 minutes to read the passage and fill in the blanks. Students were asked to put only one word in each blank and to attempt to fill every blank. They were permitted to reread as often as necessary during the 20 minutes. At the end of the permitted time, all subjects were asked to answer two rating questions dealing with interest and writing quality. The passages were then collected and returned for scoring.

Scoring Procedures

I scored the fill-ins of the Cloze passages by an acceptable word-scoring system. This system counts not only exact fill-ins, but also synonyms and other words acceptable in the context of the passage as correct answers. Blanks and unacceptable answers were all considered wrong.

The reliability of my scoring was checked by a second scorer who was informed in a general way about the study. The second scorer was given a copy of the scoring system and several passages from the pilot study were scored simultaneously by both scorers until she felt confident of her judgment. The second scorer was then given a total of 36 passages to score independently. A systematic random sampling procedure was used to select the passages from the 01 and 04 versions of each passage. The reliability check was blind; the form numbers of the passages were concealed. The second scorer did not know which forms were altered or the nature of the alterations made. An overall correlation of +.96 was obtained between the two scorers.

RESULTS

Cloze Scores

The Cloze test scores were obtained by taking an average of the scores of 20 first-year, native speaker subjects who read each form of each passage. The raw

Cloze means, standard deviations and percentages are presented in Table 7-1. There are several interesting features of these mean scores. First, keeping in mind that a raw score of about 50 is perfect, it is interesting to note that the raw scores on the 100 series are higher than the other two, that the 200 series produces a middle range, and that the scores on the 300 series are relatively low. In comparing the scores within each series, we find that the 02 and 03 forms with a single types of redundancy added produce lower mean Cloze scores than the original, unaltered version, except in the case of 302. In comparing the 04s in all cases to the scores on the other forms, the addition of both types of redundancy improves the Cloze mean in two cases, but not in the case of the 200 series. Analysis of variance was used on these Cloze means to determine the significance of these patterns.

The analysis of variance shows whether the modification in question makes a significant difference in the scores. Thus, the two forms with increased syntactic redundancy (02 and 04) are compared to the two forms without it (01 and 03). Similarly, the two forms with increased semantic redundancy (03 and 04) are compared to the two forms without the semantic change (01 and 02). If the means from Table 7-1 are combined to reflect the treatment by the analysis of variance on the addition of each type of redundancy alone, the results then appear as in Table 7-2. Note that by combining the means in this way, the presence of each type of redundancy increases Cloze scores on all forms for the 100 series and 300 series, but not for the 200 series.

Analysis of Variance

The analysis of variance is the statistical procedure of choice when more than two means are being compared, which is the case here. The analysis of variance

Table 7-1. Cloze means, standard deviation, and percentage scores

Form	*Type of R*	*Raw mean*	*Std.Dev.*	*Pct.*
101	Orig. Male dom.	34.45	5.943	71.77
102	Syntactic R inc	27.80	6.764	56.73
103	Semantic R inc	30.85	5.163	69.96
104	Both R inc	39.00	7.167	81.25
201	Orig. sports	24.90	8.296	49.80
202	Syntactic R inc	21.75	6.843	43.50
203	Semantic R inc	20.40	6.832	40.80
204	Both R inc	20.05	4.639	40.10
301	Orig. govt.perf.	15.75	7.454	31.50
302	Syntactic R inc	17.00	7.921	34.00
303	Semantic R inc	13.45	6.194	26.90
304	Both R inc	24.90	6.836	49.80

Table 7-2: Cloze means as treated by the Analysis of Variance

Cloze means:

Without syntactic redundancy		*With syntactic redundancy*	
forms	mean	forms	mean
101, 103	32.65	102, 104	33.40
201, 203	22.65	202, 204	20.90
301, 303	14.60	302, 304	20.95
Without semantic redundancy		*With semantic redundancy*	
forms	*mean*	*forms*	*mean*
101, 102	31.13	103, 104	34.93
201, 202	23.33	203, 204	20.23
301, 302	16.38	303, 304	19.20
Without any redundancy		*With both types*	
form	*mean*	*form*	*mean*
101	34.45	104	39.00
201	24.90	204	20.05
301	15.75	304	24.90

Analysis of variance

Series	*Effect*	F	*Sig. of F*
100	syntactic	.283	.999
	semantic	7.261	.008
	2way	27.537	.001
200	syntactic	1.333	.251
	semantic	4.182	.042
	2way	.853	.999
300	syntactic	15.860	.001
	semantic	3.084	.079
	2way	10.230	.002

results for each series are present in the lower portion of Table 7-2. The analysis of variance shows significant F-ratios in the 100 series in the presence of the semantic effect alone and in the two-way effect (where the 101 is compared to the 104). In the 200 series, the differences observed in the means are nonsignificant. In the 300 series, significant differences are found in the presence of syntactic redundancy alone, and in the presence of both types of redundancy. Thus in the 100 and 300 series, the additional redundancy significantly improves Cloze scores with the one or the other and with both types of redundancy. In the 200 series, the raw means drop regardless of the redundancy added, but the drops are nonsignificant in all cases.

DISCUSSION

The major conclusion to be drawn from this study is that the hypothesis that increased redundancy yields increased comprehensibility of English text for adult native speakers of English is confirmed. The conclusion is qualified by the fact that the hypothesis is true for two of the three cases studied, and appears to be consistent only when both types of redundancy are added to a text.

The results on the 200 series contrast sharply with those on the 100 and 300 series. In the 200 series, redundancy makes no significant difference at all. One explanation for this outcome lies in the Cloze scores themselves and what is known about the suitability of material at a particular Cloze level. When a reader's Cloze score is about 50%, the material used is thought to be at an appropriate level of difficulty for that reader (Bormuth, "Comparable"). Much higher Cloze scores suggest that the passage is too easy for the reader, while much lower scores suggest that material is too hard.

The results obtained here suggest that the addition of redundancy improves comprehensibility of very easy or very difficult passages, but that increased redundancy has no effect when the passage is well suited to the reader. Moreover, each type of redundancy improves comprehensibility under specific circumstances: Passages that are easy can be made more comprehensible with the addition of semantic redundancy, whereas difficult material is made more accessible to readers with increased syntactic redundancy.

The practical implication of these findings is twofold. First, it is reasonable to think that the comprehensibility of a text can be improved by specific rewriting strategies, once the Cloze scores of a group of readers are obtained. For the writers of texts, this finding points to a way in which a text can be improved. For all readers and writers, especially in these days of high speed electronic word processing, the study provides hope for texts that are much easier to comprehend.

For students learning to read, difficult texts remain a problem. The most useful insight of the present study is that difficult texts can be made more comprehensible by increasing their syntactic redundancy. Some day in the not-too-distant future, a student might select a book, do a computerized Cloze test on a passage from it, then get the text from the computer with the redundancy level adjusted for maximum comprehensibility. Much work remains to be done before we reach this point, but the present study suggests that redundancy puts us on the right path.

The study shows that adding redundancy can make a text easier to read, and that redundancy and difficulty are related to a significant degree. Though there are surely other factors that tie in to text difficulty, many of these may be extraneous to the reading process per se. Additional studies attempting to measure the difficulty level of a text in terms of redundancy are needed to confirm and expand the findings here, as well as investigation of other factors that play a role in the nature of readable writing.

The Cloze research puts pieces into a portion of the puzzle of readable writing. The study makes clear how and where the redundancy piece fits in the picture. But these data also raise the important question of why the changes that worked to improve readers' Cloze scores in the 100 and 300 series failed to work in the 200 series. Thus, as is sometimes true when working on a puzzle, it is necessary to get up and move to a different position at the table. The text analysis work in the second study views the passages and these results from a very different angle. While the present study suggests that additional research will soon solve the puzzle of text difficulty, the work on the texts themselves shows just how complex readable writing is.

CHAPTER 8

Empirical Studies: Redundancy II–Text Analysis Findings

A new seat at the table, as suggested at the end of Chapter 7, gives a fresh perspective on the complex puzzle of readable writing. From this angle, the puzzle has begun to fill in. Sometimes, after working for a period of time on a particular section, solvers lose a sense of the complete picture. Changing seats allows a new view of the puzzle that can be very helpful. The next step in the research looks at the passages more carefully from a variety of perspectives, to see how a divergent view might make the puzzle take a more complete shape. The next pieces have to do with the various strategies for text analysis, including classic readability formulas and newer alternative approaches to the analysis of texts.

I have been looking at these various approaches to text analysis in order to resolve the anomaly of the 200 series passage I have been using in my research. The study reported in Chapter 7 demonstrated that I could significantly improve comprehension as measured by Cloze scores by adding redundancy to texts written by professional writers. At least, in two of the three passages I used, my additions improved the Cloze scores. Since all three passages included enhanced redundancy, I needed to account for why my changes failed to improve the Cloze scores in the third case.

I have reexamined the texts and found that there are real differences among my passages not controlled by holding length, Dale-Chall level, and other superficial features constant. This finding supports the often-repeated point that readability is much more complex than the formulas alone suggest. My findings from both computer-based analysis and from propositional and cohesion analysis account for why my addition of redundancy did not improve the Cloze scores in my third case. Furthermore, the results of my text-based analyses show that it is complex, but possible, to take other aspects of reader-text interaction into account when analyzing a passage. In what follows, I hope to show why I obtained the results that I did, and to indicate how computer analysis of text and other strategies permit a detailed understanding of the nature of readable writing. (The passages, in their various forms, appear in Appendix 1.)

My goal here is to combine and integrate a range of approaches to the analysis of text per se. Such combining has proven helpful in analyzing data that resist other analysis like the results of the study reported in Chapter 7. Also, such combining yields an analysis that accesses both text factors and reader factors. The resulting insights provide helpful pieces for the readable writing puzzle. In this chapter, I examine approaches to text analysis that yield data on the passages from the Cloze study drawn from propositional analysis as proposed by psychological studies of text processing, as well as the cohesive tie and cohesive chain analyses some linguists and writing researchers have been trying. I have also subjected the passages to formula readability analysis using computerized programs, checking easily countable features like numbers of syllables, content words, and so forth. Some other measures of vocabulary include a measure of lexical density and a count of unique words. These and a few other measures of text elements have allowed me to investigate the following hypothesis: Text difficulty is influenced by the interaction of readability and comprehensibility factors; discourse features including redundancy and cohesion, vocabulary features, and word types interlock to affect difficulty levels.

PROPOSITIONAL ANALYSIS OF THE PASSAGES

Turning first to the propositional analysis of the original version of each passage, I have made use of the Bovair and Kieras system discussed above. This propositional analysis isolates and lists the main idea units in a passage according to a set of rules. The analysis operates chiefly at the surface level of text, and Kieras has said that by staying close to the surface, one has a greater chance of producing an accurate propositional analysis of the passage (personal communication, June 1985). In my analysis, I have stayed at this superficial level, and have produced an interesting outcome, given the Cloze results. What I have found is that the number of propositions is somewhat higher in the passage in which adding redundancy did not help (the media/sports passage, 200 series) than it was in the other two passages. And, as noted above, Kintsch's studies show clearly that more propositions increase reading time and lower recall on a passage. (See Table 8-1.)

While these differences do not reach statistical significance, they suggest that, in terms of proposition count, the 200 series passage in its original form was more difficult than either of the other two. The level of difficulty suggests that adding

Table 8-1. Proposition levels in the passages

Form	*Proposition count*
101	88
201	120
301	111

redundancy should have helped even more in this case, but that is not what the Cloze scores show. Thus, I began to look to other measures to help account for the outcome I obtained.

COHESION ANALYSIS: TIES AND CHAINS

There are other measures of difficulty, notably the cohesion analysis discussed above. My cohesion analysis follows a simplified form the system developed by Halliday and Hasan. I conducted a generalized analysis of the number of cohesive ties in each of the passages. In this case, because of the similarities in the passages due to the nature of the changes I made in adding redundancy, I was able to carry out a cohesion analysis on the increased-redundancy versions of all three passages. Several interesting findings turn up here, as presented in Table 8-2.

There are several points to be made about these figures. Overall, the mean numbers of cohesive ties suggest that the anomalous 200 series passages are less cohesive than the other two passages. And, as noted above, fewer cohesive ties in the Irwin study ("Effect") yielded longer reading times and lower recall scores,

Table 8-2. Cohesive ties in passages

Form	*Cloze %*	*Cohesive ties*	*In sent.*	*Across sent.*
101	72	40	14	26
102	57	49	22	27
103	70	45	19	26
104	81	57	31	26
		Mean 48		
201	50	40	4	36
202	44	37	7	30
203	41	43	7	36
204	40	40	10	30
		Mean 40		
301	32	54	14	40
302	34	49	9	40
303	27	55	17	38
304	49	50	12	38
		Mean 52		

thus suggesting that the 200 series is more difficult in a general way than either of the other two. The other salient finding from the cohesion analysis is that the number of cohesive ties within sentences does generally increase with the addition of redundancy, but the number of ties across sentences, which are described by Halliday and Hasan as the major type of cohesion, does not change dramatically with the addition of redundancy.

In this connection, a study of the sensitivity of Cloze to text features adds some helpful information. The report by Shanahan et al. shows that Cloze tests may not be sensitive to cross-sentence constraints in text. In the study, Shanahan and his colleagues describe three separate attempts to find Cloze tests sensitive to comprehension across sentences. Different readers were given (a) standard Cloze passages, (b) passages with sentences in scrambled order, and (c) passages where a single sentence from the standard passage was put into a wholly different context. Prior knowledge, time on task, and formula readability level were all controlled. Shanahan's results suggest that Cloze tests are not sensitive to cohesive ties. However, my data may reflect a greater sensitivity because of my Cloze methodology. In my earlier study, I used a one-word-in-six deletion formula, deleting nouns and main verbs exclusively. This procedure allowed me to delete the same words in all versions of each passage. Because I was using Cloze in this way, my task may have been more sensitive to cohesion levels, and the fact that the 200 series passages are less cohesive would be reflected in the anomalous results.

Cohesive chain analysis provides yet another way of looking at the passages, and again shows the peculiarity of the 200 series (media/sports) passage. Following Hasan's analytical method, I created a list of the lexical items in each of the original versions of the passages, and then analyzed these lists in terms of identity and similarity chains, as part of a cohesive harmony analysis. To review, cohesive harmony analysis has several steps, involving a careful look at the cohesive ties that appear in a text. The first step is to produce a lexical rendering of the text, which is simply a listing of content words. From this lexical rendering, lists or chains of related words (*tokens*) are grouped together into one of two kinds of chains: *identity chains* and *similarity chains*. For an identity chain, "every member of the chain refers to the same thing, event, or whatever. . ." (Halliday and Hasan, *Language* 84) while in similarity chains, items "refer to non-identical members of the same class of things, events, etc., or to members of non-identical but related classes of things, events, etc." (Halliday and Hasan, *Language* 84). The measurement of cohesive harmony is obtained in part by calculating the number of total tokens involved in cohesive chains.

Several concepts contribute to the other useful component of cohesive harmony:

1. Relevant tokens: All tokens that enter into identity or similarity chains; these divide into: (a) Central tokens: those relevant tokens that interact; (b) Non-central tokens: those relevant tokens that do not interact;

Table 8-3. Numbers of tokens in cohesive chains and level of coherence where larger % in chains indicates greater coherence

Passage	*Tokens in chains*	*Total tokens*	%
101	71	118	60
201	93	233	40
301	86	116	74

2. Peripheral tokens: All those tokens that do not enter into any kind of chain. . . (Halliday and Hasan, *Language* 93)

Using these categories, several calculations can be made. The first is the one described above, which provides a measure of the number of tokens in chains as opposed to those not involved in some chain. The more tokens involved in chains, the more coherent the text. A second calculation reveals the proportion of peripheral to relevant tokens in chains, where a lower proportion indicates greater coherence (Halliday and Hasan, *Language* 93-94). The data analysis is presented in Appendix 2. The resulting counts are quite revealing, as shown in Tables 8-3 and 8-4.

These findings suggest yet another way in which the 200 series passage differed from the other two. The findings show that the 200 series text was much less coherent, as defined by Hasan. These counts look at the text itself without regard to direct reader response, and are not the only distinguishing features of the passage in which the Cloze results do not show the difference I expected redundancy to make. Additional factors have also provided an explanation of the results.

COMPUTER-BASED FINDINGS ON READABILITY

In terms of features known to have an impact on difficulty as measured by reading time and recall (i.e., not Cloze), the 200 series passage is different from, and more difficult than, either of the other two. Several other measures support this finding in a more objective fashion. I have made use of the computerized readability program written by Michael Schulyer as described in Chapter 4, above. In addition, I have had my passages analyzed by the Writer's Workbench

Table 8-4. Proportion of peripheral to relevant tokens in chains where lower proportion indicates greater coherence

Passage	*Peripheral*	*Relevant*	*Proportion*
101	47	71	66
201	140	93	150
301	30	86	35

program developed by Bell Labs and in use at Colorado State University. Finally, I have analyzed the passages using the Sensible Speller program for Apple computers and the Homer program for writing assistance, and have done statistical analyses of the results of these various computer-generated counts of a variety of features in the texts. The findings presented below are more objective than those discussed already, and again bear upon the outcome of the original study and help to account for what happened.

Michael Schulyer's computerized Readability program makes counts of syllables, words, sentences, and three-syllable words, and uses these figures to calculate nine popular readability formulas. The raw numbers generated by the program are of considerable interest. The syllable count is particularly pertinent for these data. To count syllables, the program counts the number of characters in the passage and divides by a constant of 3.1127, which, according to Schulyer (personal communication, August, 1985), provides a highly accurate count of the number of syllables. The results of this count are presented in Table 8-5.

The discussion of prediction data by George Klare suggests clearly that the number of syllables is related to the difficulty or complexity of the passage (710). Here, the mean numbers of syllables in the passages show considerable variation. And, once again, the 200 series, where the addition of redundancy did not improve Cloze scores, has the largest number of syllables, suggesting that it is simply a much more complex passage.

Yet another measure of text difficulty comes from counts of content words, a task easily done by a computer. This task can be accomplished in several different ways, and two approaches applied here produced results consistent with the findings presented thus far. In the Writer's Workbench program, the computer generates a count of content words and a percentage figure representing the percentage of words in the passage that are content as opposed to function words. The count of content words represents all nouns, verbs, adjectives and non *-ly* adverbs in the passage. The results of the content word count are presented in Table 8-6.

Here again, the 200 series shows a higher count of content words and a higher percentage of content words than either of the other two, both of which are at about the same level.

Table 8-5. Mean syllable counts derived from Readability program.

Series	*Syllables (mean)*
100	455.63
200	523.10
300	503.66

Table 8-6. Mean content words and percentages by Writer's Workbench.

Series content	*Mean number of content words*	*Mean percentage of content*
100	156	52.2
200	185.8	62.07
300	161.5	53.77

LEXICAL DENSITY

Halliday's work addresses the issue of content words from a somewhat different standpoint, but his measure of lexical density also reveals clearly the key difference between the 200 series passage and the other two. The measure of lexical density is a count of the number of lexical items (i.e. content words) as a proportion of running words in the text. Halliday proposes that more "written" language has a higher level of lexical density than spoken language (Halliday, *Spoken* 64-67). In a common sense way, this helps account for the difficulty some listeners have processing a spoken text that was meant to be read silently. Conference papers read aloud at a meeting are a particularly salient example. In the passages, the measure of lexical density turns out as reported in Table 8-7.

As is true of the other measures discussed here, Halliday's lexical density figures confirm that the 200 series passage is quite different from the other two.

OTHER MEASURES

Yet another approach to content can be taken by using Sensible Speller, a program designed to correct spelling errors in texts. One feature of Sensible Speller is that it produces a count of the number of unique words in the passage it is analyzing. To produce this count, the program first counts the total number of words in the passage. It then throws out all duplicate words, producing a count of all words that appear at least once in the passage (Hartley). The resulting count of unique words, while not a count of content words per se, is a count of the number of different words in the passage, tallying only once the articles, function words, and others that recur normally in written text.

As Table 8-8 shows, the 200 series contains a larger number of unique words, and like the content words, this finding suggests that the 200 series passage was generally more complex for readers than either of the other two.

Table 8-7. Halliday's lexical density measure.

Form	*Total words*	*Lexical items*	*Proportion*
101	295	118	40%
201	304	233	77%
301	306	116	38%

Table 8-8. Mean counts of unique words, derived from Sensible Speller program.

Series	*No. of words*	*Unique words*
100	293	154
200	301.7	173.25
300	298	148.5

These data have been examined statistically to determine whether or not it is reasonable to make predictions based on the results from these small samples. Here, perhaps, is where the most interesting outcome appears. I tried correlating these various counts with one another and with my Cloze score results. I turned up very strong correlations of content words to syllable counts in the 100 and 300 series, both strong and significant in the statistical sense. In the 200 series, a weak, negative, and nonsignificant correlation appears, as shown in Table 8-9.

Logically, it seems that the numbers of syllables and the numbers of content words should correlate, particularly since the research literature shows that both are factors in text difficulty (Samuels and Eisenberg). Here, the figures suggest that the 200 series is a highly unusual passage in which the expected correlation fails to appear.

Finally, the Homer program counts prepositions, *to be* verbs, nominalizations, and "woolly words." None of these counts is particularly informative with the exception of the nominalization figures. This program counts nominalizations, as these forms have been found by researchers to require more processing in the brain, and thus to be more difficult, where difficulty is measured by reading time (Klare 716). Like the other results, these numbers again suggest a difference in the 200 series. As before, the 200 series has a larger number of nominalizations, suggesting again that the 200 series was inherently more difficult than either of the other two passages.

NEW ANGLES ON THE PUZZLE

On a number of measures, both subjective and objective, the passage that did not respond to added redundancy is different from and more difficult than the other two passages studied. My hypothesis concerning text difficulty, which

Table 8-9. Spearman correlation coefficient, content words to syllable count.

Series	*Spearman correl.*	*Significance*
100	1.0	$p<.001$
200	$-.26$	$p<.37$
300	.89	$p<.05$

Table 8-10. Mean nominalization counts derived from HOMER program.

Series	No. *of shun* words
100	11
200	14
300	8.5

suggests that it is a by-product of the interaction of readability factors and comprehensibility factors, is supported by the findings discussed here. As these results have come in, I have become more and more convinced that the 200 series passage was impervious to the addition of redundancy alone, at least as I defined it. It seems that the changes I made, based on my hypothesis that adding redundancy would improve comprehension, should have worked no matter what the nature of the passage was. Since all the passages were treated the same way, it seems as though my changes still should have worked.

However, rethinking suggests why this reasoning is incorrect. Redundancy, as I defined it (Horning, "On Defining. . ."), affects the text syntactically and semantically, tapping factors not clearly measured by any of the features reviewed thus far. That is, redundancy does not alter nominalizations, content words, syllable counts, proposition counts, or cohesive ties across sentences to any great degree. Thus, when I add redundancy, I do not alter any of these factors known to contribute to text difficulty, because increasing redundancy does not reduce any of these difficulty factors. Redundancy must, based on my results, contribute to readable writing, but its effects are mitigated to varying degrees by other difficulty factors. All these factors, both subjective and objective, which contribute to difficulty in some way, have turned out to be at much higher levels in the passage where adding redundancy did not improve Cloze scores.

Clearly, a complete understanding of the nature of readable writing must include both the predictive factors summarized here, and the productive factors like cohesion and proposition density that are in the control of writers. The research findings reported here point to the next step in solving the puzzle of readable text. First, knowing that the factors measured here, cohesion, propositions, syllable and content word counts, play a role in the inherent difficulty of text demonstrates that additional text features can and should be analyzed to make a predictive measure of difficulty. Second, these factors are now known to be significant because they tap into the interaction between text and reader. Third, production factors such as redundancy, which can be altered in a text, must also be measured and, when other factors don't interfere, can significantly reduce the difficulty of text. My findings in the text analysis study suggested to me that cohesion, particularly in combination with redundancy, might produce a fuller picture of readable text. Thus, the research done on the role of cohesion in reading suggests that the next section of the puzzle to focus on is connected to that linguistics corner where cohesion in text is pictured. We move to that corner next.

Chapter 9

Empirical Studies: Redundancy and Cohesion – Miscue Research

Text analysis research pointed clearly to the significance of cohesion. The role of cohesion is also supported by the studies reported in the chapters on reading and writing research, which strongly suggest that cohesion plays a key role in the comprehension and composition of readable writing. Since, in working on the puzzle of readable writing, I had already put redundancy in place, this second factor warranted closer examination. In addition, the Cloze procedure I used in the initial study of redundancy alone raised important methodological questions, given the need to look carefully at reader responses. To see where the cohesion piece fit in the puzzle, I needed to examine the impact of cohesion alone and in conjunction with redundancy, and to use a methodology that would allow me to focus more precisely on reader response.

One of the best methodologies for looking at individual reader response is reading miscue analysis (Goodman and Burke). Miscue analysis, focusing on deviations between a written text and readers' oral renderings, allows an investigator access to reading in progress in a way that Cloze procedure does not. And while the method has some weaknesses, this is its chief advantage. The miscue study provided an opportunity to look again at the passages with redundancy added, using the 04 version of each passage that incorporated both syntactic and semantic redundancy, and an opportunity to watch readers' responses to the increased cohesion (in the 05 versions created for this study of reading miscues) and the combination of cohesion and redundancy (in the 06 versions) in the texts I have been studying (the passages appear in Appendix 1).

For the miscue study, the passages of text were rewritten to incorporate redundancy and cohesion, and college students were asked to read these passages aloud and write brief summaries of them. Because reading miscues show readers in the process getting meaning from print, the two predictions here are that readers will produce fewer and "better" (i.e., more meaning-preserving) miscues on the versions of the passages with increased redundancy and cohesion. The results of the miscue study suggest that these rewriting strategies do indeed produce texts that are more accessible for readers.

PURPOSE AND HYPOTHESES

The variables involved in the miscue study are redundancy and cohesion. Both semantic and syntactic redundancy were increased in the passages, since earlier research shows that both together produce the greatest improvements in comprehension (except in the atypical 200 series passages). Cohesion was incorporated in a way that allowed a control for overall length of the passages. Earlier research also showed that, while redundancy and cohesion are related to each other, redundancy works chiefly within sentences, while cohesion makes the greatest difference across sentences. For this reason, a form of cohesion that links sentences very specifically, cohesive conjunctions, seemed to be the best variable. Changes in these elements were expected to produce evidence that readers got more meaning from the text.

The purpose of this study is to examine individual readers' responses to the passages through their oral reading miscues to see whether readers make fewer miscues and preserve more meaning when they read passages in which redundancy and cohesion have been enhanced. As the discussion in Chapter 4 indicated, there is some research evidence that these types of changes will create more readable writing. Miscue analysis provides a methodology for close examination of how readers interact with text by revealing the reading process in progress. For these reasons, the major hypotheses studied here state that increased redundancy and cohesion will cause readers to make fewer miscues, and that the miscues produced will reflect greater preservation of meaning.

METHODOLOGY

Subjects

Following the pattern of the redundancy study reported above (Chapter 7), 80 college students were asked to read the passages. The subjects were first-year students at Oakland University, drawn from three sources. Some subjects were members of the Academic Support Program during the summer of 1988, when the data collection began. Other students were drawn from composition courses in session during the Fall 1988 semester, and still others were enrolled in introductory psychology courses during the same term. All subjects were native speakers of English. A total of 62 females and 18 males elected to participate in the study, with a mean age of 19 (and very little variance except for two older subjects, one 38 and the other 46). A variety of academic majors and subjects of interest are represented in the subject pool. Participation in the study was strictly voluntary. Subjects were given an informed consent document before their reading and received a debriefing explanation sheet after completing the exercise.

Some consideration was given to examining the Myers-Briggs Type Indicator results for subjects in this study. However, although some entering students take the Myers-Briggs Type Indicator for advising purposes, it is not a regular part of the university's orientation and placement process. Thus, MBTI results are not available for subjects in the study, and it is not clear how the subjects' overall type results might have influenced their responses to the passages. Also, while I might speculate about the subjects' type distributions based on normative data from the U.S. population generally or from data on typical first-year college students, there are two reasons why such speculation would be necessarily tentative.

First, the MBTI is meant to be an appraisal of an individual's particular set of personality preferences. As such, it is inappropriate to generalize about a group of subjects as to their likely type distributions. Second, even if data were available from which to make such speculations, the association of a particular type to a kind of response to text would necessarily be tentative. In Chapter 10, I will present individual case studies with professional reader/writers and comment on the impact of their individual types on their responses. Finally, methodologically, the miscue study made an attempt to use another kind of individualized appraisal device to make generalizations from a group. So methodology is, here as elsewhere, a key issue in the complex appraisal of readable writing.

Many of the subjects had taken a placement test for the university's writing program, which includes the College Entrance Examination Board's test of Reading Comprehension, one part of their Descriptive Tests of Language Skills, and an optional essay portion. Experience suggests that students who score at or above 69% on the test can be successful in the second term of the university's two-term sequence of writing courses. Students who score below this level generally do best taking both writing courses, unless they elect to write the essay and demonstrate a higher level of ability. Although the placement test is nominally required, students who were members of the Academic Support Program did not, at this time, take the placement test, and some other students also do not take it for various reasons.

Among the subjects in the miscue study, of the 80 participants, CEEB test scores were available for 74 of them. Their mean score on the Reading Comprehension test was 78%, substantially higher than our 69% level required for placement in the second term writing course. Since ordinarily a relatively small proportion of entering students place into the second term course, the subject pool has a disproportionately large number of students who scored well on this test. Insofar as other research suggests that better readers will have more sensitivity to cohesion and make better use of it as they get meaning from text, the standardized test score data helps support the results I obtained.

Materials

The same three passages used in the Cloze and text analysis studies were used in this study. The first passage (100 series) deals with the history of the origins of male dominance in society. The second passage discusses the impact of mass media on sports, while the last passage concerns evaluating the performance of government (see Appendix 1 for all passages in all versions). All passages were controlled for length and formula readability level. All were suitable for college-level students. Each passage was selected because it was a self-contained discussion of one major idea, and because it was drawn from a source the subjects were unlikely to have seen before.

Each passage had four versions: the original version (01), a version with both syntactic and semantic redundancy increased (04), a version with about eight cohesive conjunctions added to the original (05), and a version with both redundancy and the cohesive conjunctions (06). Thus, there were 12 passages in all (see Appendix 1). The texts were typed triple space on plain paper, so that the readers' copies and the worksheet for marking miscues used by the researcher were identical.

The addition of redundancy has already been described (Chapter 7). Cohesive conjunctions were chosen and arranged in the text for several reasons. The cohesive elements added included words like *instead, thus, therefore, in conclusion, however, then, finally*, and several others. These items are drawn from a sample list presented by Halliday and Hasan. The cohesive conjunctions were added at points where they seemed necessary and/or helpful in the text, both at the beginnings of sentences and within sentences.

The changes made could be spread fairly even through the text, and the same changes could be made to both the original version of the passage and to the form with added redundancy, in order to study the combined effect of increased redundancy and cohesion. Only eight (in one case, nine) cohesive conjunctions were added to each passage to maintain the control on length, and conjunctions were chosen partly because they would not impinge on the control on length. Cohesive conjunctions were also chosen because they are often recommended to writers for addition in revising text.

Using the 100 series as an example, the original version of the passage appears in Appendix 1. Here is form 105, which is the original version with cohesion enhanced. The cohesive conjunctions I added appear here in capitals, though they were printed as regular text on the pages study participants saw:

> So far as the history of the origin of masculine dominance is concerned, we must call attention to the fact that this is a phenomenon which does not occur as a natural thing. INSTEAD, this is indicated by the numerous laws which are necessary to guarantee this domination to men. It is also an indication that previous to the legal enforcement of masculine domination there must BY CONTRAST have been other epochs in which the masculine privilege was not nearly so certain. History proves that such epochs actually existed FORMERLY in the days of the matriarchate, the age in which it was the mother, the woman who played the important role in life, particularly so far as the child was concerned. At that time each man in the clan was in duty bound to respect the honored position of the mother. THUS, certain customs and usages are still colored by this ancient institution, as for instance, the introduction of all strange men to a child with the title "uncle" or "cousin." THEN a terrific battle must have preceded the transition from matriarchate to masculine domination. Men who like to believe that their privileges and prerogatives are determined by nature will THEREFORE be surprised to learn that men did not possess these prerogatives from the beginning, but had to fight for them. The triumph of man was simultaneous with the subjugation of women, and IN THE END, it is especially the evidence in the development of the law which bears witness to this long process of subjugation. IN CONCLUSION, masculine dominance occurred chiefly as a result of constant battles between primitive peoples, during the course of which man assumed the more prominent role as warrior, and finally used his newly won superiority in order to retain the leadership for himself and for his own ends.

A total of eight changes were made in this passage, and this did increase the length slightly. However, again, my choice of cohesive conjunctions allowed me to make the same changes to both the original version and the version with increased redundancy.

The 06 form is the version of each passage with both kinds of redundancy increased (i.e., 04), plus cohesive conjunctions. Once again, the cohesive conjunctions appear in all capitals here for the reader's convenience, though they were not specially marked or distinguished in any way for the subjects in the study:

> We must call attention to the fact that so far as the history of the origin of masculine dominance is concerned, this phenomenon of masculine dominance does not occur as a natural thing. INSTEAD, the fact that masculine dominance is not natural is indicated by the numerous laws which are necessary to guarantee this domination to men, such as property rights and divorce laws. Previous to the legal enforcement of masculine domination, there must BY CONTRAST have

> been other epochs in which the masculine privilege was not nearly so certain, and this fact also indicates that masculine dominance is not natural. History proves that such epochs actually existed FORMERLY in the days of the matriarchate, the age in which the mother, the woman played the important role in life, particularly so far as the child was concerned. Each man in the clan was in duty bound, at that time, to respect the honored position of the mother. THUS, certain customs and usages are still colored by this ancient institution, as for instance, the introduction of all strange men to a child with the title "uncle" or "cousin." THEN a terrific battle must have preceded the transition from matriarchate to masculine domination. Men may like to believe that their privileges and prerogatives, for example their authority in the family, are determined by nature, but they will THEREFORE be surprised to learn that men did not possess these prerogatives from the beginning, but had to fight for them. The triumph of man, that is, his rise to a position of power, was simultaneous with the subjugation of women, and IN THE END the evidence in the development of the law especially bears witness to this long process of subjugation. IN CONCLUSION, masculine dominance occurred chiefly as a result of constant battles between primitive peoples.

With all the 06 forms prepared in this way, the miscue study consisted of 12 passages, four versions of each of the three I have used in all the studies reported here. The miscue study made use of the original, unaltered version (01), the version with both types of redundancy increased (04), the original version with cohesive conjunctions added (05), and a version incorporating both enhanced redundancy and cohesive conjunctions (06). All three passages were treated in a similar fashion, and are presented in Appendix 1.

The new versions of the passages, the 05 and 06 forms, were run through the Readability computer program and also analyzed by Writer's Workbench to check their consistency with the 04 version with enhanced redundancy, and no particular differences appeared. There were, of course, the minor changes in length resulting from the addition of cohesive conjunctions, but the Dale-Chall readability levels and other major features remained constant on the average for all forms of each passage.

Procedure

Subjects generally volunteered by means of a sign-up sheet distributed in class or a similar kind of sheet on a designated bulletin board in the psychology department. Some subjects forgot, and data collection could not continue during term break. Thus, the data were collected over a four month period from July to October 1988.

When subjects arrived for the study, they were given the informed consent statement to read and sign first. Any questions were answered, and then the subject was asked to complete the personal information sheet. These items were separated, and the informed consent documents were stored separately from all other materials. Each subject was assigned a number and was anonymous for the purposes of the study. Subjects also received, for each passage they read, an index card, on which their subject number and the passage number were written, and on which the subject was instructed to write a two sentence summary of the passage. The subject was then told what the exercise involved, and began reading the first passage.

While the subject read, the investigator was marking miscues on a worksheet copy of the passage, and the reading was audiotaped for later playback to confirm miscues and check the accuracy of the written record. Following the oral reading of each passage, the tape recorder was stopped while the subject wrote a two-sentence summary of the passage. The same process was followed for the second and third passages. When all three passages were completed, the subject was given the debriefing sheet explaining the study. Each subject read one version of each of the three passages. Both the order of presentation of the passages, and the particular version of each passage, were randomized. All passages were about 300 words long, with a small amount of variation due to the addition of redundancy and cohesive elements (approximately 10 words or less).

Following standard miscue analysis procedures, the subjects' oral readings were audiotaped using a small cassette recorder and microphone. The subject sat in a chair opposite the researcher, with the tape recorder and microphone on the desk between them. At the conclusion of the reading of the three passages, subjects were given a one-page description of the purpose of the study, the hypotheses under investigation, and a short list of readings in the area. This debriefing sheet was required for students in the psychology courses and was given to them when they completed the exercise. The entire procedure took about 20 minutes for each subject.

The subjects provided 240 complete oral readings of the passages and written summaries for all of the readings. The oral reading miscues are analyzed below. The miscues made by subjects in their oral readings were analyzed using standard Reading Miscue Inventory procedures (Goodman and Burke), except that only four of the nine Inventory questions were answered for each miscue (correction, grammatical and semantic acceptability, and meaning change), because these questions yield patterns of comprehension and grammatical relations that reveal how the readers responded to the passages. The results of this analysis of approximately 1,500 miscues are presented below.

Scoring of the Data

As the data collection proceeded, I scored the miscues generated by the readers. I followed the standard miscue analysis procedure as described by Goodman and Burke for the four questions of interest here: was the miscue corrected, was it grammatically and semantically acceptable in context, and did the miscue cause a change in the meaning of the text. These questions are rather subjective, and so a second scorer was asked to review a portion of the miscues and score them in a blind study of the reliability of the scoring process.

Reliability

For the reliability study, a systematic 10% sample was used, yielding 24 forms that together provided about 10% of the total miscues examined for the study. The second scorer was a colleague finishing a doctoral dissertation in reading whose dissertation research project incorporated some miscue analysis. Thus, the second scorer was fully trained in standard miscue research procedures. The scorer was generally familiar with my work and was aware of the purposes of the present study. The scorer was given the 24 forms for the reliability check, and these forms were renumbered so that the scorer did not know which version of each passage was being evaluated. The subject numbers were also obscured, even though they had no significance to the scorer.

Of the 170 miscues on the 24 forms in the reliability study, there were discrepancies between the scorers in whether or not a particular miscue was codable according to Goodman and Burke's criteria in 13 cases. These 13 discrepancies were excluded from the study, since in these cases only one of us coded the miscue, giving no basis for comparison. This process left 157 miscues to be compared. Since the total number of miscues on all forms by all readers was 1,477, the miscues in the reliability check amount to a bit more than 10% of the total miscues under study. Thus, the reliability study provided results reflective of the data overall. The results are summarized in Table 9-1.

The second scorer was asked to review the handwritten worksheets on which I had recorded the miscues and verified them using the audio tapes of each subject's oral reading. She was then asked to code the miscues she felt were codable on RMI criteria in terms of the three inventory questions used in the study: grammatical acceptability, semantic acceptability, and meaning change. For each of these questions, the scorer's possible responses are "yes," "no," or "partial." We were in complete agreement if we both evaluated the miscue

Table 9-1: Reliability check on scoring of miscues

24 forms in sample		
170 miscues total; 13 discrepancies in scoring; 157 miscues compared		
Grammatical acceptability, total or partial agreement	129	82%
Semantic acceptability, total or partial agreement	142	90%
Meaning change, total or partial agreement	144	92%
Mean level of agreement		88%

identically, partial agreement if one of us responded with the "partial" response and the other chose "yes" or "no," and opposite if one of us chose "yes" and the other "no."

Comparing the second scorer's evaluation of the miscues with my own, we were in total agreement on the average 61% of the time, and in partial agreement on the average 27% of the time, showing a reliability rate of 88% on the miscues examined. Since it is unreasonable to expect absolute agreement in the scoring of miscues, this result suggests an adequate level of consistency in the scoring.

RESULTS

My scoring of the data created a database consisting of the 1,477 miscues generated by all readers in the study. The database provided printouts of miscues by form, so that I could tally the numbers of miscues made by all subjects on each form and compare the results in the versions with redundancy and cohesion added to the results on the original passages.

Hypothesis 1: Redundancy, Cohesion, and Numbers of Miscues

The first hypothesis under study proposed that increasing redundancy and cohesion would result in texts on which readers would make fewer miscues. To examine the results in terms of this hypothesis, I used simple counts of the total numbers of miscues. The results are presented in Tables 9-2 to 9-4.

These tables show that, in two of the three passages, readers did generate fewer miscues on the 04 version with increased redundancy as well as on the

Table 9-2: Number of miscues by form

Form	*Number of miscues*	*Mean(/20)*
101	110	5.5
104	135	6.75
105	146	7.3
106	156	7.8
201	141	7.05
204	108	5.4
205	145	7.25
206	105	5.25
301	121	6.05
304	84	4.2
305	139	6.95
306	84	4.2

Table 9-3: Total numbers of miscues across all forms

Series Versions	*100*	*200*	*300*	*total*
01	110	141	121	372
04	135	108	84	327
05	146	145	139	430
06	156	105	84	345

Table 9-4. Mean miscues across all forms

Series Versions	*100*	*200*	*300*	*mean*
01	5.5	7.1	6.1	6.2
04	6.8	5.4	4.2	5.5
05	7.3	7.3	7.0	4.2
06	7.8	5.3	4.2	5.8

06 version with both redundancy and cohesion increased, and the mean figures also reflect this outcome.

Hypothesis 2: Redundancy, Cohesion, and "Better" Miscues

The second hypothesis under investigation in the study claims that readers will produce miscues demonstrating greater preservation of meaning when reading the forms with increased redundancy and cohesion. To evaluate this hypothesis, I used several different approaches to the miscues. One approach follows Goodman and Burke's analysis of comprehension patterns, looking at those miscues which show no loss of meaning or only partial loss of meaning. The results are presented in Table 9-5.

These results suggest that, in at least two of the three passages, the number as a percentage of the total number of miscues generated on the passage goes up for the 100 and 300 series when the 01 versions are compared to the 06 versions (for the 100 series, the percentage of "good" miscues goes from 55% on 101 to 63% on 106, and for the 300 series, from 80% on 301 to 82% on 306). Here again, it is useful to note that the 200 series, the passage which produced Cloze scores suggesting that redundancy alone did not improve comprehension, fails to conform to the expected percentage increase in numbers of meaning-preserving miscues. The percentage increases are small, but are present for both the 100 series and the 300 series, consistent with the hypothesis.

A different approach to analysis of the miscues for this hypothesis calls for the examination of miscues which show correction. Such miscues would indicate that readers are following the meaning quite successfully. To examine the results

Table 9-5. Comprehension patterns of miscues by form

Form	No. of miscues	No.w/no loss or partial
101	110	61 (55%)
104	135	87 (64%)
105	146	79 (54%)
106	156	99 (63%)
201	141	100 (71%)
204	108	74 (69%)
205	145	83 (57%)
206	105	64 (60%)
301	121	97 (80%)
304	84	55 (65%)
305	139	101 (73%)
306	84	69 (82%)

in this way, a simple count of the miscues showing full or partial correction is presented in Table 9-6.

These results suggest that, on a percentage basis, readers in the 100 and 300 series were able to correct fully or in part those miscues they made, and to do so more effectively on the 06 versions than on the originals. Once again, the 200 series deviates from the pattern predicted by the hypothesis. And once again, because of the nature of miscue analysis, it is inappropriate to test these results by inferential statistical methods.

Results of Reader Summaries

A key part of miscue analysis procedure is the use of a retelling following the oral reading of the passage. Such retelling is a reasonable methodology, particularly

Table 9-6. Count of miscues showing full or partial correction

Form	No. of miscues	No. corrected or partially corrected
101	110	20 (18%)
104	135	32 (23%)
105	146	29 (20%)
106	156	35 (22%)
201	141	31 (22%)
204	108	22 (20%)
205	145	19 (13%)
206	105	16 (15%)
301	121	20 (17%)
304	84	20 (24%)
305	139	26 (19%)
306	84	21 (25%)

for young readers working with stories. When readers summarize the key elements of the plot and can name the characters and so forth, the retelling provides helpful holistic information about readers' comprehension of the text. A retelling is less indicative when the material is expository in nature. The content may not be summarized fully, and even though Goodman and Burke allow for partial prompting in the recall, it is often harder to tell what readers have gleaned from a passage of nonfiction.

In the miscue study examining redundancy and cohesion, I used a slight variant of this approach, asking readers to write a brief summary of the passage immediately following their reading aloud. These summaries were written on index cards. Following Irwin, I intended to analyze these recalls for propositional content, and to compare them to the propositions in the passage itself. The prediction here is that the forms with increased redundancy and cohesion would yield recalls with more propositions.

I found the recall data extremely difficult to analyze, and my approach yielded no useful information. Quite a number of subjects drew a blank when asked to summarize the reading, and could only say very generally what the passage was about. In addition, even scholars using propositional analysis have raised many questions about it, as noted above, including its subjective nature, and the difficulty of comparing one proposition list to another (Kieras, "An Advanced"). I considered various other manipulations of the data, such as counting key words in the passages and in the recalls and comparing these, all unconventional treatments without consistency and lacking the authority of more conventional treatments of the data. Since the miscues themselves provide fairly objective data, allowing for some individual variation in the scoring (see reliability discussion above), and the recalls seem to provide no useful insight into the impact of redundancy and cohesion on readers' responses, the recalls were not considered in the study.

DISCUSSION

The miscue study supports the prominent placement of redundancy and cohesion in the puzzle of readable writing. Actually, the results presented here are in a sense similar to those I obtained on the original Cloze study, in that they support my hypotheses in a general way, but not in every case. That is, here again, two of the three passages conform to my hypotheses, but not with complete consistency across all passages. These results raise some issues that I have mentioned several times before.

The first issue has to do with methodology. Miscue research has been questioned as a means of assessing reading, because it asks readers to engage in a different kind of reading activity than is the activity we are most interested in, that is, it requires readers to read aloud rather than silently. There are other features of the situation which call miscue studies into question, such as the presence of an investigator who is taking notes, the use of a tape recorder, and the specially prepared materials. For all these reasons, miscue analysis may not be the best means for examining reader response to the texts with added redundancy and cohesion. On the other hand, it does provide an angle on text processing.

Yet another issue concerns the absence of recall material. Because the recall data have not been analyzed here, the study departs from standard miscue research procedures. However, the recall task seemed to be a significant challenge to many of the subjects in the study. I have the impression that many of them, although they were told about writing the summary at the outset, were unable to comply with this request after they had read the passages aloud. This response may be an indication of the readers' responses to the demands of the study, or it may be a human variable not anticipated in the research methodology. In any case, if the recalls were substantive and useful, they might provide a different confirmation of the readers' responses to the texts with added redundancy and cohesion, and this data is lacking from the study.

A further issue has to do with reader ability. Above, I noted in the description of the subjects that their scores on the CEEB test of Reading Comprehension suggested that they were better than average readers. There are some complications to this finding, suggesting that the subjects may not be as adept at reading as the CEEB test results suggest. Lesser reading ability might help to explain the inconsistency of the miscue results. There are several possibilities involved here.

First, the test results are not complete for the entire subject pool, since some subjects did not take the test. In particular, some results were unavailable for those who entered the university in the Academic Support Program in part because they need additional developmental work in reading. Second, an examination of the test itself shows that it provides brief passages of about four to seven sentences, followed by multiple choice questions. Many reading researchers have questioned the validity of this kind of test as a measure of reading ability.

Third, many of these readers lack experience dealing with longer passages of continuous text in which redundancy and cohesion have particular impact, as noted by Carolyn Boiarsky (131). She comments on findings by Haas and Flower that less capable readers work on text in small chunks, without awareness of the larger discourse issues that pertain to readable writing. If students are only able to work on small chunks and have no sense of the overall picture (a by-product, she proposes, of television's propensity for short segments, such as those on "Sesame Street," MTV, and perhaps in 15-second commercials), they would be insensitive or less sensitive to the presence or absence of features that help to tie texts together, like redundancy and cohesion. This analysis helps to explain why only two of the passages confirm my hypotheses in the miscue study. It is interesting to note that Boiarsky goes on to suggest teaching strategies that focus on Halliday and Hasan's cohesion, among other features, to enhance the readable quality of word-processed texts.

Finally, keep in mind that miscue research was designed and developed for use with individual readers. It provides a strategy for the diagnosis of individual reader ability with a particular text. There is no question that the Goodmans's work with miscue studies has provided significant insight into the nature of the reading process. It has also revealed the different ways that individual readers respond to texts, and has shed light on reading success. These achievements, however, do not necessarily justify the use of miscues in the kind of study reported here, since my intentions required a focus on text and were not an attempt at individual reader diagnosis. It seemed reasonable at the outset to think that miscues would give a clearer picture of how readers respond to these texts, but finally, analysis of miscues may not be the best methodology for the kind of text-based study I had in mind.

As I looked at the data resulting from this study, it became clear that I needed to look at reader response still more closely than miscue analysis would allow. Thus in the next study, I turned to a much more individualized response with an entirely different group of subjects in an attempt to focus more sharply on individual reader response. An additional consideration in the next study involves the subjects. In the Cloze and miscue studies, the subjects were all first-year college students. In thinking about those findings that show that a sensitivity to cohesion (and perhaps redundancy as well) appears only among skilled and highly proficient readers, it seemed reasonable to think that subjects with strong reading and writing skills might provide a more explicit response to the changes in the texts. As the case studies presented in Chapter 10 will show, highly skilled, professional reader/writers demonstrate a strong and consistent awareness of redundancy and cohesion in text and their impact in reading and writing.

The miscue study moves the puzzle of readable writing somewhat closer to solution, albeit with only partial support of the hypotheses I proposed. The study does so by suggesting that cohesion has some impact in the texts under study and by suggesting that cohesion combined with redundancy makes a definite difference in how readers respond to these texts. This outcome adds cohesion in the puzzle picture, and redundancy and cohesion begin to form the center of the puzzle. The pieces sit on the table, clearly fitting together with readable writing, though perhaps not firmly in place. The interlocking of the two features, as they draw on readers' and writers' knowledge of language, belong in the central sections of the puzzle of readable writing. The next step, then, is to get a close look at skilled professionals reading and responding to these texts. The cases examined in Chapter 10 show that, by using different methodology and asking different kinds of questions, the role of redundancy and cohesion in readable text becomes clear and their position in the puzzle firm.

Chapter 10

Case Studies with Professional Reader/Writers

Solving a jigsaw puzzle sometimes requires a number of different steps, like constructing the edges and then filling in various portions of the picture. In the filling-in process, it is sometimes easier or necessary to assemble a portion of the picture separately, a goal achieved by collecting all pieces of a particular color together and then assembling them outside of the puzzle itself. In some ways, the case study research represents my attempt to connect a number of pieces outside the puzzle and then to fit them into the larger picture. While I cannot say that I have all the pieces or the right pieces, or even that this puzzle is finite, these cases provide more evidence that redundancy and cohesion interlock with readable writing.

One set of pieces already placed in the puzzle comes from my prior empirical studies of the three passages that I have been testing. The previous study, the miscue project reported in Chapter 9, produced mixed results and various difficulties. For example, there are several discussions in the literature about the strengths and weaknesses of miscue research as a means of examining reading. Methodologically, moreover, there was a problem working on the recalls in the miscue study, as discussed above also. Thus, while the miscue study helped to suggest the place for redundancy and cohesion in the puzzle I have been putting together, it still did not give the broad outline of the entire picture. Similarly, the text analysis of the passages counts key elements but does not take real readers' responses into account. In addition, some aspects of text analysis seem remarkably subjective, like the exploration of cohesive chains. Finally, in the Cloze data, I could not initially account for why I got disparate results in the 200 series. So there are various missing elements.

WHY A CASE STUDY?

My work to this point had taken up different approaches and methods of addressing the nature of readable text, but all the strategies to this point involved fairly objective, quantifiable data. Some support for an alternative research strategy comes from scholars who have thought about the nature of research in these areas. North notes diversity of approach in his review of the range of research strategies he classifies in his analysis of the development of composition research. Lauer and Asher make a similar point in their review of empirical designs in composition research, as does Sternglass in her choice of retrospective accounts of reading and writing. The discipline of writing, as embodied in its professional organization, the Conference on College Composition and Communication, has formally acknowledged the importance of diverse, interdisciplinary approaches to research (*Scholarship in Composition*).

The same issue comes to light in a slightly different form in the work of Jensen and DiTiberio. In their work on the relevance of personality preferences in writing, they make a strong case for instruction in writing that helps writers develop both their preferred approaches to writing tasks and also some facility with strategies opposite from their preferences. Their claim is that such balance can help writers produce better texts more easily. Jensen and DiTiberio's view of balance in writing strategies and the research analyses together made me think about the work I had done, and the fact that, because of my preference for objective data and for numerical findings I could classify and analyze, I had not chosen to look at more subjective sorts of data. I had also been thinking about the results I had obtained in these more objective projects, which provide only suggestive data about the questions I am interested in. For these reasons, a more subjective approach that would generate data requiring one-by-one analysis, though not my preferred research strategy, offered an alternative approach to balance against the numerical data I had gathered thus far.

I decided that I ought to try to interlock some of my pieces outside the puzzle by trying a divergent approach to gathering response data. Robert Yin's *Case Study Research* was helpful in some other work I was doing, and as I read Yin against the background of these other things, the present study took form. Yin's discussion of case study methods, and clear, step-by-step approach to choosing appropriate cases and handling the data, gave me a clear procedure to follow and demonstrated how I could meet my own preference for consistency and order in data that would not be countable or objective.

A view of the puzzle pieces outside the frame sometimes provides a unique angle that moves the puzzle dramatically closer to the solution. For this reason, and because I wanted sophisticated reader/writer responses to the passages, I designed the following research study to examine individual responses to the passages in cases of individual reader/writers. In this study, professional readers and writers respond to the passages, clearly demonstrating the central role of redundancy and cohesion in readable writing.

All of the experiments reported here thus far involve first-year college students, responding to the passages in some way. The other work, reported in Chapter 8, deals with objective analysis of the text by counting various elements or making calculations of text features. Unlike these approaches, the case study approach yields different data, in the form of individualized and evaluative responses. In addition, all respondents had and were willing to give me Myers-Briggs Type Indicator results. The Type Indicator, as discussed in Chapter 3, is a psychological instrument that gives a profile of an individual's preferences on four dimensions: where people focus their attention, acquisition of information, decision-making processes, and orientation to the outer world. The instrument contributes some helpful insights into why individuals respond to texts as they do, but does not provide complete or absolute answers to the complicated nature of readable writing. The MBTI results for the subjects in the cases make possible some tentative exploration of the role of personality preferences in readers' responses to text but preferences are, like other aspects of this investigation, only one of many pieces of the puzzle.

PURPOSE AND HYPOTHESES FOR THE STUDY

There are three formal hypotheses under study here. The first of these is that professionals will judge the versions of the passages with added redundancy and with added cohesion to be "better" in some way that suggests they are more readable: more understandable, easier to follow, and so on. A second hypothesis states that professionals, giving advice toward revision of one version for use in teaching about writing, will advise strategies or changes that in one way or another add redundancy or cohesion to the passage. The third hypothesis suggests that there is a relationship between readers' responses and their MBTI type. In investigating these matters, the case study approach allowed me to examine individual responses in significant detail, and provides strong confirmation of the first two of these hypotheses and informative speculation about the third.

METHODOLOGY

Subjects

After conducting a small pilot study, I sent the materials to a total of 30 colleagues, including some at my home institution and some at institutions around the country, and asked them to volunteer to participate in the study. For the formal project, I selected as subjects people who had chosen work with language, and especially work involving reading and writing, as their professional career. Those most readily available to me are academics, all but one of whom hold Ph.D.'s in areas that entail reading and/or writing: rhetoric, literature, language studies or some closely related field. I had 10 responses, and these 10 cases are the basis of the following discussion.

The subjects who provided responses include six women and four men. The one without the Ph.D. is at work on a dissertation in reading at present. With this one exception, all have had 7 or more years of full time teaching experience and regularly teach reading, writing, or language analysis courses. All are native speakers of English. All those who responded provided data on all three passages, and several provided lengthy and detailed commentary on the materials and their reactions to the exercise. Participation in the study was strictly voluntary, and there was no payment involved. Brief sketches of the participants follow, including their Myers-Briggs types.

Subject 1. Subject 1 is different from the other cases in various ways. Like Subject 10, she had seen some of the passages previously, having served as the second scorer in the miscue study. But also like Subject 10, she had not looked at the passages themselves in a few years and had not looked at all of them taken together as was the case in this exercise. Unlike the others, she does not have full-time teaching experience that involves language production or language comprehension, and also unlike the other subjects, this subject has not completed her Ph.D. She is, however, a doctoral candidate in reading with some background in linguistics, and also has taken the Myers-Briggs Type Indicator; her type is INFP.

Subject 3. This subject is a male who completed his Ph.D. in English, with a specialization in Romanticism, in 1976. He has 14 years of full-time teaching experience, including courses in fiction, Victorian literature, the Romantics and 19th century literature. His MBTI result is INTJ.

Subject 7. This male subject holds a Ph.D. in Theology and Literary Criticism, and has 27 years of full-time teaching experience. His teaching interests center on American literature, modern drama, Irish literature, fantasy, and writing. His Ph.D. was awarded in 1965. This subject had taken the Myers-Briggs Type Indicator some years prior to my study, and retook it at my request after he responded to the passages. His type result in ENFJ.

Subject 10. Subject 10 is also male, a colleague who completed his Ph.D. in 1970 and whose dissertation is in the area of teaching English to speakers of other languages. In his 27 years of full-time teaching experience, Subject 10 has taught courses dealing with language and culture, writing, and second language testing and teaching methods. This subject chose not to use the response sheets I provided, but instead wrote lengthy comments on each passage he returned, and also wrote a three-page response to all of the passages. Perhaps this kind of response is related to his personality type, which is INTP. I will explore this possibility below in the section discussing results on the second and third hypotheses in the study.

I should indicate that this subject is a special case in some other ways, because I have consulted him in the past on various studies reported here and because he has seen the passages before in other research contexts as part of this consultation. However, it has been some years since he last looked at the actual texts and he had not, as I recall, seen the 05 and 06 versions of the passages previously. Still, his response, particularly given its length and detail, is consistent with that of other subjects.

Subject 12. Subject 12 is a male who completed his Ph.D. in 1987. ENFJ is this subject's Myers-Briggs type. He has had 7 years of full-time teaching experience. His Ph.D. focused on rhetoric and teaching writing, and he regularly teaches freshman composition, philosophy of rhetoric and a course in peer tutoring in writing. Unlike most of the other subjects, this man chose a different form as best than the one he recommended for revision.

Subject 25. A woman holding a Ph.D. in American literature and civilization, Subject 25 has 20 years of full-time teaching experience. She regularly teaches courses in American literature, poetry, writing, and American studies. Although this subject had taken the MBTI some years before participating in the study, she could not confidently recall the result, and so took the Indicator again some time after working on the passages, at my request. Her result was ISTJ, an introverted, sensing, thinking, judging type.

Subject 26. Having completed her Ph.D. in English and Rhetoric in 1987, Subject 26, a woman, has 25 years of full-time teaching experience. She teaches an array of courses in writing at various levels, in addition to a peer tutoring course for students interested in tutoring writing, and some courses in study skills. Like Subject 12, Subject 26's Myers-Briggs type is ENFJ.

Subject 27. This subject, also a female, completed her Ph.D. in English medieval literature in 1975. She has 20 years' full-time teaching experience, including various writing courses, persuasion, and English drama. Her MBTI type result is ENFJ, like Subject 12 and Subject 26.

Subject 29. Subject 29 is a woman who completed her Ph.D. in English literature in 1979. She has had 7 years of full-time teaching experience, chiefly in writing courses of various kinds and levels including freshman composition and technical writing. INTJ is Subject 29's Myers-Briggs type.

Subject 30. The subject in this case is a female who completed her Ph.D. in English literature with a specialization in modern literature and the history of drama in 1979. She has 10 years of full-time teaching experience in courses ranging from advanced composition to world literature. Subject 30 completed the MBTI at my request some months after responding to the passages; her result is INTJ.

Materials

The main materials for the study are the passages I created for the miscue study, in forms with increased redundancy and cohesion (i.e., 01, the original, 04 with redundancy alone added, 05 with cohesive conjunctions added, and 06 which incorporated both redundancy and cohesion, for each passage). The passages were accompanied by a cover letter, a set of directions, a background information form, a half-page response sheet attached to each set of passages, and some other items (see Appendix 3 for a sample of the materials used).

Procedure

Prior to collecting this data, I conducted a small pilot study with three colleagues in close fields (two linguists and a person with experience teaching college-level reading and writing, and an M.A. in reading, now working in another field). I asked these individuals to complete the exercises in the form in which I planned to give them to the subjects in the formal study, and also to respond to the clarity of the directions and to keep track of their time in completing the work. The pilot led to minor modifications in the directions and to the addition of a different kind of response sheet in a sealed envelope, included with the materials, for those who found the task challenging and/or frustrating (the "HELP" envelope). No subject in the formal study chose to make use of the "HELP" envelope. At least one subject, reading a draft of this chapter, was unable to recall the presence of the "HELP" envelope among the materials.

The materials as shown in Appendix 3 were then mailed to colleagues elsewhere in the country or hand-delivered to those at my institution. The subjects were asked to complete two main tasks. In the first part, subjects were asked to read all versions of each passage and judge which was best for a colleague to use in a hypothetical class on readable writing for first-year college students; subjects were also asked to say why they felt their choice was "best."

As a second task, they were asked to choose one version of each passage for revision prior to such classroom use, say why they chose this version and indicate the nature of the revisions on their response sheet. In addition, subjects were asked to write comments in the margins of the passage chosen for revision, to indicate changes to be made to the text. Subjects were asked to separate the response sheet and version of the passage they recommended for revision from the rest of each packet, and to return only those materials and the background form to me by a deadline date.

Each subject received the packet of materials described above, including the three passages in four versions, all in numerical order. Because I expected these subjects to read the passages more than once and in varying order, I did not randomize the order of presentation. The responses came back in varied order, confirming this expectation.

Validity Concerns

Comments on the text itself provided a useful second source of information about readers' responses, pursuant to Yin's advice on enhancing the construct validity of case study research (36). The materials were designed to provide more than one source of information on the readers' responses: Subjects were to summarize their advice to a colleague for revision and also to write on the texts themselves.

As a further enhancement to the validity of the findings, participants were asked to read a draft of this chapter of the book and respond to it in terms of my report of their responses to the passages and in terms of the overall findings. Like the designed request for more than one source of information, this process increases the validity of the results (Yin 137-38). Responses from those subjects who had comments on the draft have been integrated in the chapter.

DATA ANALYSIS AND FINDINGS

Results on Hypothesis 1

My first hypothesis in this study concerned the overall response of these professional reader/writers to the passages, and projected that the subjects would show a preference for the forms with added redundancy (04), or cohesion (05), or both (06), over the original versions (01) of all passages. To assist the reader in this chapter, these forms are followed by a letter code as they are mentioned, as a reminder of the type of modification to each form (thus, the 01/o should remind the reader that this is the original version, 04/r the form with redundancy, 05/c the form with cohesion, and 06/rc the combined form with both redundancy and cohesion added. The results for all the subjects are displayed in Table 10-1.

Table 10-1. Individual readers' choices for "best" version of each passage and for revision.

Subject	*MBTI*	*100*		*200*		*300*	
		Best	*Rev*	*Best*	*Rev*	*Best*	*Rev*
1	INFP	106	106	206	206	306	306
3	INTJ	101	105	201	206	301	306
7	ENFJ	106	106	201	201	301	301
10	INTP	–	101	–	205	–	305
12	ENFJ	104	101	205	204	301	304
25	ISTJ	104	104	206	206	301	301
26	ENFJ	104	,105	205	206	305	306
27	ENFJ	105	105	204	204	305	305
29	INTJ	106	106	206	206	305	305
30	INTJ	106	105	205	205	305	305

On the whole, any altered version was generally preferred to the original version that was lacking in added redundancy or added cohesion or both. A good number of the subjects responded consistently across all passages, choosing all 05/c or 06/rc as best. Indeed, only one subject felt 101/o was best, though three suggested it for revision; two subjects preferred 201/o and also chose it for revision; in the 300 series, half preferred the 301/o form, but only three suggested using it as the basis for revision. The results indicate confirmation of the first hypothesis. The subjects' responses are presented in detail below, as many of their extended comments pertain both to their choice of a "best version" and to their suggestions for revision.

Results on Hypothesis 2

The professionals' responses to the revision question provide results pertinent to the second hypothesis. In general, the subjects indicate, quite uniformly, a sensitivity to the redundancy and cohesion of the passages, and their revision advice and actual changes to the passages all support their view of the significance of redundancy and cohesion for the creation of readable writing. Thus, the cases also support the second hypothesis, that professional reader/writers would recommend revisions to add redundancy or cohesion or both to the texts.

To analyze the data on this hypothesis as well as the results on the third hypothesis, the subjects must speak for themselves. On both hypotheses, the most revealing aspects of the data come both from the individual choices on each set of passages and from what the subjects say about their chosen forms and what they suggest for revision. Below, I give a case-by-case discussion of readers' responses to each set of passages, commenting also on their MBTI type results and preferences among the passages. Readers may find it useful to refer to Table 10-1 above for a visual display of each subjects' preferences.

Subject 1 (INFP). Like some other subjects, Subject 1 provided some general comments on the exercise, which she had taken up late in the day. She found the task quite challenging overall, though most of her difficulty centered on her suggestions for revision rather than on her choice of passage. This response may reflect aspects of her type, since a feeling type would want to be careful about the writer's feelings in suggesting revisions, and perceivers often have difficulty making decisions of any kind. Interestingly, she chose the 06/rc version as best and also as the one to be revised, for all three passages.

On the 100 series, Subject 1 found form 106/rc better organized than the others and liked the use of transitional words and phrases in this version. Her suggestions for revision on the response sheet included adding paragraph breaks, deleting the final sentence, and adding a conclusion. She notes that she also liked form 104/r and, again typical of perceivers, had difficulty choosing between these forms.

On the text itself, she offers some additional thoughts. She recommends moving the sentence "Men may like to believe. . ." to the very beginning of the passage, suggesting that it is out of place in its current position as third from last. This sentence, because it in some ways draws together the key points of the passage, would add some discourse level redundancy not now present even in form 106/rc. Her other notes on the text relate to the paragraphing problem: She suggests that there might be a paragraph on legal issues and one on the idea of matriarchate, but that neither idea in this version of the passage is developed fully enough to comprise a paragraph. Her last note suggests deleting the last sentence.

As noted above, subject 1 chose the 06/rc version of each passage, and so chose 206/rc from the 200 series group, feeling both that it was "best" and that it was the one that might most profitably be revised before serving as the basis of a discussion on writing. In choosing form 206/rc as best, this subject indicated that she liked the transitional words and phrases, specific examples, and clear referents, a clear preference for features of redundancy and cohesion as I have defined them.

Her recommendations for revision on the response sheet ask for the addition of examples and make a minor change in the placement of *however* but she notes that she is generally satisfied with form 206/rc as is and doesn't feel it needs much work. Her request for examples draws from form 205/c, in the last paragraph where the list of "close-up, instant replay. . ." occurs. I omitted this list from the revision for length considerations, though it clearly adds redundancy to the passage.

Subject 1 also liked the 06/rc version of the 300 series, though she did not care for the topic of the passage. She found form 306/rc "warmer, friendlier" in tone, and liked again the transitions and examples. This response is consistent with the feeling aspect of her MBTI type; feeling individuals have a stronger concern with connection to a text than would a thinker type. Subject 1 wrote no suggestions on the text of form 306/rc, citing the lateness of the hour and her diligence with the other passages as a rationale for her lack of response. Thus, this response provides incomplete data on the 300 series passage, but still indicates that the subject's choice of form 306/rc resulted from her awareness of the use of transitions and examples, that is, a sensitivity to the cohesion and redundancy added to the passage.

This subject's type result, INFP, indicates an introverted, intuitive, feeling and perceiving type. Her responses are consistent with her type, as Isabel Briggs Myers notes, commenting that "People with INFP preferences have a great deal of warmth. . ."(17), hence her preference for one version of one of the passages as warmer and friendlier. As with Subject 10, whose responses are discussed below, there may be some feeling of inadequacy on the exercise, despite both subjects' consistency of response to the redundancy and cohesion of the passages.

In response to a draft of this chapter of the book, Subject 1 made several notes consistent with her personality type. First, she commented that she felt she had not done the exercise "right" and wished for the chance to do it again. This response might be consistent with her type's need for harmony and preference to be positive and not critical. She also noted that she was distinct from the rest of the group because she is not a practicing teacher of writing, but she goes on to point out that her highly unusual type (INFP's appear to be about 1% of the general population (Keirsey and Bates 176)) often feels different from others.

As a writer and reader, she indicates that she seeks to incorporate a great deal of redundancy in any text she produces, again reflecting a preference for thoroughness, but does not have the same expectations for a text when reading. In reading, she suggests that redundancy and cohesion might have different levels of impact depending on prior knowledge (where high prior knowledge is present, less redundancy and cohesion are needed), interest, and motivation (again, when high, less text support through redundancy and cohesion is needed). She observes that other readers made a number of remarks about the content of the passages, supporting her view that content makes a difference to the appraisal of readable writing and the role of text factors. The consistent response of all subjects in the study to the redundancy and cohesion of these passages, however, suggests that they are salient features of readable writing irrespective of topic.

Subject 3 (INTJ). In the 100 series, this subject found the 101/o version best, though he qualifies his comment by saying he is not sure why and that no version is good. His choice for revision is either the 101/o or 105/c version. His complaints have to do with wordiness, need for more conciseness, and with awkward phrasing and a need for more sentence structure variety. He did not find the various versions distinct. His marks on the draft for revision (he sent back form 101/o) suggest some editing for wordiness, and in particular an objection to the structure of the third sentence. It is interesting to note that the sentences he marked as "wordy" are all ones without a true subject, or ones in passive voice. These requests are met by some of my changes to add redundancy, in changing the dummy subjects to real ones and converting passives to actives.

In the 200 series, this subject found form 201/o the best in that it seemed clearest and most concise. Subject 3's thinking preference may have influenced his preference for specific content. He sent back form 201/o as his choice for revision, though on the response sheet, he indicated that either 201/o or 206/rc could be revised. His suggestion calls for more examples, a different kind of redundancy. As an additional comment, he said he also found the 200 series passages very similar to one another. His notes on form 201/o indicate a need to make the sentences in which there are examples more explicitly exemplars of the author's point. This subject's interest in the examples demonstrates his sensitivity to the redundancy level of the passage.

In the 300 series, this subject again chose the 01/o version, noting it was the "clearest?", suggesting again perhaps a focus on content as is typical of a thinking type . His comment in response to the third question on the response sheet is: "Maybe I like the 1st because it is so hard to keep reading the same info. again and again." He sent back form 301/o, urging the writer to clarify "point of view," a phrase he marked in both the first and third paragraphs, and commenting that the exact focus is not as clear as it could be. While this subject did not provide written comments on the draft of 301/o as requested, he seems to be asking for a bit more clarification in this passage. Clarification can be achieved in various ways, the addition of redundancy at both discourse and sentence levels among them.

Subject 3's INTJ Myers-Briggs type helps account for these responses to the passages. In asking for point of view, this reader may be looking for the broad vision characteristic of Ns. The INTJ is particularly good at analysis (Myers 24), and this is revealed by the subject's careful reflection on his own responses to the text. His complaints about wordiness are also characteristic of his type, as I will describe below in the section considering the interaction of NT and NF dimensions. NTs like terse and compact statements, and so this subject would make a point of asking for less wordiness in these texts.

Subject 7 (ENFJ). In the 100 series, this subject preferred form 106/rc, and like the other subjects, he chose this one to return with suggestions for revision. To account for his preference for form 106/rc, the subject wrote:

> Despite "thing" a non-word, this passage is direct, avoids "this is" but like others repeats phrases (the fact)—it could most easily be revised.

His specific suggestions for revising form 106/rc involve cutting the first sentence and working to repair "logical fallacies" and "filler." He suggests, on the text itself, deleting all of the first sentence up to the phrase "masculine dominance," and rewriting the remainder of that sentence to read "Masculine dominance does not occur naturally." He objects, like Subject 25, to unsupported generalities like "There must have been other epochs in which the masculine privilege. . ." Although he deletes *thus* at the beginning of "certain customs and usages are still colored. . ." he asks for an explanation of the example of introducing men with familiar titles.

His response to the 200 series shows that Subject 7 is looking for similar kinds of things in this text as in the 100 series. He found the various versions of the passage rather close together, but preferred 201/o and also returned that one for revision. He liked in form 201/o the details at the end, and found them relevant. In his comments on the response sheet about his advice for revision, he notes that the parallel structure of the last sentence in paragraph 1 and the last two sentences of paragraph 2 is useful. He says the structure "helps make the thought easy to follow." Parallel structure is a form of cohesion, insofar as it gives the same structure repeatedly, allowing the writer to fill in the information that varies within the structure. Two comments appear on the text itself, both concerning examples. He asks for examples to be added at the end of the sentence which begins "Sports terminology and thinking habits. . .," perhaps influenced by the addition of examples at this point in 204/r and 206/rc. This subject approved of the examples in the second to last sentence of the passage. Because examples provide additional semantic redundancy, it is clear that this subject responded strongly and positively to both the redundancy already present in the passage, and to the need for some additions to it.

In the 300 series passage, this subject had a mixed response to the cohesion of form 305/c. He chose 301/o as the preferred form, but then commented

> First sentence clear and to the point. 305 using consequently and it follows give clear signals but therefore appears to me as "overkill" (ditto "in conclusion" and "specifically") (get rid of 2-3 thus's).

His suggestions in answer to question 2 of the response sheet (which asks for the subject's choice of a version to be revised prior to using it in a writing class, and requests suggestions for revision on the response sheet and marginal notes on the text—see Appendix 3 for the materials) deal with the cohesive elements also, suggesting the use of consequently and it follows from form 305/c but limiting the use of the word thus.

On the text of form 301/o, the subject removed *thus* prior to *some demands* and replaced it with *consequently*, and removed *thus* at the beginning of the defense example, replacing it with *for example*. A third instance of *thus* in the last sentence of the first paragraph was replaced by *it follows that* by this subject. In the case of form 301/o, then, the subject appeared to want more cohesion than was provided, but not quite as much as I added to form 305/c, or not in the particular words I chose for form 305/c. Still, it seems clear that the subject was seeking additional cohesion in the passage.

The subject's Myers-Briggs result of ENFJ places him in a group of subjects who share this type. ENFJs have a strong need to make connection with other people (Myers 15) and so would naturally look in writing at the ways in which the writer tries to connect with the reader. Thus, Subject 7 is consistent with his type in his responses, asking for more cohesion or connection in the text. The same impulse may drive the subject's request for examples, a form of redundancy that tends to make writing more personal. Examples are a way that writers reach out to readers, the sort of writing tactic an ENFJ would think important.

Subject 10 (INTP). Many of Subject 10's comments in his written response pertain to his difficulty doing the task I set. He found he could not really make a decision about which passage in each series was "best." This response is consistent with his Myers-Briggs perceiving preference—Ps often find it difficult to make a decision. His insights on this problem written in the context of his reading of the 200 series demonstrate his awareness of my research questions, but also his responses to the text:

> I can't really make a decision about which is "best." Yes, certain parts of some struck me as being less "mature" than the parts of others. But I thought the easier were "better" for demonstration, but I liked reading the more "sophisticated" ones a bit better. In some, there seemed to be more examples, and I liked that, but then I checked and found that on at least two others the examples were also there. So maybe it's transitions, and sure enough, in one the transitions were standing right out there at a part of the sentence like welcome mats, and so I began to think (now more "conscious" of form, perhaps) that I "liked" this better. But reading on, it [sic] wasn't so sure that the satisfaction came from the reading as from the "Ah, hah!" feeling that I was finding out what was going on in my environment (that is, in answering your questions). In other words, I was finding it very difficult to decide how, if at all, the passages were really different. They seemed all to be "good," in many ways, and "ordinary," "normal," or even a bit "pedantic" in others.

This leads the subject to draw some analytic conclusions before attempting to read the passages again in order to complete the tasks I set:

> 1. Readability is probably affected by vocabulary. And part of what struck me as "inappropriate" in the passages is the fairly high-flying lexicon. I'd want to simplify the words.
>
> 2. I wondered if sentence length was a factor. I didn't want to count. But my sense was that that wasn't "it."
>
> 3. Transition words, examples, and explanations of vocabulary seemed different, but I could grasp their significance at neither the "feel" or the "think" levels. I did find a few "explanations" that I found totally unnecessary, and hence encumber-

ing, but reading on in the same passage, I found the examples made the passage seem less abstract.

4. The passages need to be broken up into pieces (paragraphs) to be more readable.

The subject goes on to complain, as he actually makes his choices and writes comments on the texts themselves, that none of the versions of any of the passages is really good in a sense he can identify. Like other subjects, he complains about the play of fact and opinion in the 100 series, and the lack of clarity of the point in both the 100 and 200 series. The 300 series was, for Subject 10, quite vague and "best" seemed like a contradiction to him. In light of these responses, his choices of 101/o, 205/c and 305/c are quite interesting.

On form 101/o, the subject numbered his comments, presumably in response to my request for specific suggestions. Like others, he shortened the opening sentence and asked for paragraph structure to be added though he marked only one paragraph break. His revisions add two instances of *and* as well as one of *but* along with two places where he makes use of a question-and-answer format. His paragraph break occurs at "Men who like. . ." and he adds *so* to the beginning of the sentence.

His changes set the first half of the passage, through the "uncle" and "cousin" example in contrast to the second half, which accounts for this change over time and describes the result. The additions and changes the subject made rearrange the order of information from old to new, given to new, and this pattern, according to the linguistic analysis discussed above, enhances redundancy. And as before, the addition of different conjunctions seems to me to be a matter of taste and individual perception of key concepts which supports my claim that these professionals seek added redundancy and cohesion in various ways.

Subject 10's reaction to the 200 series is consistent with these claims. His changes to the opening of form 205/c involve a reordering of sentences so that the sentence beginning "Sports terminology. . ." appears first, followed by "In fact, in no other culture. . .," followed by the opening two sentences as written. He made a number of changes to the transitional elements, deleting *however* in sentence 2 but adding *even further* at a later point in the restructured version of the sentence. He complains about *thus* at the beginning of the last sentence of the first paragraph, and circles, without commentary, several other transitional elements. He feels that this last sentence is a repetition of the earlier ideas of the passage, but does not specifically indicate its deletion.

Consistent with the subject's Myers-Briggs type is his concern with content rather than with its warmth or friendliness. His notes suggest that the point of this passage is unclear, and that either the idea that TV has affected sports or that sports have affected us is the possible point of the passage. His rewrite leaves these options open. At the end he offers a new outline that combines the two ideas in a different way that shows their relationship. It seems clear that the subject found this passage quite challenging to deal with, but despite his difficulty, his suggestions point toward enhancing cohesion.

The changes in form 305/c support this subject's attention to both redundant and cohesive elements. Again note that he chose the form to which cohesive conjunctions had been added, and while he changes those elements, he maintains the cohesion. He adds *first* to the beginning of sentence two and *second* to the beginning of sentence three. He replaces *it follows that* with *so*. All of these changes enhance cohesion, as does the addition of some parallel structure in the two sentences dealing with "prolonged unemployment." A number of changes serve to enhance redundancy as defined, chiefly moving passive voice sentences to active voice and replacing dummy subjects with real subjects in active voice structures. His notes on this passage complain about its passive and abstract qualities, and his changes serve to reduce both features by adding to the redundancy of the text.

This response is particularly important. Although the subject is generally more familiar with my research than any other participant, he was setting aside most of what he knew and simply seemed to engage in the exercise I set. His changes move the passages in the general direction of increased redundancy and increased cohesion as I have defined and described them. In addition, his choices of preferred passages, while made under the duress of the forced choice nature of the exercise, show that he found more potential in the altered forms than in their original versions, in at least two of the three cases. Thus, this subject was consistent with others in the group in his recommendations, and consistent with about half the others in his choice of altered forms.

Subject 10's MBTI result is INTP (introverted, intuitive, thinking, and perceiving). In describing this type in the *Introduction to Type*, Isabel Briggs Myers writes as follows about INTP types:

> People with INTP preferences use their thinking to find the principles underlying whatever ideas come into their awareness. They rely on thinking to develop these principles and to anticipate consequences. As a result, they are logical, analytical and objectively critical. (13)

This description may help account for some of Subject 10's critique of the passages. True to his type, Subject 10 is quite intellectually independent and has his own ideas about these passages and many other things. But also, he sees prospects and possibilities, though he encounters difficulty expressing his reaction. This response, too, is quite consistent with his type, since as Myers says

> INTPs. . .main interest lies in seeing possibilities beyond what is present, obvious or known. . . .They want to state the exact truth, but often make it so complicated that not everyone can follow them. (13)

Despite the difficulties Subject 10 reports, and his criticisms of the passages, his responses agree to a significant degree with those of other respondents in the project in terms of redundancy and cohesion.

Subject 12 (ENFJ). In the 100 series, Subject 12 chose form 104/r, claiming that, in his view, it states the central idea more powerfully and directly, and makes better use of subordination. His choice of a version to revise is form 101/o, however, and his suggestions include recasting the central concept more clearly and changing the following sentences so they are clearly subordinated to the main idea. This request for more redundancy is borne out by his comments on the text.

In the opening five lines of form 101/o, he circles *this*, *this domination*, and *it* and notes "these referents seem unclear. Readers must wander the thicket back to the idea of masculine dominance not occurring naturally." In revising to add redundancy, one of my operational steps was to replace dummy subjects like *this* and *it* with substantive subjects, so this subject seems to me to be asking clearly for additional redundancy. He also asks that the first sentence be changed so that the real subject and verb of the sentence and their relationship is more clear. These responses may follow from the subject's personality preference, particularly given his intuitive (N), feeling (F) combination. People with an NF preference are especially concerned with relationships among ideas and with a focus on the reader.

In the 200 series, the subject chose form 205/c as best because "it consistently uses transitional phrases to signal the relationship among sentences, thereby assisting readers to see how its initial concept takes root." Again, the subject's concern for the reader is clear in the comments. His suggestions for revision are intended for form 204/r, the one he returned with comments. On the response sheet, he asks for transitions, asking, again, for cohesion. His comments on the text of form 204/r ask for more explicit relationship statements between the ideas. He asks for the transitions that occur in form 204/r to be moved to the beginnings of sentences in several cases, a style point which suggests the importance of transitions among elements for this subject.

Subject 12's response to the 300 series makes this even more clear. Here, he chose form 301/o as best, citing its subordinators and connecting phrases as making this preferable, demonstrating once more his preference for cohesive text. His comments on the response sheet concerning revision of form 304/r refer specifically to this text feature. He says that form 304/r shows "no consistent control of transitions, connectives and other signals of cohesiveness: repetition of key phrases, etc." This concern for the overall shape of the text is consistent with the subject's preferences for intuition and feeling.

On the text of form 304/r, he asks that the transitional elements that do appear be moved to the beginnings of sentences, and that subordination that helps to make the connection between sentences be foregrounded. He objects to repetition of *the system* toward the end of the first paragraph, and also to repetition of *the minority's* in the last sentence of the paragraph, suggesting that the use of a pronoun would focus more attention on the subject. Actually, as Halliday and Hasan's analysis of cohesion suggests, cohesion can be achieved either through repetition or through use of pronouns, and so the subject simply has a style preference here.

This subject's responses are particularly interesting since he makes specific reference to cohesion and demonstrates a sensitivity to cohesion in his responses to the passages. While his idea of best does not cause him to choose one of the altered versions consistently (he liked 301/o best in the 300 series), it is clear from his comments that Subject 12 considers cohesion a central feature of good writing, and he makes numerous suggestions to enhance it.

Like Subject 7, Subject 12's MBTI result is ENFJ, an extraverted, intuitive, feeling, judging type. Isabel Briggs Myers describes this type as being good with language and expression of ideas, though Es prefer to demonstrate these qualities by speaking rather than by writing (15). This type has a particular interest in harmony and in valuing the views of others, and in seeing the possibilities in a situation beyond what is concretely present. These features of this type may account for this subject's particular focus on cohesion, since cohesion is a means of fostering connections among various parts of a text as well as facilitating the connection of reader and writer in the text.

Subject 25 (ISTJ). In the 100 series, this subject reported that she didn't like any of the versions, although 104/r had the advantage of more specific examples of key ideas. However, since 104/r suffered from heavy repetition, it was not clearly "best," though it was the one she returned for revision with comments. She felt all the versions had problems of organization and misplaced logical signals. However, her chief complaint concerned unsubstantiated assumptions, which she recommended modifying in the revision. This complaint may be consistent with this subject's Myers-Briggs preference that would likely lead her to focus on content as a thinker.

Having completed all three passages, this subject noted that, as a reader, she found herself comparing the various versions rather than responding to the substance of the ideas presented, as would be the case if the reader had only one draft to review. She said that, in several of the cases, she would suggest wholesale rewriting rather than advocating smaller scale changes in word order, transitions, and detail.

The 100 series seemed to provoke this reader to a strong response. She wrote a lengthy commentary (about 500 words) on the back of form 104/r, most of which addresses her substantive complaints about the content of the passage and the assumptions it makes about the relationships between men and women at different times in history. This lengthy response begins with this comment, which reflects her ISTJ concern with logic and content:

> My experience as a reader of this text in all four versions is one of being stalled by a constant impulse to resist the implied (or in some cases clearly signalled) logic. Part of the problem is that the paragraph was intended to fall within a longer discourse that would explain who "we" are and why we are presenting this quick sprint through history.

The discussion continues from this point citing the misleadingly broad character of the assumptions about gender, power, culture, history, and law that are contained in the passage.

When the subject focused on this as a writing task, however, in her commentary on the response sheet and on the text of the passage itself, she advocates revision of form 104/r. She asks for revision that will restructure, tighten, and modify the passage to eliminate unsubstantiated assumptions. To reach these goals in revision, she eliminates the first sentence and asks for definition of the term *natural* in sentence 2. She also deleted sentence 3, questioning the use of conjecture (cf. *must*) as fact. She moves the section from "Men may like to believe. . ." to "long process of subjugation" from the end to the beginning of the passage. She also asks for clarification of the custom of introducing strange men with affectionate names, in terms of tying it more clearly to the claim being made about matriarchal societies. Requests for definition and clarification are requests for redundancy and cohesion, so despite this subject's concern for the logic and substance of the paragraph, rewriting it for her involves adding these features of text.

This subject was not nearly so strongly responsive to the 200 nor to the 300 series. In the 200 series, she preferred 206/rc, saying that it contains more specific information that 201/o or 205/c. She notes that it is almost identical to form 204/r (an accurate observation, as both are forms with increased redundancy), but also notes the addition, in form 206/rc, of "transitional words that signal logical relationships among ideas." For this reason, this subject found form 206/rc preferable, confirming precisely my hypothesis about professional readers' preferences for the forms with increased redundancy and cohesion.

In revision, she advocates slight changes in the early portions of the passage, and more information in the last paragraph. On the draft, she moves the *since* and *however* portion of sentence 2 to its beginning, and asks for examples in the last sentence. The location of the conjunctive adverbs seems to me to be a matter of individual taste, as is the choice of a particular cohesive word. The request for examples is clearly a request to add redundancy, because examples provide another way of revealing the author's ideas. This subject deleted the *in addition* in the last sentence, marking it "redundant," once again demonstrating an intertwining of redundancy with the addition of a cohesive device.

Finally, in the 300 series, this subject chose passage 301/o. She says it is slightly preferable to 305/c or 306/rc, because the opening seems more clear and because of the redundancies, by which I speculate that she means simple repetition, and misleading logical signals in these forms. In her request for revision, she asks for more detail and stronger logic. Her comments on the text of form 301/o request more examples, add more transition (she adds *likewise* before "Prolonged unemployment. . ." and uses *Nonetheless* in place of "It is not unlikely, however, that. . ." in the last sentence) and replaces an omission, changing the form of cohesion from ellipsis to simple repetition of a key word.

On the back of form 301/o, the subject writes a comment on the last paragraph of all versions of the passage. In this comment, she asks for more transition between the defense example and the unemployment issue, and suggests that some ideas have been short-circuited—again, an accurate observation resulting from length constraints in my revisions of the passages. In essence, this final comment asks for a last paragraph that summarizes the point of the passage, yet another, more sophisticated kind of discourse-level redundancy.

Subject 25's personality preferences are introverted, sensing, thinking, and judging (ISTJ). Myers notes that people with this set of preferences tend to seek "facts to support their evaluations and decisions" (Myers 20) and so this subject may have been particularly bothered by her view of unsubstantiated claims in the first passage. Similarly, this type is strong on logic and clarity (Myers 20), preferences that clearly shape the subject's reaction to first and third passages. Reading a draft of the chapter, Subject 25's response was to suggest that the MBTI information was "supple enough. . .to allow various lines of argumentation," again reflecting her concern with logic. She also noted that, for reasons having to do with her current views of literary theory, she was strongly focused on demonstrable facts, but might at another point be more intuitively inclined.

Subject 26 (ENFJ). In the 100 series, this subject chose form 104/r as "best," saying it seemed most coherent, and noting that it establishes coherence through repetition of *masculine dominance* and synonyms for it, through the use of pronouns and active voice and through transitional expressions that signal time like *history* and *previous.* Note these preferences are carefully focussed on redundancy (such as active voice) and cohesion (pronouns, repetition, synonyms).

Subject 26's choice for revision is form 105/c. She makes clear what she has in mind for the revision by identifying the writer's key problem here as the insertion of

> commonly used "transition words" and "connectors" to develop coherence, but these seem artificially placed since true coherence derives from focussing the reader's attention on a central subject. It looks as though the writer was taught to insert these words so he/she does so. In most cases, they are not necessary to maintaining "flow" and in fact, often disturb the flow by calling attention to themselves and diverting attention from the subject. These words would not be so diverting if 1)the text called for such signals or 2)if they were accurately tied to the logic of the passage. These words constitute "just miss" signals because they just

> miss capturing the actual logic that is needed. In 105 the student needs to maintain a stronger lock on the subject of the passage by using more repeated words and repeated stems.

On the text of the passage, the subject deleted the opening clause of the first sentence and started it with "We must call attention," creating an active substantive subject at the beginning of the sentence. She circled a number of the transitional elements complained about in the above comments, and the *this* subject in sentence 2 and the *It* subject in sentence 3. From my point of view, the subject is responding clearly to the redundancy and cohesion of the passages and is looking, not only to rearrange these features, but to incorporate them in ways that contribute to readable writing.

This subject, like several others, provided lengthy written comments on each series, and also, like a few other subjects, chose a different passage as "best" than the one recommended for revision. In the 200 series, subject 26 chose form 205/c as best, noting the writer's appropriate use of transition words where they are needed and to signal the development of the idea of the passage. She also notes the use of parallel structure and coordination in the second paragraph. On her comments on the text she notes that the first sentence of the third paragraph gives a helpful restatement of the "first element," pointing her to a particular type of redundancy in the text that she thinks is especially noteworthy. These comments all suggest the subject's sensitivity to redundancy and cohesion as contributors to readable, coherent writing.

Her comments on the passage for revision, form 206/rc, also point this way, asking for more relationships between the ideas in the passage. She complains about misuse of the connectors and about the importance of adding clear expectations for the reader. In the opening paragraph, her notes on form 206/rc ask for stronger use of time expressions like *since World War II* and *consequently*.

In the second paragraph, she calls for more coordination, again a form of cohesion. Note that her choice for the best in both the 100 series and the 200 series are forms that have added redundancy and/or cohesion, and the subject's changes alter the form of the revisions, but not their nature.

This finding holds as well in subject 26's response to the 300 series, where her choice for the best form is form 305/c. She also liked 301/o, but found 305/c marginally better due to the use of overt connective elements. The subject finds that there are more of these than may really be needed since the passage has a clear cause and effect logic, but speculates that the writer of form 305/c may have been "more fearful that the reader may not follow that logic and so builds in more overt connectors."

Her choice for revision is form 306/rc, and here this subject demonstrates a particular sensitivity to redundancy. Her written comments suggest that the writer needs to set clearer expectations for the reader. She notes that cause-and-effect logic requires stronger if-then structure in the sentences of the passage than appear in this version. She asks for transitions to be moved to the front of the sentences, such as in "Priorities must be established in the end." "Causal logic," says Subject 26, "demands that "in the end" be placed first in order to lead the reader to appropriate conclusions."

Her final general comment is that the writer needs to work on "rhetorical notions of establishing expectations in the reader and then fulfilling them," another way of suggesting the need for more redundancy than appears here in the subject's view. Her notes on the text itself ask for rearrangement of the sequence of ideas in this way, and also for different transitional expressions. Once again, these changes are matters of taste rather than changes to a different approach to readable writing. Throughout her lengthy and detailed response, Subject 26 makes clear the need for redundancy and cohesion in readable text.

Subject 26's personality preference is extraverted, intuitive, feeling, and judging (ENFJ). As noted above for Subjects 7 and 12, this type has a preference for harmony, and such a preference might lead to a desire for cohesion and coherence, a kind of harmony or unity in the text. The ability to see possibilities, another strength of this type, may be the basis of the comments on setting up clear expectations for readers in the passages as recommended by this subject. The importance of clarity for the ENFJ is described in the *Introduction to Type* in connection with the "high value on harmonious human contacts" (15). Such clarity through connections, formed in text using redundancy and cohesion, is likely to lead to the fit of writer and reader I have been calling readable writing.

Subject 27 (ENFJ). In the 100 series, the subject's overall response to the passage appears in the "additional comments" part of the response sheet, where she says that the topic of the passage is explosive and cites a need for more examples to lend credibility to the discussion. She chose form 105/c as "best" and also returned it as the one for revision. The rationale given for her choice of form 105/c as "best" does not exactly support the choice made; instead, this subject found this version "least objectional" and liked the sentence structure of the 105/c version. Her comments on the passage suggest that it is wordy and abstract in the opening, and specifically request additional examples.

In the 200 series, the subject asks for or puts in expressions that focus on the use of examples in form 204/r. At the end of the passage, the subject adds the list of examples beginning with "the close-up, the instant replay. . ." from the other forms (omitted in 204/r due to length considerations), and also adds the example phrase at the end ("complete with statistical and personal sidelights"). Because the subjects were not restricted by length, they were free to make such choices. The subject also made some changes in the use of cohesive devices, rearranging one of them and substituting a cohesive word (*specifically*) in place of a redundant expression, again supporting the interplay of redundancy and cohesion in the creation of readable text.

In her response to the 300 series, Subject 27 chose form 305/c, despite "awkward transitions." She indicates a preference for 305/c's opening sentences. Her changes to this passage again indicate attention to the transitional words and phrases, including both a marginal complaint of "too many thus-s" and the deletion of *thus* in several places and its replacement with other conjunctive adverbs like *also* and *indeed.* Without making an issue of which conjunctive adverb is most appropriate at a given point in the passage, note that this professional noted and adjusted the use of cohesive devices in the passages she chose for revision.

Subject 27's Myers-Briggs result is ENFJ like that of Subjects 7, 12, and 26. Like those other subjects, this woman seemed particularly concerned with added cohesion in the passages, pursuing cohesive needs even in form 204/r, where cohesion was not enhanced. This subject's preference for harmonious human contacts also may be driving her requests for examples, a way that writers may try to connect with readers in their text. As noted in the chapter on writing research, Deborah Brandt has claimed that cohesion reflects readers' and writers' involvement with one another (Brandt, *Literacy* 76-77). This desire for involvement appears in the responses of the other subjects of this type as well.

Commenting on a draft version of this chapter, Subject 27 noted an important caveat about the use of type in teaching aspects of readable writing. She doubts that the Type Indicator as an instrument is completely reliable for making precise distinctions among personality types. Personality types are not absolute and, particularly since preferences may be lived out in such different ways, can be misleading. Real people, dealing with real instances of readable writing, will inevitably be more ambivalent and ambiguous than the tidy categories of the Type Indicator suggest. This critique makes the point that the MBTI does not explain everything about anyone, and as this subject has noted, responses to readable writing are complex and multidimensional. The present study, and the work of Jensen and DiTiberio, Keirsey and Bates, Kroeger and Thuesen, and others, mark the beginning of a careful exploration of the ways that type findings can provide insight into readable writing and other aspects of life.

Subject 29 (INTJ). Like most other subjects, Subject 29 chose the same form as best and as the form recommended for revision. In all cases, she preferred a revised form, either 05/c or 06/rc versions.

In form 106/rc, she observes that it is best because it makes more use of concrete examples and because the links or transitions occur more logically, even though they could be improved. The need for more work is consistent with the subject's personality preferences; Jensen suggests that, for INTJs, things can always be better. Her suggestions for revision of this version call for more focus on content, more specific information, and more careful placement of the transitions, all issues that follow from her personality preferences for focus on content and logical relationships among ideas. She feels all versions are wordy and could be more concise, striking on the text the whole of the first two lines and beginning with "Historically, masculine dominance. . ." at the beginning of line 3. She responds positively to *such as* and *for example* phrases, and asks for specifics from form 105/c to be added at the end. Her specific responses to the transitions and examples show a sensitivity to the redundancy and cohesion I added to the form she preferred.

Form 206/rc was Subject 29's preference in the 200 series, for rather similar reasons to her preference for 106/rc. She notes on the response sheet that there is more concreteness in form 206/rc and it makes better use of transitions. In particular, she notes that the reader cues are better in 206/rc than in form 204/r—and note that this is a clear preference for the added transitional expressions as well as the redundancy of 206/rc.

For revision, Subject 29 advocates clarifying the shift from newspapers to tv/radio in the second sentence, and then marks the "however, since World War II" portion of sentence 2 to be moved to the beginning of the sentence. She also suggests simplifying the structure of the last sentence of the first paragraph, saying the specifics are good but the series itself is complex. For this reason, perhaps, she suggests on the response sheet that this passage may require a very sophisticated reader. Here, I think we see some style and taste preferences inside the general response. This subject noticed and responded to the redundancy and cohesion of this passage, despite wanting to alter the form of these features somewhat.

The subject's response to the 300 series tells essentially the same story. Her preference here is for form 305/c, which she notes has a clear statement of the main idea and which has connecting links between virtually all sentences. In addition, she particularly liked the repetition of *decision* in the second sentence and the last sentence of the passage.

On the text itself, she follows up her suggestions for condensation and simplification of wording. She adds *get* to the third sentence "make their interests heard and get their demands satisfied" which clarifies the parallel structure and enhances the cohesion of this sentence. She alters the transitions a bit, and deletes a portion of the first sentence of the last paragraph, noting that having both *in conclusion* and *from an overall point of view* is an unnecessary signal of the ending. She also deletes *specifically* in the last sentence, but replaces *given* with *certain*, changes that are indicative of personal style preferences. Her overall response to this form is favorably based on the transitional expressions and repetition, elements of redundancy and cohesion.

Subject 29's MBTI result is INTJ, an introverted, intuitive, thinking, and judging type, like the type of Subject 3 and Subject 30, below. This type is highly goal directed but capable of focusing on detail (Myers 24), as is clearly the case here. The changes made in the particulars of the expression of redundancy and cohesion may relate to the preference of this type for innovation.

Subject 30 (INTJ). In the 100 series, this subject chose form 106/rc as "best" because it had more specific detail, but claimed that the logic of the paragraph obscures the idea (the passage of the 100 series is a single paragraph). She said 105/c seemed better until she took it apart because of the transition words. She sent back form 105/c as the one for revision, recommending reorganization, serious "cutting of redundancy" to reduce overall length, sentence combining and statement of the relationship between ideas. My understanding of this subject's use of 'redundancy' here is that she means simple repetition and not the more complex psycholinguistic redundancy she seeks to enhance in her changes to the passages. In addition, since the reader calls for the relationships among ideas to be clarified, she is asking clearly for more cohesion.

This subject actually rewrote form 105/c, and her changes mostly move the sentences into subject-verb-object word order, delete the dummy subjects *this* and *it* and make several other changes that are consistent with my operational definition of redundancy. In addition to combining two sentences, this writer also broke up the last sentence and put in a pronoun subject instead of the cohesive conjunction *finally*, showing clearly how redundancy and cohesion work together in a passage. Interestingly, this subject's revision of the passage reduced it from about 300 words to 145 words in length (she provided the count).

Though she chose not to provide a rewrite of form 205/c, she chose it as best, noting the detail, and transitional words that flag logical relationships, i.e. cohesion. Her recommendations for revision show a preference for some of the changes of the other forms, advocating a substitution of paragraph 2 from form 204/r and the incorporation of examples from 206/rc in paragraph 1. At the end, she adds the word *through* before the list of "close-up, instant replay," etc. and complains of wordiness through much of the passage.

In the 300 series, this subject chose 306/rc as "best" because it begins well, but actually thought 305/c was better in stating the relationships among ideas, presumably a response to the added cohesive elements in the 05 versions. This subject found the last paragraph weak in all four versions of the 300 passage.

In her advice on revision of form 305/c, which she returned, she asked specifically for more accuracy with transitions, divided paragraph 2 in half at "Thus, if defense is the highest demand. . .," and requested more articulation of the relationships among the ideas in this passage. In this passage, she changed several of the conjunctive words used, substituting *for example* in place of *by the same token* and *however* for *but since* as well as *likewise* for *therefore*. The play with transitional expressions seems to me to be more a matter of taste or individual reader perception of the connections among the ideas at a given point in the passage; the key is that professional writers seek explicit statement of such relationships and add them as they work on a piece of writing. This response is consistent across all the professionals in this study.

Subject 30's rewrite of form 105/c may fit with her personality type, INTJ, which characteristically focuses on goals and inspirations. Perhaps she thought she saw what was needed and went ahead to produce it rather than just making suggestions for revision. Also, like Subject 3, she complains of wordiness, again typical of her personality type with its preference for directness. Subject 30 read a draft of this chapter, and her comments interestingly focus on several points in the opening segment of the chapter where she suggests editorial changes to condense the text and make it more efficient. Though she had no comments on this particular section, her revision suggestions for the chapter are similarly consistent with her type. There are some other features of this subject's response that fit with her NT combination, to be discussed below.

There are a number of points to be made about these cases taken together as a group, in terms of the hypotheses under study here. The most important finding is that all of the cases show professionals' clear preferences for redundancy and cohesion, as indicated by the versions of the passages they chose as best or by their recommendations for changes to the passages. Every subject asked specifically for either redundancy or cohesion or both to be enhanced in the passages, as the second hypothesis proposed.

Results on Hypothesis 3

The third hypothesis under investigation in the case study project proposed that there is a relationship between professional reader/writers' responses to texts and their type preferences as indicated by their results on the Myers-Briggs Type Indicator. On this hypothesis, only limited speculation is possible here, since not all types are represented in the cases. I have made some comments about type in the descriptions of the subjects' responses to the passages in the individual cases above. However, the overall consistency of the subjects' requests for enhanced redundancy and stronger cohesion demonstrates that these preferences appear among readers of at least several different types. I will take up type preferences among the subjects as they fall into groups, particularly the predominance of N (intuitive) types among them and the interaction of sensing-intuition and thinking-feeling dimensions that bear on the subjects' responses to this exercise.

The first issue concerns the prevalence of Ns and their responses to these texts. Among the subjects, all but one are Ns; this is not surprising since, as I will detail below, NFs and NTs have a particular interest in language and communication. The N or intuitive preference pertains to how a person prefers to take in information, a particularly strong element in how people respond to writing. The N prefers to find out about things through intuition, which shows you the meanings,

> relationships, and possibilities that go beyond the information from your senses. Intuition looks at the big picture and tries to grasp the essential patterns. (Myers 5).

The N would naturally be interested in cohesion, because it supports the relationships among ideas in a text, and also in redundancy, because, at least at the discourse level, the use of such redundancy is precisely to reveal the larger pattern of the ideas in the text.

Considering another dimension, half of the subjects here are thinkers, and some of their responses are true to type, as they seek a more linear and explicit kind of structure. At the other end of this dimension, the feeling subjects respond more to the flow or interaction of the ideas as they perceive them than to their list like quality. My view of the responses on this dimension of preference is that it is interesting to note that both preferences call for structure, albeit of different kinds. Moreover, what appears crucial is less the type of structure wanted than that the structure be clearly signalled or indicated in the text. Such signals, I have argued, arise from cohesion and redundancy, and the subjects, at both ends of the dimension, seem to be calling for these salient contributors to readable writing.

In responding to a draft of this manuscript, George Jensen has shared several interesting insights about the thinking-feeling dimension as these preferences appear in the subjects' responses to the passages. Thinking types, according to Jensen, tend to set up text as though it were a plan for a building, using lists or topics as focal points. Feeling types are more likely to use chronology, or association, often relying on narrative structures, so their character does not seem linear or spatial in nature. Jensen says that structure is thus variable with the meeting ground of reader and writer (letter to the author). Jensen's views are supported by some empirical findings reported by Marti Singer. As I have noted, both ends of this dimension seek structure in different forms, and redundancy and cohesion are salient ways in which writers can signal their structure to readers, thereby creating readable writing.

A different view of the subjects in the cases arises from an understanding of the combinations of particular dimensions on the Type Indicator. In this view, presented in Keirsey and Bates's *Please Understand Me: Character and Temperament Types*, the keys to understanding people's preferences lie in the sensing-intuition continuum, and the thinking-feeling continuum. These two dimensions are said to interact to create a person's temperament in Keirsey and Bates's analysis. The analysis of temperament yields four characterizations of key preferences. Thus, temperament is somewhat less complex than considering all 16 types derived from the Type Indicator, so that it can sometimes provide a short cut to the relevance of type for particular kinds of activities, like producing and understanding readable writing.

Among my subjects, four fit into the NT temperament, termed by Keirsey and Bates the "Promethean"(47). Their remarks on how this temperament deals with language are quite pertinent to these subjects' responses to the passages:

> In his communications the NT is likely to speak with little or no redundancy. His communications tend to be terse, compact and logical. He has a deep reluctance to

> state the obvious, restricting his verbal communications because, he believes, 'Of course, everyone knows that. . .' And, it follows, for the NT, that if he did state the obvious, his listeners surely would be bored. . . .The NT is inclined to be precise in his choice of language and hopes that others will be the same. . .
>
> . . .NTs as a group tend to enjoy playing with words, finding pleasure in exploring verbal intricacies. Convoluted phrases and paradoxical statements fascinate them. (Keirsey and Bates 52, 55)

The four subjects who are NTs in my cases mention in their responses a number of features of the texts that fit with this description, suggesting reactions consistent with aspects of their personality type as I proposed in the third hypothesis. Subject 3 seeks to make the passages more concise, while Subject 10 pays particular attention to the need for logic and analysis, along with precision in expression. Subject 29 complains of the passages' wordiness, probably what Keirsey and Bates mean by redundancy. Subject 29 also suggests making the passages more concise and logical. Subject 30 shares this view as well.

A second group of subjects' Type Indicator results are intuitive and feeling (NF), placing them in a group Keirsey and Bates identify as having an "Apollonian" temperament (57). Five subjects have the intuitive (N)-feeling (F) combination as part of their MBTI results: Subjects 1, 7, 12, 26, and 27. Keirsey and Bates describe this temperament with regard to written language as follows:

> . . .their influence on the minds of the populace is massive, for most writers come from this group. Novelists, dramatists, television writers, playwrights, journalists, poets and biographers are almost exclusively NFs. . . .(W)riters who wish to inspire and persuade, who produce literature, most often are NFs. (60)
>
> More than any other group NFs can speak and write fluently, often with poetic flair. (61)
>
> NFs. . .prefer to work with words, and need and want to be directly or indirectly in communication with people (63).

As a group, subjects with this temperament are particularly concerned with making connections with readers and seeing the overall shape of a text. This concern is a marked contrast to that of the ST subject (Subject 25), whose major focus was on demonstrable facts. These subjects frequently comment on the need for more or different transitions and clear relationships among the ideas in the text. In addition, Subject 27 makes a point of commenting on the "flow" of the text, an issue of special concern to those with a literary or poetic talent as suggested by Keirsey and Bates.

The other point to be made about this temperament is the interest of intuitive (N)-feeling (F) types in "communication with people," so that many of the comments reflect a concern with consideration for the reader and for making the connection of reader to writer that I have been saying occurs with readable writing. Subjects 12 and 26 raise this point in a number of their responses to the passages.

I want to mention one more point. Jensen and DiTiberio, in their chapter on the evaluation of writing, suggest that personality preferences shape how teachers respond to student writing (Jensen and DiTiberio 139-40). Both researchers had some comments to add to my discussion. DiTiberio notes that, while "instructors *may* have a natural tendency to more highly value and reward the writing of students whose personality type is similar to their own" (140, emphasis added), there is also evidence that instructors value other kinds of writing for reasons shaped by type (letter to the author). For his part, Jensen agrees that the situation is more complicated than their discussion in *Personality and the Teaching of Composition* would suggest (letter to the author). Among other things, teachers and writers are under the influence of the shared ideology of their discourse communities, and are also under the influence of affect, i.e., their feelings about their own writing and that of others. Thus, personality preferences contribute to the intricate web of features that comprise readable writing, but they, like other matters considered in this book, are only part of the picture.

Overall, then, the situation is much more complex than my necessarily tentative speculations may indicate, since the actual levels of scoring on the Indicator make a difference (a higher number indicates how sure the subject is of a preference, and/or, according to some researchers, how sure the Indicator is of the subject's preference). Another point concerns an individual's dominant process, a more highly developed preference on either the sensing-intuition dimension or the thinking-feeling dimension (Jensen and DiTiberio 16). The dominant process colors how the preferences on the other two dimensions are played out, and also has an impact on the kinds of responses here. Moreover, there may be a difference in how reader/writers actually respond to writing, just as there may be differences in how two people with similar preferences live out those preferences. Finally, the interaction of all the dimensions has an influence on the overall response. More research with an array of all 16 types may show more generalized support for redundancy and cohesion as central features of readable writing, as suggested by the limited assortment of types in this study.

CROSS-CASE ANALYSIS

Several other commonalities appear among the respondents. First, with only two exceptions, the subjects chose the same form as "best" and as the one they recommended for revision. This result was not what I anticipated from the respondents, and yet it is consistent with the view of a number of subjects that no version of any passage was really a "best" version. One subject, commenting on this outcome, suggested that a consistent choice of "best" as the one for revision resulted from the desire to use a pretty good piece of writing and improve on it. Most subjects did not comment on this point specifically.

Subjects were also consistent in their desire for more examples to be added to the passages and were consistent in their recognition of the importance of transitional expressions, even though in many cases there were disagreements over which expression was warranted and at exactly what point in the text. Moreover, there was a fairly consistent desire among the subjects for explicit statement of the relationships among the key ideas in the passages, and perhaps this is a reflection of these professionals' preference for the use of transitional expressions. While it is possible that these readers concentrated their attention on transitions because they appear so overtly in the 05 and 06 versions of the passages, it seems to me that the consistency of the request for enhanced cohesion comes as a result of how professional readers view texts generally.

My analysis of the cases in this final study constitute an effort to put together some pieces outside of the puzzle of the nature of readable text. Fitting them into the larger picture now seems straightforward. The consistency of the findings in the case study suggests to me that professional reader/writers have a clear view of text factors and look for particular features in the text itself: The features they seek, respond to favorably, and advise adding are those I have described as redundancy and cohesion. The strong findings provided by these individual cases, supported by other pieces of suggestive evidence from different kinds of studies, all fit together in the puzzle of readable writing. In this picture, redundancy and cohesion figure prominently and interlock strongly to create readable writing.

CHAPTER 11

Readable Writing and Critical Literacy

As we have seen in this book, readable writing, though a complex and still incomplete jigsaw puzzle picture, draws on knowledge of language as analyzed by linguists, on the nature of how people respond to text both in terms of psychological processing and as filtered by individual personality preferences, and on our understandings of reading and writing processes. These four sources have provided a base for research that demonstrates the centrality of two key textual features of readable writing, psycholinguistic redundancy and cohesion, features which can contribute to the critical literacy taught and learned in higher education's multicultural classrooms. To draw the discussion to a close, I will bring the many disciplines and varied research methodologies together to position a final piece in the puzzle: An understanding of readable writing is central to critical literacy in the culturally diverse classrooms of contemporary higher education.

A REVIEW OF DEFINITIONS AND RESEARCH

In readable writing, readers and writers commingle, their expectations and intentions meeting and merging. This meeting in text is facilitated by two key characteristics, redundancy and cohesion. Readable writing entails both readability issues that address the countable components of text, tangible features like vocabulary, syllable count and sentence length, and comprehensibility, less tangible features like discourse conventions used by writers, as well as readers' interest, motivation, and aptitude. Readable writing also draws in the concept of difficulty, the relative ease of a particular text. Readable writing focuses on the text itself but presupposes the readers and writers who meet there.

The first characteristic essential to readable writing, *psycholinguistic redundancy*, is most simply defined as a feature of text that insures that the message sent is the message received. It is said to be present whenever the same information is available from more than one source. The last two sentences provide a simple example of redundancy, in that I have given two definitions of redundancy with essentially the same meaning. In general, simple repetition alone can easily lead to too much redundancy. However, while redundancy may derive from simple repetition or restatement, its more pervasive and necessary sources lie in predictable syntactic and semantic features. Redundancy comes additionally from both discourse structure and text content, which brings to mind such prior knowledge as the reader may have including cultural knowledge and expectations about text form, as well as various other sources.

The companion feature that interlocks with redundancy to create readable writing is *cohesion*. Cohesion is the feature of a string of sentences that makes it a text rather than a disconnected set of sentences. Cohesion appears in texts in a variety of different forms; some simple examples include pronouns and their antecedents, and, in two of my research studies, the use of various kinds of transitional expressions.

These two features of text, redundancy and cohesion, must be present in readable writing. Their basis is linguistic and psychological, and they pervade the processes of reading and writing, appearing in varied forms across diverse cultures, ethnic groups, and individuals, as reflected in personality preference variation. What we know about redundancy and cohesion must be viewed specifically through the wide-angle lens of several alternative research methodologies and different disciplinary views. This perspective makes clear the relevance of readable writing to critical literacy in higher education.

MULTICULTURAL DIMENSIONS OF READABLE WRITING

Some research in linguistics, psychology, reading, and writing discussed in the early chapters of this book relates to the multicultural aspects of readable writing. For example, Halliday's work has several characteristics that make it particularly pertinent for a multicultural understanding of readable writing. The first of these is that, unlike a number of competing theories of transformational and posttransformational linguistics, functional-systemic grammar is one of the few theories that looks at language at the level of discourse. Moreover, in his examination of discourse, Halliday focuses closely on the "context of situation" in which a text occurs. He looks, not only at the language per se, but also at the activity occurring as the language is produced, and the roles of the speakers or writers as well as the relevance of the language to the situation. Such attention contributes to multicultural studies of writers' choices in their context of situation; this work, thus, has special relevance to the increasingly diverse classrooms of American higher education, comprised, perhaps, of speakers of various dialects of English as well as speakers of other languages.

Propositional analysis from psycholinguistics has several advantages for the study of readable writing in diverse settings. First, as discussed in Chapter 3, it provides some insights from empirical research about how individuals produce and understand readable text. One such insight is that propositions seem to be processed by readers in terms of their prior knowledge, called a schema in propositional analysis (Kintsch). A schema gives an indication of the readers' prior knowledge and expectations about a text, a specific way of finding out whether particular readers have prior knowledge that is pertinent to reading a certain kind of text or a text on a particular topic. A reader's cultural and ethnic background may influence both the form and content of the schema. A second insight is that, through the use of propositional analysis as a research tool, some psycholinguists have found that the text features I have described, cohesion and redundancy, produce writing that readers read more quickly and remember more fully (Kintsch, Irwin). A third key feature of propositional analysis, because it focuses on the *meaning* of a continuous text or discourse, is that it is generally impartial about writers and thus has no essential cultural bias.

Research involving the Myers-Briggs Type Indicator gives writers and writing teachers additional ways to understand their own and one another's individual preferences, and better access to an awareness of differences. In work with the Type Indicator, no preference is thought to be inherently right or wrong, and this view leads to a rich appreciation of individual strengths (Myers). This appreciation is necessary in the increasingly multicultural classrooms of American higher education, and ultimately in our society generally (a broad discussion of some of the relevant issues can be found in D'Souza). Multicultural understanding as it pertains to readable writing is also one of the keys to critical literacy as broadly envisioned in several recent discussions (Clifford, Rexford Brown, "Schooling").

Additional research on reading addresses cultural variation in a different way. As our understanding of text processing in reading has improved, scholars have noted some differences between reading in a first language and reading in a second language. These differences pertain to the nature of readable writing in multicultural educational settings. Readers working in a second language may not be literate in their first language, or even if they are, they may not be strong or fluent readers, and/or they may not be well motivated toward reading generally. Even if readers are literate and skilled at reading in the L1, they may not be able to transfer their abilities easily to L2. Finally, differences in orthography, where applicable, and differences in overall knowledge of the language can make a significant difference to the ability to read effectively in L2 (Grabe). Insofar as research in second language reading has noted these differences and suggested that teaching reading be based on an interactive model of the reading process (i.e., one that draws on both bottom-up skills like word attack and sentence structure analysis as well as top-down comprehension skills), there is support for the analysis of the text features I have described across languages and cultures (Carrell, Swaffar), and for their incorporation in texts intended for diverse audiences inside the classroom and outside as well.

William Grabe's work in the area of contrastive analysis of text types has concentrated on the nature of different kinds of texts within a language and across languages. His text-based individual work, and the research he has done with Robert Kaplan, support the role of redundancy and cohesion in helping to understand differing text types across languages, and provide an avenue for understanding and appreciating diverse approaches to the production of readable writing. The research on contrastive rhetoric, some of it text based and some of it more empirical in nature, points up the contribution of shared cultural knowledge to the prior knowledge component of redundancy. Like the Myers-Briggs preferences, which do not judge right and wrong, contrastive rhetoric is a means for understanding differences and appreciating individual strengths in readable writing.

In a multicultural classroom, teachers can use these approaches to the nature of readable writing to help themselves and their students appreciate differing approaches and welcome the virtues of alternative views of how one might best present ideas in written form. In a multicultural setting, my series of studies with diverse students and with professional reader/writers provide evidence of the importance of what is in the text itself. My studies and those of others, employing assorted methods, demonstrate that redundancy and cohesion are the central features of readable writing. Linguistically, psychologically, through reading and writing: A kaleidoscope of views of readable writing support the findings of my studies. A focus on the redundancy and cohesion of texts makes it possible for readers and writers in multicultural settings to assemble the pieces of the readable writing picture essential to the development of critical literacy urgently needed by every member of our society.

In his brilliant and beautifully written autobiography, *Lives on the Boundary*, Mike Rose discusses the "struggles and achievements of America's underprepared," as I noted at the beginning of this book. The students Rose describes are the sort of ethnically and culturally diverse students found in increasing numbers in multicultural classrooms in American higher education. Rose's own educational experiences, as well as those of the students he has worked with over the years, provide a clear picture of the diversity and challenge of working with such students. In addition, however, Rose makes clear the broadest need such students have, for literacy: They need the ability to read efficiently and critically and write clearly. The potential for higher education to meet the need for critical literacy will be enhanced by our multidisciplinary exploration of the nature of readable writing.

APPENDIX 1

All Passages in All Versions

FORM 101

So far as the history of the origin of masculine dominance is concerned, we must call attention to the fact that this is a phenomenon which does not occur as a natural thing. This is indicated by the numerous laws which are necessary to guarantee this domination to men. It is also an indication that previous to the legal enforcement of masculine domination there must have been other epochs in which the masculine privilege was not nearly so certain. History proves that such epochs actually existed in the days of the matriarchate, the age in which it was the mother, the woman who played the important role in life, particularly so far as the child was concerned. At that time each man in the clan was in duty bound to respect the honored position of the mother. Certain customs and usages are still colored by this ancient institution, as for instance, the introduction of all strange men to a child with the title "uncle" or "cousin." A terrific battle must have preceded the transition from matriarchate to masculine domination. Men who like to believe that their privileges and prerogatives are determined by nature will be surprised to learn that men did not possess these prerogatives from the beginning, but had to fight for them. The triumph of man was simultaneous with the subjugation of women, and it is especially the evidence in the development of the law which bears witness to this long process of subjugation. Masculine dominance occurred chiefly as a result of constant battles between primitive peoples, during the course of which man assumed the more prominent role as warrior, and finally used his newly won superiority in order to retain the leadership for himself and for his own ends.

FORM 102

We must call attention to the fact that so far as the history of the origin of masculine dominance is concerned, this phenomenon of masculine dominance does not occur as a natural thing. The fact that masculine dominance is not natural is indicated by the numerous laws which are necessary to guarantee this domination to men. Previous to the legal enforcement of masculine domination, there must have been other epochs in which the masculine privilege was not nearly so certain, and this fact also indicates that masculine dominance is not natural. History proves that such epochs actually existed in the days of the matriarchate, the age in which the mother, the woman played the important role in life, particularly so far as the child was concerned. Each man in the clan was in duty bound, at that time, to respect the honored position of the mother. Certain customs and usages are still colored by this ancient institution, as for instance, the introduction of all strange men to a child with the title "uncle" or "cousin." A terrific battle must have preceded the transition from matriarchate to masculine domination. Men may like to believe that their privileges and prerogatives are determined by nature, but they will be surprised to learn that men did not possess these prerogatives from the beginning, but had to fight for them. The triumph of man was simultaneous with the subjugation of women, and the evidence in the development of the law especially bears witness to this long process of subjugation. Masculine dominance occurred chiefly as a result of constant battles between primitive peoples, during the course of which man assumed the more prominent role as warrior, and finally used his newly won superiority in order to retain the leadership for himself.

FORM 103

So far as the history of the origin of masculine dominance is concerned, we must call attention to the fact that this is a phenomenon which does not occur as a natural thing. This is indicated by the numerous laws which are necessary to guar antee this domination to men, such as property rights and divorce laws. It is also an indication that previous to the legal enforcement of masculine domination there must have been other epochs in which the masculine privilege was not nearly so certain. History proves that such epochs actually existed in the days of the matriarchate, the age in which it was the mother, the woman, who played the important role in life, particularly so far as the child was concerned. At that time, each man in the clan was in duty bound to respect the honored position of the mother. Certain customs and usages are still colored by this ancient institution, as for instance, the introduction of all strange men to a child with the title "uncle" or "cousin." A terrific battle must have preceded the transition from matriarchate to masculine domination. Men who like to believe that their privileges and prerogatives, for example, their authority in the family, are determined by nature will be surprised to learn that men did not possess these prerogatives from the beginning, but had to fight for them. The triumph of man, that is, his rise to a position of power, was simultaneous with the subjugation of women, and it is especially the evidence in the development of the law which bears witness to this long process of subjugation. Masculine dominance occurred chiefly as a result of constant battles between primitive peoples, during the course of which man assumed the more prominent role as warrior.

FORM 104

We must call attention to the fact that so far as the history of the origin of masculine dominance is concerned, this phenomenon of masculine dominance does not occur as a natural thing. The fact that masculine dominance is not natural is indicated by the numerous laws which are necessary to guarantee this domination to men, such as property rights and divorce laws. Previous to the legal enforcement of masculine domination, there must have been other epochs in which the masculine privilege was not nearly so certain, and this fact also indicates that masculine dominance is not natural. History proves that such epochs actually existed in the days of the matriarchate, the age in which the mother, the woman played the important role in life, particularly so far as the child was concerned. Each man in the clan was in duty bound, at that time, to respect the honored position of the mother. Certain customs and usages are still colored by this ancient institution, as for instance, the introduction of all strange men to a child with the title "uncle" or "cousin." A terrific battle must have preceded the transition from matriarchate to masculine domination. Men may like to believe that their privileges and prerogatives, for example their authority in the family, are determined by nature, but they will be surprised to learn that men did not possess these prerogatives from the beginning, but had to fight for them. The triumph of man, that is, his rise to a position of power, was simultaneous with the subjugation of women, and the evidence in the development of the law especially bears witness to this long process of subjugation. Masculine dominance occurred chiefly as a result of constant battles between primitive peoples.

FORM 105

So far as the history of the origin of masculine dominance is concerned, we must call attention to the fact that this is a phenomenon which does not occur as a natural thing. Instead, this is indicated by the numerous laws which are necessary to guarantee this domination to men. It is also an indication that previous to the legal enforcement of masculine domination there must by contrast have been other epochs in which the masculine privilege was not nearly so certain. History proves that such epochs actually existed formerly in the days of the matriarchate, the age in which it was the mother, the woman who played the important role in life, particularly so far as the child was concerned. At that time each man in the clan was in duty bound to respect the honored position of the mother. Thus, certain customs and usages are still colored by this ancient institution, as for instance, the introduction of all strange men to a child with the title "uncle" or "cousin." Then a terrific battle must have preceded the transition from matriarchate to masculine domination. Men who like to believe that their privileges and prerogatives are determined by nature will therefore be surprised to learn that men did not possess these prerogatives from the beginning, but had to fight for them. The triumph of man was simultaneous with the subjugation of women, and in the end, it is especially the evidence in the development of the law which bears witness to this long process of subjugation. In conclusion, masculine dominance occurred chiefly as a result of constant battles between primitive peoples, during the course of which man assumed the more prominent role as warrior, and finally used his newly won superiority in order to retain the leadership for himself and for his own ends.

FORM 106

We must call attention to the fact that so far as the history of the origin of masculine dominance is concerned, this phenomenon of masculine dominance does not occur as a natural thing. Instead, the fact that masculine dominance is not natural is indicated by the numerous laws which are necessary to guarantee this domination to men, such as property rights and divorce laws. Previous to the legal enforcement of masculine domination, there must by contrast have been other epochs in which the masculine privilege was not nearly so certain, and this fact also indicates that masculine dominance is not natural. History proves that such epochs actually existed formerly in the days of the matriarchate, the age in which the mother, the woman played the important role in life, particularly so far as the child was concerned. Each man in the clan was in duty bound, at that time, to respect the honored position of the mother. Thus, certain customs and usages are still colored by this ancient institution, as for instance, the introduction of all strange men to a child with the title "uncle" or "cousin." Then a terrific battle must have preceded the transition from matriarchate to masculine domination. Men may like to believe that their privileges and prerogatives, for example their authority in the family, are determined by nature, but they will therefore be surprised to learn that men did not possess these prerogatives from the beginning, but had to fight for them. The triumph of man, that is, his rise to a position of power, was simultaneous with the subjugation of women, and in the end the evidence in the development of the law especially bears witness to this long process of subjugation. In conclusion, masculine dominance occurred chiefly as a result of constant battles between primitive peoples.

FORM 201

American newspapers created, nurtured and shaped mass spectator sports between the end of the Civil War and World War II. Since World War II, radio and television have become more important in spreading the interest and determining the form of these activities. In no other culture have the commonplace aspects of popular games so permeated daily life, even for those who pay no direct attention. Sports terminology and thinking habits have become an inseparable, often unrecognized, part of our language and even our philosophy. In man-hours devoted to sports activities, in dollars generated by direct and allied sports business, in sheer amount of recreational attention devoted to playing, watching, reading about and listening to organized sports events, American sports have a hold on American civilization unmatched in any other time or place.

Spectator interest rests on three pillars: intimate knowledge (or at least the illusion of it) of the nature of the game and the identity of the participants, some degree of emotional alliance to one side or the other, and willingness to spend money for this sort of entertainment. Without the first, mental involvement is not possible; without the second, the first quickly becomes meaningless. But without both, the motivation for the crucial third element can't be maintained, and without the commercial element the staging of sufficiently skilled and significant contests would not be possible.

The growth of television and radio, however, has meant an important difference to the first element, the spectator's knowledge. Television has changed this knowledge in two directions. On the one hand it is immeasurably more informative than newspaper and magazine stories ever were: the close-up, the instant replay, the right camera angle, slow motion. Furthermore, television (and even radio) carries with it instantaneous commentary on what is happening, complete with statistical and personal sidelights.

FORM 202

American newspapers created, nurtured and shaped mass spectator sports between the end of the Civil War and World War II. Radio and television have become more important in spreading interest and determining the form of these activities since World War II. The commonplace aspects of popular games have permeated daily life in our culture as in no other, even for those who pay no direct attention. Sports terminology and thinking habits have become an inseparable, often unrecognized, part of our language and even our philosophy. American sports have a hold on American civilization unmatched in any other time or place, in man-hours devoted to sports activity, in dollars generated by direct and allied sports businesses, and in sheer amount of recreational attention devoted to playing, watching, reading about and listening to organized sports events.

Spectator interest rests on three pillars: intimate knowledge (or at least the illusion of knowledge) of the nature of the game and the identity of the participants, some degree of emotional alliance to one side or the other, and willingness to spend money for this sort of entertainment. Mental involvement is not possible without the knowledge; the knowledge becomes meaningless quickly without emotional alliance to a side. The motivation for the crucial commercial element can't be maintained without knowledge and emotional alliance, and with the commercial element, the staging of sufficiently skilled and significant contests would not be possible.

The growth of television and radio has meant an important difference to the spectator's knowledge, however. Television has changed this knowledge in two directions. First, television is immeasurably more informative than newspaper and magazine stories ever were: the close-up, the instant replay, the right camera angle, slow motion. Second, television (and even radio) carries with it instantaneous commentary on what is happening, complete with statistical and personal sidelights.

FORM 203

American newspapers created, nurtured and shaped mass spectator sports such as football and baseball between the end of the Civil War and World War II. Since World War II, radio and television have become more important in spreading the inte rest and determining the form of these activities. In no other culture have the commonplace aspects of popular games so permeated daily life, even for those who pay no direct attention. Sports terminology and thinking habits have become an inseparable, often unrecognized, part of our language and even our philosophy, as in, for example, taking a rain check or getting to first base. In man-hours devoted to sports activities, in dollars generated by direct and allied sports business, in sheer amount of recreational attention devoted to playing, watching, reading about and listening to organized sports events, American sports have a hold on American civilization unmatched in any other time or place.

Spectator interest rests on three pillars: intimate knowledge (or at least the illusion of it) of the nature of the game and the identity of the participants, some degree of emotional alliance to one side or the other, and willingness to spend money for this sort of entertainment. Without the first, mental involvement is not possible; without the second, the first quickly becomes meaningless. But without both, the motivation for the crucial third element can't be maintained, and without the commercial element the staging of sufficiently skilled and significant contests would not be possible.

The growth of television and radio, however, has meant an important difference to the first element, the spectator's knowledge. Television has changed this knowledge, that is, has increased it, in two directions. On the one hand it is immeasurably more informative than newspaper and magazine stories ever were. Furthermore, television (and even radio) carries with it instantaneous commentary on what is happening.

FORM 204

American newspapers created, nurtured and shaped mass spectator sports such as football and baseball between the end of the Civil War and World War II. Radio and television have become more important in spreading interest and determining the form of these activities since World War II. The commonplace aspects of popular games have permeated daily life in our culture as in no other, even for those who pay no direct attention. Sports terminology and thinking habits have become an inseparable, often unrecognized, part of our language and even our philosophy, as in, for example, taking a rain check or getting to first base. American sports have a hold on American civilization unmatched in any other time or place, in man-hours devoted to sports activity, in dollars generated by direct and allied sports businesses, and in sheer amount of recreational attention devoted to playing, watching, reading about and listening to organized sports events.

Spectator interest rests on three pillars: intimate knowledge (or at least the illusion of knowledge) of the nature of the game and the identity of the participants, some degree of emotional alliance to one side or the other, and willingness to spend money for this sort of entertainment. Mental involvement is not possible without the knowledge; the knowledge becomes meaningless quickly without emotional alliance to a side. The motivation for the crucial commercial element can't be maintained without knowledge and emotional alliance, and without the commercial element, the staging of sufficiently skilled and significant contests would not be possible.

The growth of television and radio has meant an important difference to the spectator's knowledge, however. Television has changed this knowledge, that is, has increased it, in two directions. First, television is immeasurably more informative than newspaper and magazine stories ever were. Furthermore, television (and even radio) carries with it instantaneous commentary on what is happening.

FORM 205

American newspapers created, nurtured and shaped mass spectator sports between the end of the Civil War and World War II. Since World War II, however, radio and television have become more important in spreading the interest and determining the form of these activities. In fact, in no other culture have the commonplace aspects of popular games so permeated daily life, even for those who pay no direct attention. Sports terminology and thinking habits consequently have become an inseparable, often unrecognized, part of our language and even our philosophy. Thus, in man-hours devoted to sports activities, in dollars generated by direct and allied sports business, in sheer amount of recreational attention devoted to playing, watching, reading about and listening to organized sports events, American sports have a hold on American civilization unmatched in any other time or place.

Spectator interest rests on three pillars: intimate knowledge (or at least the illusion of it) of the nature of the game and the identity of the participants, some degree of emotional alliance to one side or the other, and willingness to spend money for this sort of entertainment. Without the first, mental involvement is not possible, and likewise, without the second, the first quickly becomes meaningless. But without both, the motivation for the crucial third element can't be maintained, and then without the commercial element the staging of sufficiently skilled and significant contests would not be possible.

The growth of television and radio, however, has meant an important difference to the first element, that is the spectator's knowledge. Television has changed this knowledge specifically in two directions. On the one hand it is immeasurably more informative than newspaper and magazine stores ever were: the close-up, the instant replay, the right camera angle, slow motion. Furthermore, television (and even radio) carries with it in addition instantaneous commentary on what is happening, complete with statistical and personal sidelights.

FORM 206

American newspapers created, nurtured and shaped mass spectator sports such as football and baseball between the end of the Civil War and World War II. Radio and television have become more important in spreading interest and determining the form of these activities, however, since World War II. In fact, the commonplace aspects of popular games have permeated daily life in our culture as in no other, even for those who pay no direct attention. Sports terminology and thinking habits consequently have become an inseparable, often unrecognized, part of our language and even our philosophy, as in, for example, taking a rain check or getting to first base. Thus, American sports have a hold on American civilization unmatched in any other time or place, in man-hours devoted to sports activity, in dollars generated by direct and allied sports businesses, and in sheer amount of recreational attention devoted to playing, watching, reading about and listening to organized sports events.

Spectator interest rests on three pillars: intimate knowledge (or at least the illusion of knowledge) of the nature of the game and the identity of the participants, some degree of emotional alliance to one side or the other, and willingness to spend money for this sort of entertainment. Mental involvement is not possible without the knowledge; and likewise, the knowledge becomes meaningless quickly without emotional alliance to a side. The motivation for the crucial commercial element can't be maintained without knowledge and emotional alliance, and then, without the commercial element, the staging of sufficiently skilled and significant contests would not be possible.

The growth of television and radio has meant an important difference to the spectator's knowledge, however. Television has changed this knowledge, that is, has increased it, specifically in two directions. First, television is immeasurably more informative than newspaper and magazine stories ever were. Furthermore, television (and even radio) carries with it in addition instantaneous commentary on what is happening.

FORM 301

It is not easy to evaluate the performance of government. From a general point of view, performance correlates with responsiveness: the more the decision-making machinery responds to the demands and the interests articulated within the system, the higher the level of performance. By the same token, the more the government allows new socioeconomic groups to participate in the system and make their interests heard and their demands satisfied, the greater the legitimacy and stability of the system. But since governmental decisions are made about the allocation of scarce resources or benefits priorities must be established. Some may get more and others less. Thus, some demands are likely to be fully met, others only in part, and some not at all. The greater the number of demands satisfied, the greater the rate of governmental performance. Thus, if defense is the highest demand, failure to be prepared against aggression would be an indicator of nonperformance. Prolonged unemployment (i.e., failure to meet the demand for full employment) would amount to nonperformance. Prolonged nonperformance would lower the attachment of many groups to the government and ultimately to the system, thus providing for instability that takes the form of a widespread rejection, not only of the government but of the system itself. Thus, failure to heed the interests and demands of a minority may account for its disaffection and the ultimate rejection of the political system on its part.

From an overall point of view, government performance relates to the manner in which over a given period of time the government meets and copes with specific social and environmental problems and also anticipates them. It is not unlikely, however, that careful study might indicate that interests and individual pressures for a given decision may be difficult or impossible or even unwise to heed.

FORM 302

Evaluating the performance of government is not easy. Performance correlates with responsiveness from a general point of view: the more the decision-making machinery responds to the demands and the interests articulated within the system, the higher the level of performance. By the same token, the more the government allows new socioeconomic groups to participate in the system and make their interests heard and get their demands satisfied, the greater the legitimacy and stability of the system. Priorities must be established, since governmental decisions are made about the allocation of scarce resources or benefits. Some groups may get more and others less. Thus, some demands are likely to be fully met, other demands only in part, and some not at all. The greater the number of demands satisfied, the greater the rate of governmental performance. Thus failure to be prepared against aggression would be an indicator of nonperformance, if defense is the highest demand. Prolonged unemployment would amount to nonperformance (i.e., failure to meet the demand for full employment). Prolonged nonperformance would lower the attachment of many groups to the government and ultimately to the system, thus providing for instability that takes the form of a widespread rejection, not only of the government but of the system itself. Thus, failure to heed the interests and demands of a minority may account for the minority's disaffection and ultimate rejection of the political system on the minority's part.

From an overall point of view, governmental performance relates to the manner in which over a given period of time the government meets and copes with specific social and environmental problems and also anticipates those problems. Careful study is likely to indicate, however, that interests and individual pressures for a given decision may be difficult or impossible or even unwise to heed.

FORM 303

It is not easy to evaluate, that is, to judge and appraise the performance of government. From a general point of view, performance correlates with responsiveness: the more the decision-making machinery responds to the demands and the interests articulated within the system, the higher the level of performance. By the same token, the more the government allows new socioeconomic groups to participate in the system and make their interests heard and their demands satisfied, the greater the legitimacy and stability of the system. But since governmental decisions are made about the allocation of scarce resources or benefits, such as money and manpower, priorities must be established. Some may get more and others less. Thus, some demands are likely to be fully met, others only in part, and some not at all. The greater the number of demands satisfied, the greater the rate of governmental performance. Thus, if defense is the highest demand, failure to be prepared against aggression would be an indicator of nonperformance. Prolonged unemployment (i.e., failure to meet the demand for full employment) would amount to nonperformance. Prolonged nonperformance, for example, continued high unemployment and inflation, would lower the attachment of many groups to the government and ultimately to the system, thus providing for instability that takes the form of a widespread rejection, not only of the government but of the system itself. Thus, failure to heed the interests and demands of a minority may account for its disaffection and the ultimate rejection of the political system on its part.

From an overall point of view, government performance relates to the manner in which over a given period of time the government meets and copes with specific social and environmental problems and also anticipates them. Interests and individual pressures for a given decision may be difficult or impossible or even unwise to heed.

FORM 304

Evaluating, that is, judging and appraising, the performance of government is not easy. Performance correlates with responsiveness from a general point of view: the more the decision-making machinery responds to the demands and the interests articulated within the system, the higher the level of performance. By the same token, the more the government allows new socioeconomic groups to participate in the system and make their interests heard and get their demands satisfied, the greater the legitimacy and stability of the system. Priorities must be established, since governmental decisions are made about the allocation of scarce resources or benefits, such as money and manpower. Some groups may get more and others less. Thus, some demands are likely to be fully met, other demands only in part, and some not at all. The greater the number of demands satisfied, the greater the rate of governmental performance. Thus failure to be prepared against aggression would be an indicator of nonperformance, if defense is the highest demand. Prolonged unemployment would amount to nonperformance (i.e., failure to meet the demand for full employment). Prolonged nonperformance, for example, continued high unemployment and inflation, would lower the attachment of many groups to the government and ultimately to the system, thus providing for instability that takes the form of a widespread rejection, not only of the government but of the system itself. Thus, failure to heed the interests and demands of a minority may account for the minority's disaffection and ultimate rejection of the political system on the minority's part.

From an overall point of view, governmental performance relates to the manner in which over a given period of time the government meets and copes with specific social and environmental problems and also anticipates those problems. Interests and individual pressures for a given decision may be difficult or unwise to heed.

FORM 305

It is not easy to evaluate the performance of government. From a general point of view, surely performance correlates with responsiveness: the more the decision-making machinery responds to the demands and the interests articulated within the system, the higher the level of performance. By the same token, the more the government allows new socioeconomic groups to participate in the system and make their interests heard and their demands satisfied, the greater the legitimacy and stability of the system. But since governmental decisions are made about the allocation of scarce resources or benefits, in the end priorities must be established. Consequently, some may get more and others less. Thus, some demands are likely to be fully met, others only in part, and some not at all. It follows that the greater the number of demands satisfied, the greater the rate of governmental performance. Thus, if defense is the highest demand, failure to be prepared against aggression would be an indicator of nonperformance. Therefore, prolonged unemployment (i.e., failure to meet the demand for full employment) would amount to nonperformance. Prolonged nonperformance would lower the attachment of many groups to the government and ultimately to the system, thus providing for instability that takes the form of a widespread rejection, not only of the government but of the system itself. Thus, failure to heed the interests and demands of a minority may account for its disaffection and finally, the ultimate rejection of the political system on its part.

In conclusion, from an overall point of view, government performance relates to the manner in which over a given period of time the government meets and copes with specific social and environmental problems and also anticipates them. It is not unlikely, however, that careful study might indicate specifically that interests and individual pressures for a given decision may be difficult or impossible or even unwise to heed.

FORM 306

Evaluating, that is, judging and appraising the performance of government is not easy. Surely, performance correlates with responsiveness from a general point of view: the more the decision-making machinery responds to the demands and the interests articulated within the system, the higher the level of performance. By the same token, the more the government allows new socioeconomic groups to participate in the system and make their interests heard and get their demands satisfied, the greater the legitimacy and stability of the system. Priorities must be established in the end, since governmental decisions are made about the allocation of scarce resources or benefits, such as money and manpower. Consequently, some groups may get more and others less. Thus, some demands are likely to be fully met, other demands only in part, and some not at all. It follows that the greater the number of demands satisfied, the greater the rate of governmental performance. Thus failure to be prepared against aggression would be an indicator of nonperformance, if defense is the highest demand. Therefore, prolonged unemployment would amount to nonperformance (i.e., failure to meet the demand for full employment). Prolonged nonperformance, for example, continued high unemployment and inflation, would lower the attachment of many groups to the government and ultimately to the system, thus providing for instability that takes the form of a widespread rejection, not only of the government but of the system itself. Thus, failure to heed the interests and demands of a minority may account for the minority's disaffection and finally, the ultimate rejection of the political system on the minority's part.

In conclusion, from an overall point of view, governmental performance relates to the manner in which over a given period of time the government meets and copes with specific social and environmental problems and also anticipates those problems. Specific interests and individual pressures for a given decision may be difficult or unwise to heed.

APPENDIX 2

Cohesive Chain Analysis, Procedure, and Data

1. Lexical rendering of text—separate all content words
2. Sort identity and similarity chains
3. Count total number of tokens and count tokens in chains
4. Sort relevant tokens, those in chains, from peripheral tokens, not in any chain
5. Evaluations
   more in chains, more coherent text
   lower proportion of peripheral to relevant, more coherent

Form 101 chain analysis

1]history
origin
masculine dominance
concerned
call
attention
fact
phenomenon
occur
natural
thing

2]indicated
numerous

laws
necessary
guarantee
domination
men

3]indication
previous
legal
enforcement
masculine domination
epochs
masculine privilege
nearly
certain

4]History
proves
epochs
actually
existed
days
matriarchate
age
mother
woman
played
important
role
life
particularly
child
concerned

5]each
man
clan
duty
bound
respect
honored
position
mother

6]Certain
customs
usages
colored
ancient
institution
introduction
strange
men
child
title
"uncle"
"cousin"

7]terrific
battle
preceded
transition
matriarchate
masculine domination.

8]Men
believe
privileges
prerogatives
nature
surprised
learn
men
possess
prerogatives
beginning
fight

9]triumph
man
simultaneous
subjugation
women
evidence
development
law
bears

witness
long
process
subjugation

10]Masculine dominance
occurred
chiefly
result
constant
battles
primitive
peoples
course
man
assumed
prominent
role
warrior
used
newly
won
superiority
retain
leadership
himself
ends

Total tokens = 118

Identity chains—tokens in identity chains = 26

Male dominance: masculine dominance 2, domination, masculine domination, masculine privilege, masculine domination
Law: law(s) 2, guarantee, legal, evidence
Man/men: man 4, men 3, uncle, cousin
Woman: matriarchate 2, mother 2, woman/women 2

Similarity chains—tokens in similarity chains = 45

Time: history 2, origin, indicated, indication, previous, epochs 2, days, age, ancient, preceded, transition, beginning, simultaneous, development, long, process, occurred, constant primitive, course.

Animosity: duty, bound, battle, possess, fight, triumph, battles, warrior.

Superior/Inferior: phenomenon, enforcement, important, respect, honored, position, title, privileges, prerogatives 2, subjugation 2, prominent, superiority, leadership.

Form 201 chain analysis

1]American
newspapers
created
nurtured
shaped
mass
spectator
sports
end
Civil War
World War II

2]World War II
radio
television
become
important
spreading
interest
determining
form
activities

3]culture
commonplace
aspects
popular
games
permeated
daily
life
pay
direct
attention

4]Sports
terminology

thinking
habits
become
inseparable
unrecognized
part
language
philosophy

5]man-hours
devoted
sports
activities
dollars
generated
direct
allied
sports
business
sheer
amount
recreational
attention
devoted
playing
watching
reading
listening
organized
sports
events
American
sports
hold
American
civilization
unmatched
time
place

6]Spectator
interest
rests

three
pillars
intimate
knowledge
illusion
nature
game
identity
participants
degree
emotional
alliance
side
willingness
spend
money
entertainment

7]mental
involvement
possible
quickly
becomes
meaningless

8]motivation
crucial
element
maintained
commercial
element
staging
skilled
significant
contests
possible

9]growth
television
radio
meant
important
difference

element
spectator's
knowledge

10]Television
knowledge
two
directions

11]immeasurably
informative
newspaper
magazine
stories
close-up
instant
replay
right
camera
angle
slow
motion

12]television
radio
carries
instantaneous
commentary
happening
complete
statistical
personal
sidelights.

Total tokens = 233

Identity chains—total in identity chains = 25

Sports: sports 6, activities 2, games 2, events, contests
Media: newspapers 2, radio 3, television 4, magazine
American: American 3

Similarity chains—total in similarity chains = 68

Time: end, become(s) 2, time, degree, growth, instant, instantaneous, maintained

Culture/civilization: Civil War, World War II 2, culture, philosophy, civilization
Business: man-hours, dollars, allied, business, amount, spend, commercial, staging, money
Activity: created, nurtured, shaped, spreading, devoted, entertainment, listening, playing, reading, watching
People: mass, spectator 3, popular, organized, participants, emotional, alliance, mental, involvement, motivation, personal
Knowledge/information: terminology, thinking, language, attention, interest, knowledge 3, nature, identity, informative, commentary, statistical
Media related: stories, close-up, replay, camera, angle, slow, motion, sidelights

Form 301 chain analysis

1]easy
evaluate
performance
government

2]general
performance
correlates
responsiveness
decision-making
machinery
responds
demands
interests
articulated
system
level
performance

3]government
allows
new
socio-economic
groups
participate
system
interests
heard

demands
satisfied
greater
legitimacy
stability
system

4]governmental
decisions
allocation
scarce
resources
benefits
priorities
established

5]

6]demands
likely
met

7]number
demands
satisfied
rate
governmental
performance

8]defense
highest
demand
failure
prepared
aggression
indicator
nonperformance

9]prolonged
unemployment
failure
meet
demand

full
employment
nonperformance

10]prolonged
nonperformance
lower
attachment
groups
government
ultimately
system
providing
instability
takes
form
widespread
rejection
government
system

11]failure
heed
interests
demands
minority
account
disaffection
ultimate
rejection
political
system

12]government
performance
relates
period of time
government
meets
copes
specific
social
environmental

problems
anticipates

13]careful
study
indicate
interests
individual
pressures
given
decision
difficult
impossible
unwise
heed

Total tokens = 116

Identity chains—total in identity chains = 36

Performance: performance 5
Government: government 6, governmental 2, political
Demand: demand(s) 7, interests 4, problems, pressures
System: system 6
Nonperformance: nonperformance 3

Similarity chains—total in similarity chains = 50

Measurement: evaluate, correlates, level, greater, scarce, benefits, number, rate, highest, meet, lower, account, ultimate(ly) 2, period of time, indicator, prolonged, allocation

People/groups: socio-economic, groups 2, minority, individual

Problems: resources, defense, aggression, unemployment, employment, failure, social, environmental, pressures, instability

Affiliation/rejection: participate, satisfied 2, legitimacy, stability, attachment, rejection 2, disaffection, copes

Choices: decision making, decision(s) 2, priorities, heed 2, meets

Appendix 3

Case Study Materials

The material for the case study includes the passages in the forms with increased redundancy and cohesion (i.e., 01, 04, 05, and 06 for each passage; see Appendix 1 for texts). The passages were accompanied by a letter, a background information form, a set of directions, and a half-page response sheet attached to each set of passages. In addition, each packet contained a plain white envelope marked HELP on the outside. These materials are shown here. (Each subject also received an envelope for the return of the materials.)

1. Cover letter

Dear Colleague:

As many of you know, I am continuing to conduct research on the nature of readable writing. My current interest calls for some assistance on your part. I would be grateful if you would take a break from your regular work to complete the enclosed exercise. The entire project may take you a couple of hours, but you can work on it in sections, and I think it will give you an interesting respite.

To give you a general idea of my work, I can say that I have been trying to analyze the particular features of texts which contribute to their readability. Readability is a complex matter, chiefly because it hinges on the interaction of reader and writer in a text. The text itself has been my focus because it seems possible that specific features of text can increase readability, and when we know what those features are, they can be taught to people interested in writing more readable texts. Until now, I have been having first-year college students respond in various ways to passages of text which incorporate certain features I have been studying. In the present study, I am focusing more on writing and teaching writing, and I need responses from professional readers and writers like you.

There are three sets of passages enclosed here, in addition to brief directions and a short set of background questions. For each set of passages, there is a half-page response form and a request for written comments on one version of each passage. If you wish to provide additional comments about the passages, I will be glad to have them. Please note that your response and background sheets are coded by number, so that for my purposes you will be anonymous. If you send me signed comments, I will treat them confidentially.

I would be grateful if you could complete the exercise and return it to me no later than April 10. A return envelope is enclosed for your convenience.

Thank you very much for your participation.

Yours,
Alice Horning

2. Background question sheet

Sex: M F
Highest degree and year of award:
Subject area of thesis:
Undergraduate major:
Graduate major if specified:

Years of full-time teaching experience:
List here the courses you typically teach (by title or subject matter) or have taught in an academic year:

3. Directions

Please respond to the background question sheet first.
Please read the following passages, one set at a time.
For each set, a half page form is attached with some brief questions to answer.

For the version of each passage you recommend revising, please also write at least three brief constructive suggestions in the margins of the text to help your colleague revise the passage.

If you wish to make additional comments on the passages, on the back of the question sheet or on separate pages, in any form, I will be happy to have them and will treat them confidentially. In the enclosed envelope, please send back only your half-page response sheets (3), your responses to the background questions, and the pages containing the three passages you recommend revising with your specific handwritten suggestions. I will be grateful for any additional comments about the passages, their readability, style or other aspects. I would also be grateful for citations to writing texts you use or would have your colleague read for advice on revising the passages. Alternatively, if you have handouts for students which deal with revising strategies or style matters, I would appreciate copies of those.

IF YOU RUN INTO PROBLEMS OR FEEL FRUSTRATED, PLEASE OPEN AND RESPOND TO THE PAGE IN THE ENCLOSED ENVELOPE, OR, IF CONVENIENT, CALL ME (home: 123-456-7890, office: 123-456-1122). Otherwise, disregard the envelope. Thanks very much for your help!

4. Response sheet (typed on a half page and attached to each set of passages, one for each series)

Subject Series _____

A colleague is preparing some prose passages to use to discuss readable writing with first-year college students in a writing course. You are asked to respond to two questions from your colleague about the four versions of this passage.

1. Which version is best in your opinion and why?
2. If you were advising the colleague to revise one version further, prior to use with students, which version would you suggest working from, and what 2 or 3 specific suggestions would you make for the revision? Please note your suggestions here and make marginal notes on the text itself.
3. Additional comments and responses most welcome.

Separate this sheet from the rest of the material, and return it in the enclosed envelope with the one version from this set on which you have written comments. Thanks!

5. The HELP envelope contained the following page:

If you have found the exercise extremely frustrating and challenging, here is an alternative series of questions to respond to on as many of the passages as you can manage. If it seems preferable, call me or see me to discuss the exercise.

1. Describe how you set about doing the exercise.
2. What was the initial source of your difficulty or frustration?

3. What responses did you have to passage 1?
4. What responses did you have to passage 2?
5. What responses did you have to passage 3?
6. How much time have you spent on this task thus far (approximately)? Describe how you have spent the time.
7. If you were able to choose one version of a passage to suggest revising, can you say why that version seemed unclear to you?
8. Any other comments, response, feedback you care to provide? (Use the back or additional sheets if necessary; handwritten notes on scratch paper or any other format perfectly ok.)

References

Adler, Alfred. *Understanding Human Nature.* New York: Fawcett World Library, 1954.

Anderson, Gordon. "Applying Discourse Analysis, Miscue and Cohesive Analysis to Reader and Text: Classroom Implications Related to Comprehension." International Reading Association Annual Convention. New Orleans, 5-9 May 1985. ERIC ED 269 726.

Atkinson, Dwight. "Discourse Analysis and Written Discourse Conventions." *Annual Review of Applied Linguistics* 11 (1990): 57-76.

Bailey, Mary and Colin Harrison. "Cloze Procedure as a Measure of Reading Comprehension: the Effects of Variations in Subject Matter on Textual Redundancy." *Human Learning* 3 (1984): 185-201.

Baker, Eva, Nancy Atwood and Thomas Duffy. "Cognitive Approaches to Assessing the Readability of Text." Davison and Green 55-84.

Bamberg, Betty. "What Makes a Text Coherent?" *College Composition and Communication* 34 (1983): 417-429.

Beach, Richard and Susan Hynds, eds. *Developing Discourse Practices in Adolescence and Adulthood.* Norwood, NJ: Ablex, 1990.

Bensoussan, Marsha. "Aspects of Cohesion and Coherence in Context: Investigating Causes of Difficulty for Israeli University Students Reading Texts in English." Diss. Hebrew U, 1984.

Biber, Douglas. *Variation Across Speech and Writing.* Cambridge: Cambridge UP, 1988.

Bingham, Adelaide Bates. "Readers' and Listeners' Use of Cohesive Ties in Processing Relational Meaning." *Language Sciences* 8 (1986): 49-61.

Binkert, Peter J. *The Cognitive Basis of Syntax.* Troy, MI: The Residential Grammar Corporation, 1989.

______ *Generative Grammar Without Transformations.* Berlin: Mouton, 1984.

Boiarsky, Carolyn. "Fluency, Fluidity, and Word Processing." *Journal of Advanced Composition* 11.1 (1991): 123-131.

Bormuth, John. "Comparable Cloze and Multiple-choice Comprehension Test Scores." *Journal of Reading* 10 (1967): 291-299.

______ "Readability: A New Approach." *Reading Research Quarterly* 1 (1966): 79-132.

Bovair, Susan and David Kieras. "A Guide to Propositional Analysis for Research on Technical Prose." Britton and Black 315-62.

Brand, Alice G. *The Psychology of Writing: The Affective Experience*. New York: Greenwood, 1989.
Brandt, Deborah. *Literacy as Involvement: The Acts of Writers, Readers, and Texts*. Carbondale, IL: Southern Illinois UP, 1990.
______ "The Message is the Massage." *Written Communication* 6 (1989): 31-44.
______ "Text and Context: How Writers Come to Mean." Couture 93-107.
Britton, Bruce K. and John B. Black, eds. *Understanding Expository Text: A Theoretical and Practical Handbook for Analyzing Expository Text*. Hillsdale, NJ: Erlbaum, 1985.
Broselow, Ellen. "Second Language Acquisition." Newmeyer, 3: 194-209.
Brown, H. Douglas. *Principles of Language Learning and Teaching*. 2nd ed. Englewood Cliffs, NJ: Prentice-Hall, 1987.
Brown, Rexford. "Schooling and Thoughtfulness." *Journal of Basic Writing* 10.1 (1991): 3-15.
______ *Schools of Thought: How the Politics of Literacy Shape Thinking in the Classroom*. San Francisco: Jossey-Bass, 1991.
Bruce, Bertram and Andee Rubin. "Readability Formulas: Matching Tool and Task." Davison and Green 5-22.
Carrell, Patricia. "Cohesion is Not Coherence." *TESOL Quarterly* 16 (1982): 470-488.
______ "Content and Formal Schemata in ESL Reading." *TESOL Quarterly* 21 (1987): 461-481.
______ "Facilitating ESL Reading by Teaching Text Structure." *TESOL Quarterly* 19 (1985): 727-752.
______ "Schema Theory and ESL Reading: Classroom Implications and Applications." *Modern Language Journal* 68 (1984): 332-343.
______ "SLA and Classroom Instruction: Reading." *Annual Review of Applied Linguistics* 9 (1988): 223-242.
______ "Text as Interaction: Some Implications of Text Analysis and Reading Research for ESL Composition." Connor and Kaplan 47-56.
Carrell, Patricia, Joanne Devine and David Eskey, eds. *Interactive Approaches to Second Language Reading*. Cambridge: Cambridge UP, 1988.
Chall, Jeanne. "Readability and Prose Comprehension: Continuities and Discontinuities." Flood 233-246.
Chapman, L. John. *Reading Development and Cohesion*. London: Heinemann, 1983.
______ *Reading: From 5 to 11 Years*. Milton Keynes, England: Open UP, 1987.
Charrow, Veda. "Readability Vs. Comprehensibility: A Case Study in Improving a Real Document." Davison and Green 85-114.
Chomsky, Noam. "Language, Politics, and Composition: A Conversation with Noam Chomsky." By Gary A. Olson and Lester Faigley. *Journal of Advanced Composition* 11.1 (Winter, 1991): 1-35.
Clarke, Mark. "Reading in Spanish and English: Evidence from Adult ESL Students." Hudelson 69-92.
Clifford, John. "Enacting Critical Literacy." *The Right to Literacy*. Ed. Andrea A. Lunsford, Helene Moglen and James Slevin. New York: Modern Language Association, 1990. 255-261.
Coe, Richard M. *Toward a Grammar of Passages*. Carbondale, IL: Southern Illinois U P, 1988.
Colomb, Gregory and Joseph Williams. "A Comment on 'Textual Research and Coherence: Findings, Intuition, Application'." *College English* 52 (1990): 211-212.
Conference on College Composition and Communication. *Scholarship in Composition: Guidelines for Faculty, Deans and Department Chairs*. Urbana, IL: Conference on College Composition and Communication, n.d.
Connor, Ulla and Robert B. Kaplan, eds. *Writing Across Languages: Analysis of L2 Text*. Reading, MA: Addison-Wesley, 1986.
Connor, Ulla and Ann Johns, eds. *Coherence in Writing*. Washington, D.C.: TESOL Publications, 1990.
Connor, Ulla and Joseph Keller. "Directions in Cross-Cultural Writing Research: A Cognitive-Cultural Approach." Academic Session, Research Interest Group. TESOL Convention. New York, 25 March 1991.

Couture, Barbara. "Effective Ideation in Written Text: A Functional Approach to Clarity and Exigence." Couture 69-92.

______ "A Systemic Network for Analyzing Writing Quality." *Systemic Perspectives on Discourse*. Ed. James D. Benson and William S. Greaves. 2 vols. Norwood, NJ: Ablex, 1985. 2: 67-87.

______ , ed. *Functional Approaches to Writing*. London: Frances Pinter, 1986.

Crain, Stephen and Donald Shankweiler. "Syntactic Complexity and Reading Acquisition." Davison and Green 167-192.

Crowley, Sharon. *A Teacher's Introduction to Deconstruction*. Urbana, IL: National Council of Teachers of English, 1989.

Dale, Edgar and Jeanne Chall. "A Formula for Predicting Readability." *Educational Research Bulletin* 28 (1948): 11-20, 37-54.

Darian, Steven. "The Role of Redundancy in Language and Language Teaching." *System* 7 (1979): 47-59.

Davison, Alice and Georgia M. Green, eds. *Linguistic Complexity and Text Comprehension: Readability Issues Reconsidered*. Hillsdale, NJ: Erlbaum, 1988.

Davison, Alice and R. N. Kantor. "On the Failure of Readability Formulas to Define Readable Texts: A Case Study from Adaptations." *Reading Research Quarterly* 17 (1982): 187- 208.

deBeaugrande, Robert. "Text, Attention and Memory in Reading Research." Tierney, Anders and Mitchell 15-58.

DePalma, Anthony. "Higher Education Feels the Heat." *New York Times* 2 June 1991, national ed., sec. 4: 1+.

deVilliers, Peter and Jill deVilliers. *Language Acquisition*. Cambridge: Harvard UP, 1978.

Devine, Joanne, Patricia Carrell and David Eskey, eds. *Readings on Reading English as a Second Language*. Washington: TESOL, 1987.

DiTiberio, John K. Letter to the author. 14 June 1991.

Donahoe, John and Michael Wessells. *Learning, Language and Memory*. New York: Harper and Row, 1980.

Douglas, Dan. "An Exploratory Study of Bilingual Reading Proficiency." Hudelson 93-102.

D'Souza, Dinesh. *Illiberal Education: The Politics of Race and Sex on Campus*. New York: Free Press, 1991.

Dulay, Heidi, Marina Burt and Stephen Krashen. *Language Two*. New York: Oxford UP, 1982.

Fahnestock, Jeanne. "Semantic and Lexical Coherence." *College Composition and Communication* 34 (1983): 400-416.

Flood, James, ed. *Understanding Reading Comprehension*. Newark, DE: International Reading Association, 1984.

Flower, Linda. *Problem-Solving Strategies for Writing*. 3rd ed. New York: Harcourt, 1989.

Foss, Donald and David Hakes. *Psycholinguistics: An Introduction to the Psychology of Language*. Englewood Cliffs, NJ: Prentice-Hall, 1978.

Frazier, Lyn. "The Study of Linguistic Complexity." Davison and Green 193-222.

Fries, Peter. "Language Features, Textual Coherence and Reading." Paper presented at the Second University of Texas at Arlington Conference on Linguistics and the Humanities: The Text as Convergence of Concerns. Arlington, TX, Mar. 1985.

Goodman, Kenneth S. "A Linguistic Study of Cues and Miscues in Reading." Gollasch I: 115-122.

______ "Reading: A Psycholinguistic Guessing Game." Gollasch I: 33-44.

Goodman, Yetta and Carolyn Burke. *Reading Miscue Inventory Manual: Procedure for Diagnosis and Evaluation*. New York: Macmillan, 1972.

Gollasch, Frederick V., ed. *Language and Literacy: The Selected Writings of Kenneth S. Goodman*. Boston: Routledge and Kegan Paul, 1982.

Grabe, William. "Contrastive Rhetoric and Text-Type Research." Connor and Kaplan 115-138.

______ "Current Developments in Second Language Reading Research." *TESOL Quarterly* 25.3 (1991): 375-406.

______ "Current Developments in Written Discourse Analysis." *Lenguas Modernas* 17 (1990): 35-56.

______ "Reassessing the term 'Interactive'." Carrell, Devine and Eskey 56-70.

Grabe, William and Robert Kaplan. "Writing in a Second Language: Contrastive Rhetoric." Johnson and Roen 263-283.

Grant-Davie, Keith. "Models of Reading and Writing." Conference on College Composition and Communication. Chicago, 21-24 Mar. 1990.

Grammatik IV. Computer software. San Francisco: Reference Software International, 1991. IBM PC-DOS 2.0, 512KB, disk.

Green, Georgia and Margaret Olsen. "Preferences for and Comprehension of Original and Readability Adapted Materials." Davison and Green 115-140.

Haas, Christina and Linda Flower. "Rhetorical Reading Strategies and the Construction of Meaning." *College Composition and Communication* 39 (1988): 167-183.

Haber, Lyn R. and Ralph N. Haber. "Perceptual Processes in Reading: An Analysis-by-Synthesis Model." *Neuropsychological and Cognitive Processes in Reading*. Ed. F.J. Pirozzolo and M.C. Wittrock. New York: Academic Press, 1981. 167-200.

Halliday, M.A.K. *An Introduction to Functional Grammar*. Victoria, Australia: Edward Arnold, 1985.

______ *Spoken and Written Language*. 2nd ed. Oxford: Oxford UP: 1989.

Halliday, M.A.K. and Ruqaiya Hasan. *Cohesion in English*. London: Longman, 1976.

Halliday, M.A.K. and Ruqaiya Hasan. *Language, Context, and Text: Aspects of Language in a Social-Semiotic Perspective*. Oxford: Oxford UP, 1989.

Hartley, Charles A. *Sensible Speller IV*. Computer software. Oak Park, MI: Sensible Software, 1983. Apple 2e, 256KB, disk. (Program operation is explained in accompanying manual, pp. 26-27.)

Hasan, Ruqaiya and James Martin, eds. *Language Development: Learning Language, Learning Culture*. Norwood, NJ: Ablex, 1988.

Haswell, Richard H. "Textual Research and Coherence: Findings, Intuition, Application." *College English* 51 (1989): 305-19.

HBJ Writer. Computer software. San Diego, CA: Harcourt, 1986. IBM PC, 256K.

Hinds, J. "Inductive, Deductive, Quasi-inductive: Expository Writing in Japanese, Korean, Chinese and Thai." Connor and Johns 89-109.

Hoey, Michael. *On the Surface of Discourse*. London: George Allen and Unwin, 1983.

Hoey, Michael and Eugene Winter. "Clause Relations and the Writer's Communicative Task." Couture 120-141.

Holland, V. M. Psycholinguistic Alternatives to Readability Formulas. Document Design Project Technical Report 12, 1981. ERIC ED 214 370.

Horning, Alice S. "On Defining Redundancy in Language: Case Notes." *Journal of Reading* 22 (1979): 312-22.

______ "Propositional Analysis and the Teaching of Reading with Writing." *Journal of Advanced Composition* 6 (1985-86): 49-64.

______ *Teaching Writing as a Second Language*. Carbondale, IL: Southern Illinois UP, 1987.

Horowitz, Rosalind. "Rhetorical Structure in Discourse Processing." *Comprehending Oral and Written Language*. Ed. Rosalind Horowitz and S. J. Samuels. New York: Academic Press, 1987. 117-160.

Hoskins, Suzanne. "Discourse Structure Analysis: An Introduction to Procedures and Implications for Instruction." *Reading World* 24 (1985): 30-40.

Hsia, H.J. "Redundancy: Is Is the Lost Key to Better Communication?" *AV Communication Review* 25 (1977): 63-85.

Hudelson, Sarah, ed. *Learning to Read in Different Languages*. Washington, D.C.: Center for Applied Linguistics, 1981.

______ "Writing in a Second Language." *Annual Review of Applied Linguistics* 9 (1988): 210-222.

Irwin, Judith. "Cohesion and Comprehension: A Research Review." *Understanding and Teaching Cohesion Comprehension*. Ed. Judith Irwin. Newark, DE: International Reading Association, 1986. 31-43.

______ "The Effect of Linguistic Cohesion on Prose Comprehension." *Journal of Reading Behavior* 12 (1980): 325-32.

______ "Linguistic Cohesion and the Developing Reader/Writer." *Topics in Language Disorders* 8 (1988): 14-23.

Jensen, George. Letter to the author. 22 June 1991.

Jensen, George and John DiTiberio. *Personality and the Teaching of Composition*. Norwood, NJ: Ablex, 1989.

Johnson, Donna M. and Duane H. Roen, eds. *Richness in Writing: Empowering ESL Students*. New York: Longman, 1989.

Jonz, John. "Another Turn in the Conversation: What Does Cloze Measure?" *TESOL Quarterly* 24 (1990): 61-83.

Keenan, Janice, Susan Baillet and Polly Brown. "The Effects of Causal Cohesion on Comprehension and Memory." *Journal of Verbal Learning and Verbal Behavior* 23 (1984): 115-126.

Keirsey, David and Marilyn Bates. *Please Understand Me: Character and Temperament Types*. Del Mar, CA: Prometheus Nemesis Book Company, 1984.

Kemper, Susan. "Inferential Complexity and the Readability of Tests." Davison and Green 141-166.

Kiefer, Kathleen. *Readers as Writers: A Basic Rhetoric*. New York: Holt, 1986.

Kieras, David. "An Advanced Computerized Aid For the Writing of Comprehensible Technical Documents." *Computer Writing Environments: Theory, Research and Design*. Ed. Bruce K. Britton and Shawn M. Glynn. Hillsdale, NJ: Erlbaum, 1989. 143-168.

______ "Good and Bad Structure in Simple Paragraphs: Effects on Apparent Theme, Reading Time and Recall." *Journal of Verbal Learning and Verbal Behavior* 17 (1978): 13-28.

______ "Thematic Processes in Comprehension of Technical Prose." Britton and Black 89-108.

Kintsch, Walter. "Comprehension and Memory of Text." *Handbook of Learning and Cognitive Processes*. Ed. W. K. Estes. Hillsdale, NJ: Erlbaum, 1978. VI: 57-86.

______ "Learning from Text." *Cognition and Instruction* 3 (1986): 87-108.

______ *The Representation of Meaning in Memory*. Hillsdale, NJ: Erlbaum, 1974.

Kintsch, Walter and Craig Yarbrough. "Role of Rhetorical Structure in Text Comprehension." *Journal of Educational Psychology* 74 (1982): 828-834.

Klare, George. "Readability." *Handbook of Reading Research*. Ed. P. David Pearson. New York: Longman, 1984. 681-744.

Koppett, Leonard. *New York Times Guide to Spectator Sports*. New York: New York Times Publishing, 1976.

Krashen, Stephen. *The Input Hypothesis: Issues and Implications*. London: Longman, 1985.

Kroeger, Otto and Janet M. Thuesen. *Type Talk, Or How to Determine Your Personality Type and Change Your Life*. New York: Delacorte, 1988.

Larson, Richard. "Structure and Form in Non-Narrative Prose." *Teaching Composition: 12 Bibliographical Essays*. Ed. Gary Tate. Revised ed. Fort Worth: Texas Christian U P, 1987. 39-82.

Lauer, Janice M. and J. William Asher. *Composition Research: Empirical Designs*. New York: Oxford UP, 1988.

Lawrence, Gordon. "A Synthesis of Learning Style Research Involving the MBTI." *Journal of Psychological Type* 8 (1984): 2-15.

Lowen, Walter. *Dichotomies of the Mind: A Systems Science Model of the Mind and Personality*. New York: Wiley, 1982.

Macridis, R.C. and R.E. Ward. *Modern Political Systems: Europe*. 2nd ed. Englewood Cliffs, NJ: Prentice-Hall, 1968.

Markels, Robin Bell. "Cohesion Paradigms in Paragraphs." *College English* 45 (1983): 450-464.

______ *A New Perspective on Cohesion in Expository Paragraphs*. Carbondale, IL: Southern Illinois UP, 1984.

McKay, Sandra Lee. "Topic Development and Written Discourse Accent." Johnson and Roen 253-264.

Moe, Alden J. and Judith Irwin. "Cohesion, Coherence and Comprehension." *Understanding and Teaching Cohesion Comprehension*. Ed. Judith Irwin. Newark, DE: International Reading Association, 1986. 3-8.

Mosenthal, James and Robert Tierney. "Cohesion: Problems with Talking about Text." *Reading Research Quarterly* 19 (1984): 240-244.

Myers, Isabel Briggs. *Introduction to Type*. Palo Alto, CA: Consulting Psychologists Press, 1987.

Neuner, Jerome L. "Cohesive Ties and Chains in Good and Poor Freshman Essays." *Research in the Teaching of English* 21 (1987): 92-105.

Newmeyer, Frederick, ed. *Linguistics: The Cambridge Survey*. 4 vols. Cambridge: Cambridge UP, 1988.

North, Stephen M. *The Making of Knowledge in Composition: Portrait of an Emerging Field*. Upper Montclair, NJ: Boynton/Cook, 1987.

Nystrand, Martin. "Using Readability Research to Investigate Writing." *Research in the Teaching of English* 13 (1979): 231-242.

Ochsner, Robert. *Physical Eloquence and the Biology of Writing*. Albany, NY: State University of New York Press, 1990.

Olsen, Leslie and Rod Johnson. "A Discourse-based Approach to the Assessment of Readability." *Linguistics and Education* 1 (1989): 207-231.

Olson, Gary, Susan Duffy and Robert Mack. "Applying Knowledge of Writing Conventions in Prose Comprehension and Composition." *New Directions for Teaching and Learning* 2 (1980): 67-84.

Purves, Alan, ed. *Writing Across Languages and Cultures: Issues in Contrastive Rhetoric*. Beverly Hills, CA: Sage, 1988.

Purves, Alan and Gail Hawisher. "Writers, Judges, and Text Models." Beach and Hynds 183-199.

Randall, Janet. "Of Butchers and Bakers and Candlestick-Makers: The Problem of Morphology in Understanding Words." Davison and Green 223-246.

Rayner, Keith and Alexander Pollatsek. *The Psychology of Reading*. Englewood Cliffs, NJ: Prentice-Hall, 1989.

Reid, Joy M. "English as a Second Language Composition in Higher Education: The Expectations of the Academic Audience." Johnson and Roen 220-234.

______ "Responding to Different Topic Types: A Quantitative Analysis from a Contrastive Rhetoric Perspective." *Second Language Writing: Research Insights for the Classroom*. Ed. Barbara Kroll. Cambridge: Cambridge UP, 1990. 191-210.

Renfrow, Donata. "Cohesive Ties, Cloze, and Teacher Ratings as Measures of Readability and Writing Quality." Diss. Georgia State U, 1982.

Robins, R.H. *A Short History of Linguistics*. Bloomington, IN: Indiana UP, 1967.

Rose, Mike. *Lives on the Boundary: The Struggles and Achievements of America's Underprepared*. New York: The Free Press, 1989.

Ruddell, Robert. "Reading Comprehension and Structural Redundancy in Written Material." *Reading and Inquiry*. Ed. J.A. Figurel. Newark, DE: International Reading Association, 1965. 308-311.

Rumelhart, David E. and James McClelland. "Interactive Processing through Spreading Activation." *Interactive Processes in Reading*. Ed. Alan Lesgold and Charles Perfetti. Hillsdale, NJ: Erlbaum, 1981. 37–60.

Samuels, S. Jay and M. Eisenberg. "A Framework for Understanding the Reading Process." *Neuropsychological and Cognitive Processes in Reading*. Ed. F.J. Pirozzolo and M.C. Wittrock. New York: Academic Press, 1981. 31-67.

Samuels, S. Jay and Michael Kamil. "Models of the Reading Process." Carrell, Devine and Eskey 22-36.

Schafer, John. "Coupling as a Text-building, Myth-evoking Strategy in Vietnamese: Implications for Second Language Reading." Hudelson 115-126.

Schulyer, Michael. "A Readability Formula for Use on Microcomputers." *Journal of Reading* 26 (1982): 560-91.

Schumann, John. *The Pidginization Process: A Model for Second Language Acquisition*. Rowley, MA: Newbury House, 1978.

Shanahan, Timothy, M.L. Kamil and A. W. Tobin. "Cloze as a Measure of Intersentential Comprehension." *Reading Research Quarterly* 17 (1982): 229-55.

Singer, Marti. "Cognitive Style and Reading Comprehension." *Journal of Psychological Type* 17 (1989): 31-35.

Smith, Carlota. "Factors of Linguistic Complexity and Performance." Davison and Green 247-280.

Smith, Frank. *Understanding Reading*. 4th ed. Hillsdale, NJ: Erlbaum, 1988.

______ *Writing and the Writer*. New York: Holt, 1982.

Stanovich, Keith E. "Toward an Interactive-Compensatory Model of Individual Differences in the Development of Reading Fluency." *Reading Research Quarterly* 15 (1980): 32–71.

Sternglass, Marilyn S. *The Presence of Thought: Introspective Accounts of Reading and Writing*. Norwood, NJ: Ablex, 1988.

Stotsky, Sandra. "Types of Lexical Cohesion in Expository Writing: Implications for Developing the Vocabulary of Academic Discourse." *College Composition and Communication* 34 (1983): 430-446.

Sudol, Ronald. *Textfiles: A Rhetoric for Word Processing*. San Diego: Harcourt, 1987.

Swaffar, Janet. "Readers, Texts and Second Languages: The Interactive Processes." *Modern Language Journal* 72 (1988): 123-146.

Tamor, Lynne. "Subjective Text Difficulty: An Alternative Approach to Defining the Difficulty Level of Written Text." *Journal of Reading Behavior* 13 (1981): 165-172.

Tanenhaus, Michael. "Psycholinguistics: An Overview." Newmeyer 3: 1-37.

Taylor, Wilson L. "Cloze Procedure: A New Tool for Measuring Readability." *Journalism Quarterly* 30 (1953): 415-533.

Tierney, Robert, Patricia Anders and Judy Mitchell, eds. *Understanding Readers' Understanding*. Hillsdale, NJ: Erlbaum, 1987.

______ and Jill LaZansky, T. Raphael and P. Cohen. "Author's Intentions and Readers' Interpretations." Tierney, Anders and Mitchell 205-226.

______ and James Mosenthal. "The Cohesion Concept's Relationship to the Coherence of Text." Center for the Study of Reading, Technical Report number 221. Urbana-Champaign: University of Illinois, 1981. ERIC ED 212 991.

______ and James Mosenthal. "Discourse Comprehension and Production: Analyzing Text Structure and Cohesion." *Reader Meets Author: Bridging the Gap*. Ed. Judith A. Langer and M. Trika Smith-Burke. Newark, DE: International Reading Association, 1982. 55-104.

______ and P. David Pearson. "Toward a Composing Model of Reading." *Contexts of Reading*. Ed. Carolyn N. Hedley and Anthony N. Baratta. Norwood, NJ: Ablex, 1985. 63-78.

Turner, Althea and Edith Greene. *The Construction and Use of a Propositional Text Base*. Boulder, CO: University of Colorado Institute for the Study of Intellectual Behavior, 1977. Technical report number 63.

United States. Dept. of Labor. *Workforce 2000: Work and Workers for the 21st Century*. Indianapolis: Hudson Institute, 1987.

Vande Kopple, William J. "Given and New Information and Some Aspects of the Structures, Semantics and Pragmatics of Written Texts." *Studying Writing: Linguistic Approaches*. Ed. Charles R. Cooper and Sidney Greenbaum. Beverly Hills, CA: Sage Publications, 1986.

Wardell, David. Cloze Procedure: An Historical Review. Ed.D. qualifying paper, Portland State University, 1985. ERIC ED 264 306.

Wasow, Thomas. Postscript. *Lectures on Contemporary Syntactic Theories*. By Peter Sells. Palo Alto, CA: Center for the Study of Language and Information, 1985. 193-205.

Weiser, Irwin. "(Inter)textuality, Semantics, and Coherence." Conference on College Composition and Communication Annual Convention. St. Louis, 17-19 Mar. 1988. ERIC ED 293 132.

Wilson, Paul T. and Richard C. Anderson. "What They Don't Know Will Hurt Them: The Role of Prior Knowledge in Comprehension." *Reading Comprehension: From Research to Practice*. Ed. Judith Orasanu. Hillsdale, NJ: Erlbaum, 1986. 31-48.

Winterowd, W. Ross. "The Grammar of Coherence." *College English* 31 (1970): 828-35.
______ Introduction. *A Teacher's Introduction to Deconstruction*. By Sharon Crowley. Urbana, IL: National Council of Teachers of English, 1989.
Witte, Stephen and Lester Faigley. "Coherence, Cohesion and Writing Quality." *College Composition and Communication* 32 (1981): 189-204.
Wolff, Dieter. "Some Assumptions about Second Language Text Comprehension." *Studies in Second Language Acquisition* 9 (1987): 307-326.
Yang, Agnes Weiyun. "Cohesive Chains and Writing Quality." International Systemics Conference. East Lansing, MI, August, 1988.
Yin, Robert. *Case Study Research*. Beverly Hills, CA: Sage Publications, 1984.

Author Index

M

N

O

P

R

S

T

V

W

Y

Subject Index

www.ingramcontent.com/pod-product-compliance
Ingram Content Group UK Ltd.
Pitfield, Milton Keynes, MK11 3LW, UK
UKHW020141290926
15471UKWH00003B/620

9 780893 919979